A FRIEND
IN THE
MUSIC
BUSINESS

A FRIEND IN THE MUSIC BUSINESS

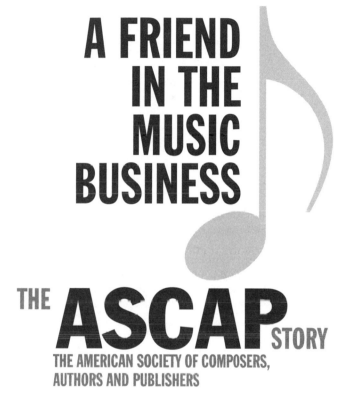

THE ASCAP STORY

THE AMERICAN SOCIETY OF COMPOSERS, AUTHORS AND PUBLISHERS

Bruce Pollock

Hal Leonard Books
An Imprint of Hal Leonard Corporation

Published in 2014 by Hal Leonard Books
An Imprint of Hal Leonard Corporation
7777 West Bluemound Road
Milwaukee, WI 53213

Trade Book Division Editorial Offices
33 Plymouth St., Montclair, NJ 07042

While every reasonable effort has been made to contact copyright holders and secure permission for all materials reproduced in this work, we offer apologies for any instances in which this was not possible and for any inadvertent omissions. Any omissions brought to our attention will be remedied in future editions.

Printed in the United States of America

Book design by Publishers' Design and Production Services, Inc.

Library of Congress Cataloging-in-Publication Data
Pollock, Bruce.
    A friend in the music business : the ASCAP story / Bruce Pollock.
       pages   cm
    Includes bibliographical references and index.
    ISBN 978-1-4234-9221-4
1. American Society of Composers, Authors and Publishers.   2. Music trade—
United States.   I. Title.
    ML3790.P66 2014
    338.7'61780973—dc23
                                                                    2013042806

www.halleonardbooks.com

CONTENTS

Foreword: Why ASCAP Matters by Quincy Jones   vii

Preface by Lyle Lovett   xi

Acknowledgments   xiii

CHAPTER 1   Herbert's Victory   1

CHAPTER 2   Buck Stops Here   19

CHAPTER 3   Radio Waves   33

CHAPTER 4   TV vs. Rock 'n' Roll   49

CHAPTER 5   The Comeback   65

CHAPTER 6   Seeding the Garden of Creativity   79

CHAPTER 7   New Blood, Nashville, and Capitol Hill   101

CHAPTER 8   Gridlock, Grants, and Gigabytes   115

CHAPTER 9   A Common Cause   135

CHAPTER 10   Follow the Dollar   149

CHAPTER 11   Playback and Fast Forward   169

APPENDIX A   ASCAP Leadership Through the Years   189

APPENDIX B   ASCAP Membership Activities   196

APPENDIX C **The ASCAP Foundation and Its Programs** 202

APPENDIX D **ASCAP and Oscar** 226

APPENDIX E **ASCAP Recipients of the Pulitzer Prize** 233

APPENDIX F **ASCAP and Tony** 236

APPENDIX G **ASCAP and Grammy** 244

Notes 249

Selected Bibliography 285

Index 291

FOREWORD
Why ASCAP Matters

I first joined ASCAP in 1955. I had previously spent a lot of time in France, and I knew about SACEM (Société des Auteurs, Compositeurs et Éditeurs de Musique), the French equivalent of ASCAP. I heard the United States had their own version of it, so that's why I became a member. Also, many other composers and songwriters that I was familiar with were members too, like Duke Ellington and Count Basie.

For nearly 60 years, I've worked as a producer, arranger, songwriter, and composer in almost every musical style including pop, jazz, R&B, rock 'n' roll, and classical—and in all media forms, including records, film, and TV. It's been an amazing journey. And through it all, ASCAP has always been there for me, making sure I received fair compensation for my work, thereby ensuring I could continue to work and grow as a creative artist. This has always been their main role—to be the champion for all their member songwriters and composers.

But in today's music business, there is a proliferation of piracy everywhere in the world. Songwriters and music industry professionals are challenged to stave off this epidemic, because the means for producing, replicating, and disseminating intellectual property such as music is so quick, easy, and accessible to everyone. In this climate, the challenge is, how do songwriters and composers continue to be properly compensated for their work? The solutions are not easy to find, but if we don't discover them, there aren't going to be songwriters to write the great songs of the future. That's why ASCAP is absolutely as essential now as it ever was and maybe even more so. It's a game-changing time throughout the business, with people reluctant to pay for various uses of music. That's why it's important for ASCAP to persevere—to make every effort to work with the entire music industry, as well as legislative bodies, in making sure songwriters continue to be treated fairly in terms of appropriate compensation. So far, for the first 100 years of their existence, they've done a great job; they've consistently worked very hard to represent us at every turn, whenever there's been a challenge to our right to make a living from our creative work. ASCAP has their hands full, but they keep working at it and finding solutions. As songwriters, we certainly need them. They are essential to our existence.

I talk to young songwriters all the time. I tell them don't forget God's rules, and that's to have humility with your creativity and grace with your success. Start with that. That's very important. Then I tell them join ASCAP and you'll get protected from piracy, because ASCAP is a rights protection organization. I tell them ASCAP will champion your right to earn a living on your creative work, and what's more, will collect revenue on your behalf for that work.

Right now, as a society, we are not respecting the rights of songwriters—that they need to be compensated for their intellectual property, which is their songs and compositions. The world is running outside the boundaries of the concept of intellectual property rights, and we've got to get back in them, because it's about respect for people's property and the morality of not just stealing it because it is so easy to do. But even though the business is in trouble, young songwriters are creating great music. Music and water will be the last things to disappear from this planet. People can't live without music. So we'll need ASCAP to be doing their job until the very end.

I was so honored when I received the ASCAP Founders Award in 2013. Some incredible musicians have been recipients of this prestigious honor. ASCAP has an amazing legacy and a long heritage of nurturing and supporting the creative process. That's why I try to do as many ASCAP events as my schedule permits. We all need to do our part to keep ASCAP visible and in the public's eye, so everyone knows how important it is that they are there.

I was elected to be on the board of ASCAP, but at the time I was in the middle of an incredibly heavy workload, especially working with Michael Jackson and all my other endeavors in the '80s. So I wrote a long letter to ASCAP recommending that Marilyn Bergman take my place on the board—which she did, and not surprisingly, she later became an awesome president and chairman of ASCAP for a period of fifteen years, until 2009. (Currently, Paul Williams has taken the reins and is continuing to do a wonderful job.) I've known Marilyn and Alan Bergman since we were next-door neighbors and worked together on the songs for *In the Heat of the Night* in 1967. She's like family. I knew she'd be right for the board because I knew her soul, her mind, and her God-given gifts. She definitely has a leader's mind. She's brilliant. You can hear it in her lyrics.

If you want to know what ASCAP's mission is and always has been, just read the first few lines of "How Do You Keep the Music Playing?" with music by Michel Legrand and lyrics by Marilyn and Alan Bergman:

How do you keep the music playing?
How do you make it last?
How do you keep the song from fading too fast?

Quincy Jones
November 2013

PREFACE

Because of my admiration for great ASCAP songwriters, I decided to join the Society in 1984. ASCAP members and fellow Texans Guy Clark, Townes Van Zandt, Steven Fromholz, Willis Alan Ramsey, and Rodney Crowell were all songwriters I listened to and admired greatly. And there were non-Texans I admired who formed a circle of songwriting royalty at ASCAP: George Gershwin, Burt Bacharach and Hal David, Billy Joel, and Stevie Wonder. What an amazing pedigree ASCAP boasted, and what a tremendous job this organization did in safeguarding the rights of songwriters and music publishers, making it possible for its songwriters to make a living writing music. That was my impression when I joined ASCAP, and in the years that have followed, that impression has been reinforced many times over.

I consider myself fortunate to have had the opportunity to interact with ASCAP and its people on many levels. The ASCAP office in Nashville was a point of entry for me and for so many others. It was a place we aspiring songwriters could go when we needed encouragement, inspiration, and even a few dollars to keep going. I, and many songwriters like me, were allowed space there to practice and were given advice that went a long way in making progress in our careers. ASCAP's doors were always open.

As I started to make recordings, ASCAP was a constant partner in ensuring that I received proper compensation for the songs I wrote and also made sure I received recognition at ASCAP awards events. I felt as though I was part of a close-knit family. I made friends in both ASCAP management and leadership. I've had the great privilege of spending time with several ASCAP presidents: Hal David, Morton Gould, Marilyn Bergman, and Paul Williams. They deserve our heartfelt thanks for being advocates for all songwriters.

I'll always remember the time I was asked to testify for ASCAP in Washington, DC. I addressed the House Subcommittee on Courts, the Internet, and Intellectual Property in May 2001 on the Internet uses of music. It was my job to give the songwriter's perspective. I remember asking, "Have you ever seen in the classified section of any newspaper an ad that reads: 'Songwriter wanted. Good salary. Paid vacation. Health benefits and many other perks'"? I went on to point out that most songwriters are independent entrepreneurs, trying again and again to write the hit that will help them take care of their families and keep them writing in the hopes of another hit down the road, so that songwriting can be a career, not a part-time unpaid struggle. It was a heady experience, going toe to toe with those who make the laws.

That's why I've never hesitated to appear at musical events ASCAP produces in Washington, DC, that highlight the value of music before our legislators. At ASCAP's concert celebrating the bicentennial of American copyright at the National Building Museum in 1990, the bill of performers I was astounded to share the stage with included Henry Mancini, Leiber & Stoller, Sammy Cahn, Cy Coleman, Ashford & Simpson, and Johnny Mandel. I was also invited to sing for President and Mrs. Clinton at the White House for an international evening ASCAP helped put together, and more recently, I performed at the Library of Congress as part of ASCAP's "We Write the Songs." Each event was a once-in-a-lifetime evening to remember and was a chance to underscore to lawmakers the importance of songwriters.

In 2014, ASCAP celebrates its 100th birthday. Although *A Friend in the Music Business: The ASCAP Story* certainly outlines the evolution of the many and various vehicles for delivery of music, what remains remarkably constant is the struggle to convince music users and our lawmakers that songs still need to be safeguarded and songwriters still need to get paid fairly for what they do. It is our goal that songwriters not have to fight quite so hard in years to come; it would be an accomplishment if, on the occasion of our next centennial, songwriters didn't have to fight at all.

Lyle Lovett
December 2013

ACKNOWLEDGMENTS

As usual with a project of this magnitude, many hands took part in bringing my book to fruition. Special thanks go to the team at Hal Leonard Corporation, who worked wonders with the manuscript, including Keith Mardak, Jessica Burr, John Cerullo, and Zahra Brown.

I would also like to acknowledge Karen Sherry and Jim Steinblatt at ASCAP for their wealth of editorial and historical expertise and perspective. Thanks again to Jim for all the research he did putting together the various appendices at the back of the book and finding the many classic photographs that adorn these pages.

I would like to thank the following people, who graciously took part in interviews for this book:

Paul Adler, Marty Bandier, Mary Ellin Barrett, Chad Beguelin, Richard Bellis, Marilyn Bergman, Caroline Bienstock, Jenn Bostic, Peter Boyle, Todd Brabec, Connie Bradley, Michael Brettler, Kenny Burrell, Bob Candela, Vince Candilora, Ted Chapin, Jerome Charyn, Barry Coburn, John Corigliano, Phil Crosland, Hal David, Bob Doyle, Roger Faxon, Nicholas Firth, Dan Foliart, Alec French, Roger Greenaway, Randy Grimmett, Dorothy Gullish, Arthur Hamilton, Wayland Holyfield, Lauren Iossa, David Israelite, John A. Jackson, Jimmy Jam, Dean Kay, Josh Kear, Jim Kendrick, Michael Kerker, Nancy Knutsen, Fred Koenigsberg, Leeds Levy, John LoFrumento, Keith Mardak, John Mayer, Jonathan McHugh, Harriet Melvin, Gloria Messinger, Jay Morgenstern, Jason Mraz, Brendan Okrent, Robert Ellis Orrall, Ben Palumbo, Stephen Paulus, Rufus Reid, Richard Reimer, Fran Richard, Irwin Z. Robinson, Debbie Rose, Earl Rose, Seth Saltzman, Dave Sanjek, Don Schlitz, Hans Schuman, Stephen Schwartz, Karen Sherry, Valerie Simpson, Ricky Skaggs, Matt Sklar, Billy Steinberg, Cameron Strang,

Charles Strouse, Michael Todd, Jimmy Webb, Paul Williams, and Toni Winter.

As always, thanks to my family for being there to keep me from disappearing under the various books, articles, public documents, transcripts, and assorted scattered notes that made up the research for this book. And to Walter Wager; I owed you another one. Too bad you didn't live to see it.

CHAPTER 1

HERBERT'S VICTORY

When pinpointing some of the most transformative moments in the evolution of American popular music, February 13, 1914, rarely if ever comes up. That was the day a group of the nation's most distinguished and popular songwriters, among them Irving Berlin, Jerome Kern, Victor Herbert, and Raymond Hubbell, arrived en masse at the Hotel Claridge in New York City to support the mission of a new organization for songwriters and publishers called ASCAP. Unless you are or once were a songwriter, chances are those initials are meaningless. But the American Society of Composers, Authors and Publishers has surely been, over the course of its 100-year history, the most prominent collective force for the advancement and nurture and financial well-being of songwriters and composers.

That they were convening that day (several months after nine of their number had braved a winter storm only to table the meeting) to implement a notion, already gaining favor abroad, that songwriters deserved a royalty whenever one of their tunes was played in public for profit—a *performance royalty*—was alone enough to mark their mission as both improbably noble and impossibly foolhardy. A notion that would slap the very hands that fed, albeit poorly, these songwriters—bandleaders, restaurant and club owners, music publishers, movie theater operators. "A tax on music," the attack ads of the day read, while the boos thundered down on the proud head of no less accomplished a figure than Victor Herbert as he tried to explain this position to the members of the American Federation of Musicians (AFM) at their annual meeting in Bridgeport, Connecticut, at the end of 1914.

It was quite a radical agenda in a world where aspiring Stephen Fosters routinely sold all their rights to publishers just to get their songs in print—whereupon publishers slipped those songs to touring troubadours, along with other informal gifts, just to get them heard. It was such a breach of protocol that in order for it to come into effect, it would literally take a ten-year pitched battle with Congress; a presidential memo signed by Theodore Roosevelt on his last day in office; many lawsuits, both lost and won; and finally a decision handed down from the Supreme Court itself, eloquently written by Oliver Wendell Holmes Jr., just to put it in motion. After which not a year would go by without further lawsuits to test the validity of what constituted a "public performance," what constituted "for profit," and why one particular constituency or another should be exempt from it—lawsuits that continue to this day, and will undoubtedly continue for the next hundred years.

Seven years after its existence was applauded and ratified in 1914, and four years after it was given the judicial seal of approval in 1917, ASCAP distributed its first royalty payments of approximately $82,000 to its hungry membership, which had dwindled by then to only a handful of dues-paying diehards. It is to these diehards the current roster of close to 500,000 songwriters, composers, and publishers must nod and give thanks when analyzing the complexities of their current royalty statements, which in total in 2012 amounted to just shy of $830 million. For thus creating a system where several generations of songwriters could at least aspire to make a living, ASCAP has performed an invaluable service to the history of popular music.

Having owed its existence for so many years to a legal premise, and starting out as a licensing and collection organization, ASCAP has ultimately found its greatest strength in its ability to recognize the changing times and adapt to them. In so doing, it expanded its mission for its members to include an enticing menu of songwriting awards, professional workshops, hands-on tutorials, and networking events that pay homage to the past while celebrating the future. By offering a willing ear to the newcomer; a stipend for the coffeehouse performer; and unlimited access to contacts and legal, business, and technical advice,

ASCAP has truly become, for every type of songwriter and composer, "a friend in the music business."

As the Society faces its second hundred years, poised atop a music business in turmoil, with fractured audiences and diminishing prospects for success, ruled by business models and new delivery systems determined to reduce the compensation of those who provide them with their content or to outright steal it, ASCAP's mission is more important than ever. In the face of unprecedented challenges, as recent events in the courts have shown, no one will miss the irony of a nation's songwriters cast adrift in the same boat they were in over a hundred years ago. . . .

It was in the Copyright Act of 1897, in fact, that American composers and lyricists first gained the right to receive payment for a public performance of their work, but if any of them were aware of it, no songwriter or music publisher chose to pursue such a hopeless, lonely quest. Even when this right was affirmed in the revised Copyright Act of 1909, this time adding significant monetary penalties for each infringing performance "for profit," the customs of doing business went on unchanged. Ever since the songwriting trade had become more visible around the time of the Civil War, most songwriters had customarily assigned all their rights to the publishers. One of America's greatest songwriters, Stephen Foster ("Jeanie with the Light Brown Hair," "My Old Kentucky Home"), reportedly never made more than $100 for any of his songs and is said to have died penniless in 1864. In the 1880s, when music publishing began to become big business, among the first to aggressively market his catalogue was Chicago's Will Rossiter, who in buying songs outright from songwriters—common practice at the time—spared himself the expense of paying royalties on tunes like "Meet Me Tonight in Dreamland."

By the last decade of the century, however, some enterprising songwriters had begun to take matters into their own hands. One young banjo player from Milwaukee named Charles K. Harris was so enraged by his royalty check of $0.85 from the House of Witmark for his worthy tune "When the Sun Has Set" that he decided to publish his next song himself. That song turned out to be "After the Ball," a multimillion-selling weeper credited with inventing the Tin Pan Alley genre before it was even named. Exhibiting the pluck of a journeyman plugger, with song in hand, Harris wangled his way backstage when the touring musical *A Trip to Chinatown*, featuring the popular ballad singer J. Aldrich Libby, rolled into Milwaukee. After having been turned down on the song by several performers, Harris happened upon the very tactic that was to prove essential in doing business in the brave new world approaching. Posing as a reporter for a local paper, he promised the singer a rave review should he put the song immediately into the show; even more to the point, he offered him the generous stipend of $500, plus continuing royalties on the sheet music sales of "After the Ball." Gladly pocketing the first payment, Libby proceeded to stun the audience into several encores. Over in New York City, the equally stunned Witmarks then offered to buy the song outright from Harris for an unprecedented sum of $10,000, but Harris had learned his lessons well. Before the first million sheet music copies were sold, he had opened a branch office of his publishing company on or near Broadway.

Irving Berlin had made a total of $0.37 in royalties in the four years since penning the lyrics to "Marie from Sunny Italy" in 1907, when he was a singing waiter at the Chatham on Doyers Street near the Bowery and the Pelham Café on Pell Street in Chinatown. In 1911 he moved out of the service professions for keeps, having come up with "Alexander's Rag Time Band" and gone into business with its publisher, the Ted Snyder Company.

Harry Von Tilzer started out as a staff writer for the publishing company Shapiro Bernstein, which in 1900 began as Shapiro Bernstein & Von Tilzer, before branching out on his own with "Down Where the Wurzburger Flows" a couple of years later. Equally typical of the songwriter's emerging new career path in those days was that of E. B. Marks, a former button salesman from Chicago. Soon after he wrote the weepy "The Little Lost Child," he went into business with Joseph W. Stern, also a salesman. Before the first decade of the new century was through, Joseph W. Stern & Company would publish classics like "Ballin' the Jack," "The Glow-Worm," "Lazy Moon," and "Ida! Sweet as Apple Cider."

Jerome Kern worked for Stern as a shipping clerk. He moved up to the position of sheet music salesman and occasional plugger at another publisher, T. B. Harms, in 1904, in which capacity he might have been seen at Macy's warbling "How'd You Like to Spoon with Me," the tune he'd written for Edward Lasca's lyrics and placed in the musical *The Earl and the Girl*. Once it became a hit for Corrine Morgan and the Haydn Quartet on the Victor label in 1906, he was able to gain part ownership of the company, run by the legendary talent spotter Max Dreyfus, ponying up a bit of his inheritance to do so.

The black composer Scott Joplin was a pioneer in more ways than one when he got the publisher John Stillwell Stark in Sedalia, Missouri, to cut him in on the royalties for his groundbreaking "Maple Leaf Rag," the first rag to be published in sheet music form, in 1899. By 1908, a year after hit cover versions by the United States Marine Band and banjo virtuoso Vess Ossman, Joplin was living at 252 W. 47th Street in New York City, just off Broadway. Did it bother him that popular journals like the *Musical Courier* and established unions like the American Federation of Musicians were decrying his pride, ragtime, as the ruination of polite society in general and teenagers in particular? Or that Irving Berlin and a few other white guys were poised to mutate ragtime into a national dance craze whose face and form would be the debonair duo of Vernon and Irene Castle? Probably not; he was too busy running through his royalties writing the operatic masterwork *Treemonisha*, which would not become a success until long after his death.

In the early part of the 20th century, many of the top freelance songwriters of the day were in the pocket of Florenz Ziegfeld, whose *Ziegfeld Follies* and *Midnight Frolic* would come to define not only the musical theater of the era but the American notion of architectural style and feminine beauty. As Jerome Charyn wrote in his book *Gangsters and Gold Diggers: Old New York, the Jazz Age, and the Birth of Broadway*: "The *Follies* would accurately mirror the preoccupations of their time, like a slightly surreal never-never land of New York and the nation. Ziggy would provide his own atmosphere. Dubbing the roof of the New York Theater the 'Jardin de Paris,' he cobbled together a variety show that was four hours long. . . . The *Follies* caught on like a house on fire and soon Ziegfeld was as famous as the *Follies* itself."

To have a song performed in the *Follies* by an Al Jolson or a Nora Bayes or Ziegfeld's main squeeze, the sexy Anna Held, could mean a lot of lunches at Lüchow's or Rector's. But the real money for the writers who didn't sell their songs outright was elsewhere. In the parlors of the rich, in the foyers of the middle class, in the crowded bedrooms of the poor, sheet music was the currency of the bustling entertainment economy, where families gathered nightly around the piano player or the player piano to sing the hits of the day. Many a popular tune, if it was well placed and well promoted, resulted in sheet music sales of a million copies or more. (As far as royalties from the piano roll companies, that was another story, soon to be decided in court.)

Losing out on the chance to collect on all these performance rights was thought of by publishers at the time as a necessary cost of doing business. Live performances of a song, after all, were free publicity for future sheet music sales. Even had they the smarts and temerity to attempt to collect on their lawful rights, most songwriters feared upsetting the historic balance and alienating the very places that exposed their music. But even major music publishers would have found keeping track of all legitimate public performances of their current as well as past catalogues that were suddenly cropping up at the turn of the century to be a logistical nightmare. In New York City alone it meant an exhausting itinerary of vaudeville and nightclub, restaurant and saloon hopping that surely would have deadened the soul and flattened the bank account of almost any publisher before producing a dime of profit. The only people in that era physically and morally equipped and recompensed to follow such a schedule were the notorious song pluggers of the day, who not only appeared regularly at most of the growing list of places where their employers' tunes were apt to be performed, but also often wound up performing one or two of them themselves.

At theaters during intermission, in restaurants between courses, at department stores between mannequins, they could hardly be avoided, these scruffy gents in fedoras holding cold cigars, who would pop up as if pulled by a force greater than destiny, but actually paid by the House of Witmark or J. W. Stern or Leo Feist or T. B. Harms or Shapiro Bernstein, to warble a ballad, run through a ditty, or demonstrate a rag. Sometimes aided by pictures or lyrics previously pressed into the unsuspecting palms of patrons or passersby, the best of them would wind up leading the throngs in wild sing-alongs and then collecting tribute through sales of the sheet music they just happened to have with them.

Often a famous personage from the Broadway stage, the vaudeville circuit, or Europe would be corralled à la J. Aldrich Libby for an under-the-table fee, and encouraged to perform the song—perhaps to take it back to the theater, on tour from coast to coast, or to the old country, thus propelling sheet music sales worldwide for several years. Al Jolson himself went straight from the synagogue choir to singing "Ma Blushing Rosie" for his supper at McGurk's on the Bowery. Many of these performers made more money accepting gratuities from publishers than they were being paid to sing on stage, a niggling affair the vaudeville managers would soon themselves convene to discuss, deride, condemn, but ultimately fail in their attempt to stamp out. And who knows how many unauthorized performances by restaurant orchestras, skinny chanteuses, and tank town belters posing as waiters and waitresses were going unchallenged on any given night?

But in 1909, when the new Copyright Act was passed, there was no performing rights organization (PRO) established in the States to collect the fees owed whenever a breach of the law occurred. Two years later, when the French society, SACEM (Société des Auteurs, Compositeurs et Éditeurs de Musique), opened a branch in New York City for American writers and publishers interested in following up on their public performances in Paris and elsewhere in Europe, they failed to generate a spark of interest, even from the songwriting community, no matter how strapped for cash most songwriters may have been. It was a situation that certainly would have appalled a foreign writer, especially someone of the international stature of Giacomo Puccini, composer of *Madama Butterfly*, who was visiting New York City in December 1910 to promote his latest opera, *La Fanciulla del West* (The Girl of the Golden West). As he was wined and dined on the arm and the tab of his publisher's US representative, George Maxwell, he was shocked to hear an unauthorized performance of his music, and doubly shocked when he was informed he was not to receive a royalty for it. Three years later, in the fall of 1913, Puccini was lunching with his good friend Victor Herbert at the opulent Shanley's restaurant on 43rd and Broadway, on one of the rare occasions when Herbert couldn't be found at that hour at his regular table at Lüchow's. Perhaps in tribute to their sometime guest, the orchestra assembled to entertain the patrons featured tunes from Herbert's new operetta, *Sweethearts*, which had opened in September and would disappointingly close in January (but not before producing a number two single of the title song for Christie MacDonald on

Victor). Hearing his friend's music, Puccini then went into the same diatribe he'd trotted out before George Maxwell in 1910, additionally fueled, no doubt, by the knowledge that nothing had been done in the three intervening years to alleviate the travesty perpetrated on lowly American composers and lyricists as well as their usually savvy patrons, the music publishers.

This time he was fulminating in front of the right party. One published account has Herbert rushing from Puccini's side to immediately entreat his songwriting buddies at their famed watering hole, the Lambs Club, to create a "performance rights" society on the spot, for the express purpose of launching a lawsuit against Shanley's. While the exact date of Puccini's fall visit has not been confirmed, and the suit against Shanley's wasn't launched until 1915, the story does dovetail nicely with a more official account of ASCAP's formation. In October 1913, 35 of the city's most respected music industry figures were set to meet at Lüchow's to discuss the parameters of the proposed society; it turned out to be a hellishly stormy night, however, and only nine of the invited guests appeared. Whether or not Victor Herbert came fresh from a revelatory luncheon with Puccini, he brought quite a bit to the table on that night, including his librettist (Glen McDonough), his publisher (Jay Witmark), and his lawyer (Nathan Burkan).

Herbert's friendship with the bookish New York City lawyer Nathan Burkan had begun in court, when Herbert sued the *Musical Courier* and its smug editor for slander in 1901 and won the extravagant sum of $15,000. Sitting at his side during that lawsuit, Burkan, an assistant at the trial, would go on to make a career for himself defending cases in front of the highest courts in the land, as well as serving as counsel to major celebrities, among them Charlie Chaplin, Al Jolson, and Mae West. His relationship with Herbert was further solidified at the Congressional hearings in Washington held from 1906 through 1908, leading up to the 1909 revisions to the Copyright Act.

At the contentious hearings, these two advocates of the songwriting art, along with several of their fellows, took on the manufacturers of piano rolls and word rolls, who were attempting to stifle an amendment to the Copyright Act that would require a "mechanical" royalty to be paid to a song's creators every time it was used on one of these new-fangled inventions. Along with the phonographic record and cylinder industry and the restaurant and nightclub owners of America, the piano roll boys were not shy in proclaiming their love of music and musicians. Why couldn't these songwriters see they were already doing them a favor, these veritable patrons of the arts, by showcasing their material in this revolutionary fashion? To demand a royalty for the use of their music would only be to jeopardize what they already had—as they put it, to create "a tax on music."

To the music publishers who joined the proceedings to lobby in favor of the amendment, it must have seemed the height of irony that they were hearing arguments from the manufacturing and nightlife communities similar to the ones they themselves had used against struggling songwriters reluctant to sign away all their rights to a particular title, citing common practice dating back to the Revolutionary War days of "Yankee Doodle." It is simply not in the nature of a businessman to want to part with a penny for something he used to get for free. Which is why, in addition to Burkan and Herbert, songwriters were lucky to have another ally working for them in an unlikely place: the White House.

As early as 1905, President Theodore Roosevelt could be heard lecturing the philistines in Congress on the finer points of the copyright law in his annual address. "Our copyright laws urgently need revision," he intoned, as he went on to explain the proposed legislation. "In form this bill would replace the existing insufficient and inconsistent laws by one general copyright statute. It will be presented to the Congress at the coming session. It deserves prompt consideration."

It would take a few more years and many sessions, several different bills, and the impassioned speeches of some of the greatest writers, poets, painters, composers, and interested international philanthropists of the era to bring the issue to a head. Offering a careful reading of *The Arguments Before the Committees on Patents of the Senate and House of Representatives, Conjointly, on the Bills S. 6630 and H.R. 19853 to Amend and Consolidate the Acts Respecting Copyright,* Edward Waters, in his biography of Victor Herbert, quotes at length from the public transcripts of a June 1906 session. While Herbert was prepared to roar, stomp, and harangue, his contemporary, the marching band maestro John Philip Sousa, led off with a nuanced approach when dealing with the weary old men in suits with whom he shared some insights in the Old Senate Reading Room of the Library of Congress: "When these perforated roll companies and these phonograph companies take my property and put it on their records they take something that I am interested in and give me no interest in it. When they make money out of my pieces I want a share of it."

Next up, Herbert easily drove Sousa home from second base.

> I would like to say that Mr. Sousa and I are not here representing ourselves as individuals and our personal interests, but we stand here for many hundreds of poor fellows who have not been able to come here . . . brother composers whose names figure on the advertisements of these companies who make perforated rolls and talking machines and who have never received a cent, just as is the case with Mr. Sousa and myself. Morally, there is only one side to it.

Unfortunately, there turned out to be many sides to this lengthy and bitter debate. An inventor named G. Howlett Davis suggested that it was he, not the composer, who actually brought music to the heart of the heartland, through his mechanical devices. He accused Herbert and Sousa of trying to steal the bread from his family's table. "This law attempts to reach out and take away from the inventor the product of his brain and to deliver it over to the composer."

Davis also accused the piano roll maker the Aeolian Company of trying to become a monopoly and to control the marketplace by signing deals with the major publishers for the use of their material, a tangential issue still at that point tangled up in the courts, but one that resonated with the opposition. This opposition included a representative from a group of independent piano roll makers, who also opposed the composers. S. T. Cameron of the American Gramophone Company ingeniously compared songwriters to instrument manufacturers. "Suppose I should come here and say to you that every time one of Mr. Sousa's cornet players played the cornet that I had sold to him that he should pay me [a] royalty for having played it! That is what he is asking of you."

Six months later, when the hearings reconvened, a representative of the manufacturers, F. W. Hedgeland, feared that compensating the composers would result in a public hardship borne by the poor consumer, an outcome he could not bear to witness. Herbert's contemporary in the classical field, Reginald De Koven, author of "Oh, Promise Me," took up the composers' chalice with uncommon bile. Because he was too ill to deliver his speech in person, his comments were read into the record: "This clause, as you doubtless are aware, was inserted into the bill to give a long-needed protection to composers, who for years have suffered from the depredations of a number of mercantile companies and corporations . . . who have taken—I had almost said stolen—their copyright works without so much as saying 'by your leave' and grown rich on the sale of them."

By 1907 there were two bills competing for consideration, one from Republican Representative Frank Currier from New Hampshire, favoring the manufacturers, and the other from Republican Senator Alfred Kittredge of South Dakota, favoring songwriters. Here again the tireless Herbert shouldered the load for his peers. Now president of the nascent and short-lived Authors' and Composers' Copyright League (with John Philip Sousa as treasurer and the eloquent De Koven as secretary), Herbert wrote educational letters, articles, and essays for national publications, collared congressmen, and eventually represented the American Federation of Musicians at further hearings.

Herbert was concerned not only with the ongoing copyright seminars in Washington but also with the progress of a suit brought by the White-Smith Publishing Company against the Apollo Company, manufacturers of piano rolls, for infringing the copyrights on two of their songs, "Kentucky Babe" and "Little Cotton Dolly," written by the blind composer Adam Geibel. As with most cases involving their rights up to this point in time, songwriters were poised to take a drubbing. If recent legal history held true, the courts would agree with the businessmen: that each newfangled invention designed to appropriate the songwriter's work for profit was immune from the copyright law as it now existed and its owners need not return a penny to the songwriter. The lawyer for the White-Smith Publishing Company summed up the feelings of his client, and the feelings of songwriters everywhere, with this defining statement from the public record:

> On behalf of the appellant it is insisted that it is the intention of the copyright act to protect the intellectual conception which has resulted in the compilation of notes which, when properly

played, produce the melody, which is the real invention of the composer. . . . It is the intention of the copyright act to prevent the multiplication of every means of reproducing the music of the composer to the ear.

But precedent favored the piano roll industry. In 1892 Judge LeBaron Bradford Colt had decided in their favor in *Kennedy v. McTammany*. Similarly, the British court system ruled against songwriters. Thus, when the *White-Smith v. Apollo* decision in favor of the piano roll manufacturers finally rolled down from Justice William R. Day in February of 1908, it came as no great shock to the songwriters. Day did, however, add, almost as a sidebar, a slight window through which the hefty Herbert and his cronies would later attempt to climb, aided and abetted by another unlikely booster.

It may be true that the use of these perforated rolls in the absence of statutory protection enables the manufacturers thereof to enjoy the use of musical compositions for which they pay no value. But such considerations properly address themselves to the legislative and not to the judicial branch of the government. As the act of Congress now stands we believe it does not include these records as copies or publications of the copyrighted music involved in these cases.

On the heels of Day's declamation came the concurring opinion of the famed Supreme Court jurist, poet, and son of a writer, Oliver Wendell Holmes Jr. Although on the surface agreeing with Day's decision in *White-Smith v. Apollo*, he immensely furthered the songwriters' cause in rhapsodic language the great Victor Herbert must have appreciated:

The result is to give to copyright less scope than its rational significance and the ground on which it is granted seem to me to demand. The ground of this extraordinary right is that the person to whom it is given has invented some new collocation of visible or audible points—of lines, colors, sounds, or words. On principle, anything that mechanically reproduces that collocation of sounds ought to be held a copy, or if the statute is too narrow, ought to be made so by further act.

Whether as a result of Holmes' poetry or Herbert's relentless vociferousness, the revised copyright bill was signed into law in March of 1909, on President Roosevelt's last day in office. The two-cents-per-copy royalty gained for all songwriters on the sale of their creations on mechanical devices both known and unknown, though less than what they wanted, was a whole lot more than they expected.

Less publicly pondered and fought over, also tucked into this bill, down in section 32B, was the clause that affirmed the songwriters' right to authorize and collect royalties for public performances of their work. But with the addition of the simple phrase "for profit," meant to grant immunity to certain charitable, church, and educational groups, the difficulty of gaining and executing the rights granted to songwriters in 1897 increased immeasurably.

It was this essential task, with all its apparent impossibility, that drove the nine founding members of ASCAP to a table at Lüchow's that rainy night in October 1913 to discuss the formation of America's first performing rights society. Seated beside Victor Herbert's powerful contingent were four of the more gifted theater writers of the day. Raymond Hubbell was the composer of the enduring classic "Poor Butterfly" and the more topical gem "If a Table at Rector's Could Talk," about the popular networking palace. Louis A. Hirsch's "The Bacchanal Rag" had been performed twice in *The Passing Show of 1912*, a *Ziegfeld Follies* knockoff. Silvio Hein was cocomposer of the classic "He's a Cousin of Mine," introduced by Marie Cahill in *Marrying Mary* and later made more famous by Bert Williams, the blackface comic who just happened to be black. Gustave Kerker had written *The Belle of New York*, in which Edna May had become a star singing "She Is the Belle of New York" (she would then play the same part in the film remake of 1916, entitled *Salvation Joan*). All of them were more than founders; they would serve ASCAP and the cause of songwriters everywhere nobly until they died.

Rounding out the nine was Puccini's American publisher at Ricordi, George Maxwell, who responded to the original challenge laid out by his opinionated Italian client by assuming the presidency of ASCAP, a position he held for the first ten years of the Society's existence.

That existence became official on February 13, 1914. At the Hotel Claridge, in front of a hundred songwriters, Maxwell was elected president and Burkan laid out the Articles of Association—based initially on the earlier French society, SACEM, but revised, over the course of the four months leading up to that meeting, to reflect American realities. Informally convening at Rector's or the Lambs Club during that period, the various founders, propelled by the hard-charging Herbert, the eloquent Hubbell, his "Poor Butterfly" collaborator John Golden, and the tireless Burkan, hashed out the basics of ASCAP, adopting the European principle of distributing royalties to all members based on performances, with each type of performance, from a song to a symphony, gaining a numeric value. Also adopted was the European system of allotting royalties: one-third to composers, one-third to lyricists, and one-third to publishers.

Meanwhile, the founders began collaring the lion's share of the city's songwriters and publishers at their various haunts and hangouts up and down Broadway, until by February such eminences as Irving Berlin, Jerome Kern, Charles Harris, and Gene Buck had started believing that such an organization could be possible, even in the face of its daunting mission. For while it was one thing to collect a licensing fee from the restaurants, bars, movie theaters, and cabarets that lured in customers with their lavish floor shows featuring the popular tunes of the day, it was quite another to unite under one roof a pair of historic antagonists: songwriters and music publishers. Certainly, on the songwriters' part, there was not a lot of trust built up over the course of doing business for the last thirty years. To put them in the same room together with their benevolent bankers was only asking for trouble.

It fell to treasurer-elect John Golden to find ASCAP's first office, six rooms above the Fulton Theatre at 46th Street and Broadway. Events continued favoring ASCAP that summer, when the Southern District Court of New York ruled for John Philip Sousa against the Vanderbilt Hotel in the first lawsuit to test ASCAP's assumed power to collect on infringements through public performances for profit. Sousa and his publisher, the John Church Company, had sued the Vanderbilt for their unauthorized performance of the tune "From Maine to Oregon" in the hotel dining room. "The hotel would not have paid for the playing of the piece unless in some way or other they were to gain thereby," wrote Judge Emile Lacombe, establishing the Vanderbilt's "for profit" motive. By the end of the year general manager John Loeffler had signed up 85 New York City hotels and restaurants, which paid an average of $8.23 a month for the right to use ASCAP music—including, of course, Victor Herbert's favorite eatery, Lüchow's.

But the heady rush of mission accomplished subsided when the Second Circuit Court of Appeals heard the hotel's appeal in February 1915, a month after ASCAP's first anniversary, and Judge Henry Ward reversed the decision.

> We are not convinced . . . that the defendants played "From Maine to Oregon" for profit within the meaning of those words in our copyright act. If the complainant's construction of it is right, then a church in which a copyrighted anthem is played is liable, together with the organist and every member of the choir, not only to injunction, but in damages . . . and the individuals perhaps to fine and imprisonment.

With the image of frightened parishioners being hauled off to the penitentiary for singing songs of praise and worship, not for the last time ASCAP's moral foundation, business ethics, and public relations persona were shaken to the core.

Despite the chilling precedent set by the Vanderbilt case, Burkan showed his mettle by going forward with Victor Herbert's case against Shanley's restaurant a month later. But in light of the Vanderbilt decision, and in the face of the rage ASCAP's collection mandate inspired, the new Society was hemorrhaging members left and right, especially among the publisher segment. Of the 22 signed up in 1914, by 1920 only six remained (Leo Feist, the House of Witmark, Harms, Charles Harris, Shapiro Bernstein, and Maxwell's employer, G. Ricordi & Co.) who hadn't been scared off by the American Federation of Musicians' outcries in all the trade publications that ASCAP's newly ordained performance royalties would be taken straight from their pockets, since the Hotel and Restaurant Association was threatening to reduce the number of musicians in their house orchestras. The leader of the AFM suggested that no union orchestras should play ASCAP songs. When he tried to appeal to their finer instincts, even Victor Herbert was booed off the stage at their annual meeting in Bridgeport, Connecticut, at the end of 1914. In court Herbert fared just as dismally, first losing his case in the district court in May of 1915 and then, on appeal, in January of 1916.

By that time, ASCAP's original office manager and staff, John Loeffler, had departed, replaced by a Burkan apprentice, Julius Rosenthal, who relocated the office to the top floor of 56 W. 45th Street. As staunch and determined as "Rosey" turned out to be, at first he had little to do but sit at his table in a broken-down chair and stare out the window as licensing activities dried up. Even the typist he'd hired was reduced to tears because ASCAP couldn't provide her with a typewriter.

The songwriters had put up a fight, but every wag on the street expected they'd soon be back at square one, dependent on the whims of chance to supplement the pittance they were paid by the publishers of Tin Pan Alley and the theatrical producers of Broadway. None of them took into account the fortitude of Herbert or the eloquence of Burkan, or the ace in the hole waiting in robes on the Supreme Court.

Oliver Wendell Holmes Jr., already the author of a favorable opinion in *White-Smith v. Apollo* in 1908, approached the *Herbert v. Shanley* decision in January of 1917 having been in 1899 the plaintiff on the losing side of his late father's copyright battle over his book of essays, *The Autocrat of the Breakfast-Table*, which had fallen into the public domain over a technicality of the law. (Had he recused himself due to his personal feelings on the subject, would ASCAP, let alone popular music, have recovered and thrived?)

On the day the fateful decision was rendered, informal ASCAP historian and songwriter Raymond Hubbell was being lectured on the niceties of the case by feared Broadway producer Abe Erlanger in Erlanger's office. He ducked out in the middle of this diatribe to take a call from fellow composer Silvio Hein informing him that Holmes had reversed the Court of Appeals decision, "giving Burkan a 100 percent victory for ASCAP."

Holmes' decision read in part,

If the rights under the copyright are infringed only by a performance where money is taken at the door, they are very imperfectly protected. Performances not different in kind from those of the defendant could be given that might compete with and even destroy the success of the monopoly the law intends the plaintiff to have. It is enough to say that there is no need to construe the statute so narrowly. It is true that the music is not the sole object, but neither is the food, which probably could be got cheaper elsewhere. The object is a repast in surroundings that to people having limited powers of conversation, or disliking the rival noise, give a luxurious pleasure not to be had from eating a silent meal. If music did not pay it would be given up. If it pays, it pays out of the public's pocket. Whether it pays or not, the purpose of employing it is profit, and that is enough.

Decree reversed.

While the Holmes decision gave ASCAP a crucial right to a continued existence and the renewed ability to collect money for performances, as Hubbell recounted, the world did not change overnight. "Did the phones start ringing? Did a single publisher who'd banqueted together with us when we were all one family offer congratulations on a victory which reestablished their ownership of the performing rights in their catalogues, or make any gestures towards a return to the fold? They did not." In fact, it took a huge conciliatory act by Burkan, much to the chagrin of ASCAP's songwriting core, to get the publisher members back to the table at all.

It was only when Burkan amended the bylaws in 1920 to give publishers half of the performance royalties, instead of the prevailing one-third, that they began en masse to swell the ASCAP rolls, joining their counterparts in the songwriting trade to make ASCAP a viable entity at last.

CHAPTER 2

BUCK STOPS HERE

D espite ASCAP's mandate from the Supreme Court given in the decision of 1917, it would take three more years before the organization started earning enough income to make its first royalty distribution to its writer and publisher members. In the meantime, it was left to Nathan Burkan to appoint lawyers he knew to oversee the momentous task of licensing movie theaters, hotels, nightclubs, and restaurants throughout the country, as well as carnivals, circuses, steamships, bowling alleys, and anywhere else a performance of music was apt to be heard. In Chicago, Manny Hartman helmed the first ASCAP field force in the Midwest. Philip Cohen handled Southern California. While the hotel industry was no pushover, movie theater operators were an even stauncher opponent. Before any of these reluctant potential clients could really test ASCAP's resolve, the war in Europe came along to shutter the leisure trades.

As the 1920s commenced, Prohibition put another damper on the nightlife of a nation, driving it underground, into the hands of criminals. Ironically, by attempting to collect their fees during this period, ASCAP representatives were often more reviled and feared than the Feds who closed down the speakeasies.

Writing in the *ASCAP Journal* in 1937, Herman Greenberg detailed his first years as a field representative in the early '20s.

Outside of New York there were at that time very few, if any, licenses in effect. Because of continuous, deliberate, and willful defiance of ASCAP's lawful rights, it was necessary to institute a great many infringement actions in the federal courts against unlicensed users of music in public performance for a profit. As time went on and case after case was decided favorably to us, exhibitors became more tolerant in their views and more receptive to the idea of operating lawfully.

However, the millennium had by no means arrived, and constant vigilance was required to induce licensees to fulfill the terms of their licenses, particularly as to payment of the stipulated fees. I was constantly in Federal and other courts. In 1921, after my first year with the Society, our gross income was $250,000.

Sustaining ASCAP in its first years in business were the restaurant, hotel, and nightclub performances taking place on "The Great White Way," a term eventually used to describe the glittering dozen-block theater district radiating from Times Square and Broadway.

"The most important thing was that all the show business people in the late teens and early '20s, whether it was Fanny Brice or Al Jolson, lived right on Broadway, so it was a village," said Jerome Charyn, author of the elegiac *Gangsters and Gold Diggers*. "There was a sense of community. Broadway had a tremendous creative energy. A lot of that had to do with growing up poor, whether it's Irving Berlin or the Gershwins. You have to rise out of poverty. That was very important."

By the time he joined ASCAP in 1914, Irving Berlin was already the most famous songwriter in America, and among its most prosperous publishers. "ASCAP was one of the great central things of his life," said his daughter, Mary Ellin Barrett. "He loved ASCAP. He fought its battles; he was excited by its triumphs."

An instinctive, prolific, and exacting writer, Berlin didn't reach his exalted status by ignoring musical trends. So although he was not crazy about Tommy Dorsey's 1937 revival of "Marie from Sunny Italy," according to his daughter, who was born in 1926,

he certainly didn't sit around deploring swing. When I was 14, he and my mother would take me and my friends to these hotel rooms where the big bands we loved were playing, like Tommy Dorsey, Benny Goodman, and Glenn Miller. At the parties I went to, and later on, in the nightclubs, they not only played brand-new songs, but they would play the old songs as if they were current. So you would hear "Blue Skies" or "Just One of Those Things" or "The Man I Love," like they'd been written yesterday.

The period starting in 1914 and lasting through the end of World War II is considered by critics as the Golden Age of pop songwriting. It was also a Golden Age for ASCAP. "The work of some of the composers for the musical stage is consistently ranked among the greatest songwriting of all, and inspired the best of the rest, setting a standard to aim at," Donald Clarke wrote in *The Rise and Fall of Popular Music* in 1995. "The American musical theater was a phenomenon second in importance only to jazz in establishing the commercial dominance of American popular music in the 20th century. Irving Berlin, Jerome Kern, George Gershwin, Vincent Youmans, Cole Porter, Richard Rodgers, and others broke the mold of operetta and turned the musical comedy into something as American as baseball."

The 1920s are also known as the Jazz Age. While ASCAP may have had its problems licensing speakeasies during the lawless 1920s, the jazz musicians of the era thrived there. "There would have been no Jazz Age and very little jazz without the white gangsters who took black and white musicians under their wing," wrote Jerome Charyn in *Gangsters and Gold Diggers*. "Legs Diamond once tipped Duke Ellington a couple of grand to play 'St. Louis Blues.' . . . Al Capone idolized Gershwin and could whistle every note of 'Rhapsody in Blue.'"

"The clubs were all owned by underworld figures, who supported everything to do with music," Charyn elaborated. "You have to remember, at this point the gangsters, because of the speakeasy, were able to enter into high society. So they invested in things they would not have ordinarily, from the ownership of the New York Giants baseball team to *Show Boat*."

Reporting in *The Night Club Era* (1933), Stanley Walker wrote, "During the first years of Prohibition, the new children of the night wanted swift dance music and no curfew. Moreover, they were able to pay for what they got. The Palais Royal had Paul Whiteman, the

Moulin Rouge was in its prime, and there were the Bal Tabarin, the Beaux Arts Café, the old Little Club, the Montmartre, the Tent, and the Monte Carlo."

One of the most important clubs of the era was the El Fey, on West 54th Street, where, according to Charyn, "café society was born, that curious mingling of high and low—sophomores from Yale, chorus girls, crime and sports reporters, impresarios, white jazz singers, bootleggers, millionaires, movie stars, playboys, heiresses, gamblers, politicians, composers, and playwrights."

When its legendary hostess, Mary Louise Cecilia (a.k.a. Texas) Guinan, was famously arrested and led away to the orchestra's rendition of "The Prisoner's Song," one assumes an ASCAP royalty wasn't paid. Guinan was not held in captivity very long; she would go on to stamp her brand of sassy entertainment on the Del Fey, the 300 Club, the Club Intime, and Tex Guinan's. *The New York Times* described her clientele as "out of town buyers, theatrical celebrities, and a sprinkling of the social and underworld elite."

One place where blues and jazz were conspicuously missing was on the radio networks just beginning to take flight in the '20s as the most important purveyor of music. Since the networks, by the terms of ASCAP's blanket license, paid for the use of ASCAP music whether they used one tune or a hundred, they had little incentive to sample the wares of anyone not a member. And since ASCAP membership depended on the kind of popularity and record sales that only sustained airplay could provide, early jazz musicians were caught in a career-altering catch-22. While it's arguable whether ASCAP membership alone would have guaranteed regular radio play, the key point for the struggling jazz musician on the outside looking in was that only songwriters who were members of ASCAP were allowed to collect their performance royalties.

As time went on, ASCAP unquestionably became an important player in the development of jazz, eventually signing up most of the best jazz songwriters of the '20s and '30s—some at the peak of their careers, but many only after years of petitioning.

In the first category, Noble Sissle and Eubie Blake, who brought *Shuffle Along*, the first jazz musical, to Broadway in 1921 for 504 performances, became ASCAP members in 1922. That year, Henry Creamer (ASCAP, 1924) and Turner Layton introduced their future standard,

"Way Down Yonder in New Orleans," and Clarence Williams (ASCAP, 1927) wrote "'Tain't Nobody's Biz-ness If I Do," with Porter Grainger and Robert Graham Prince. In 1923, Richard C. McPherson, a.k.a. Cecil Mack (ASCAP, 1925), and James P. Johnson (ASCAP, 1926) wrote "The Charleston," introduced by Elisabeth Welch in the musical *Runnin' Wild*.

Other greats took longer to win acknowledgment. In 1923 Fletcher Henderson's group took over as the house band at the Roseland Ballroom. In 1924 he added New Orleans trumpeter Louis Armstrong to his line-up. Since jazz was ignored as a source for material by many of the major publishing companies, Henderson started writing his own songs, but he didn't become an ASCAP member until 1948. Ferdinand "Jelly Roll" Morton had a big 1923, with "Kansas City Stomp," "London Blues," "Mr. Jelly Lord," and "Wolverine Blues"—but it was not big enough to gain him membership in the Society before 1938. William Christopher Handy came into the ASCAP fold in 1924. Louis Armstrong broke through on his own in 1926, with many of his lyrics scripted by his second wife, Lillian Hardin Armstrong (ASCAP, 1957); Louis himself did not become a member until 1939. Edward "Duke" Ellington, who would join the Society in 1935, was scoring hits with "Black and Tan Fantasy," "Immigration Blues," and "Birmingham Breakdown" back in 1927. That same year, one of the great black lyricists of all time, Andy Razaf (ASCAP, 1929), collaborated with James P. Johnson and Thomas "Fats" Waller (ASCAP, 1931) on "Willow Tree." In 1930, he worked with Waller and Harry Brooks (who joined that year) on the classic "Ain't Misbehavin'," for *Connie's Hot Chocolates*, in which Louis Armstrong would emerge from the pit to take the solo. Also that year he cowrote Eubie Blake's much-beloved "Memories of You" and teamed with Don Redman (ASCAP, 1942) on "Gee, Baby, Ain't I Good to You," introduced by McKinney's Cotton Pickers, and with Fats Waller on "Honeysuckle Rose," introduced in the nightclub revue *Load of Coal*.

The ASCAP members who benefited most from the system as it was back then were the founders and their brethren, the theater and Tin Pan Alley writers of Broadway. And there could have been no better person to represent them than the Society's second president, Gene Buck, who took over for George Maxwell in 1924—within days, according to Raymond Hubbell, of several board members learning that the first president of the American Society of Composers, Authors and Publishers was in fact not an American citizen. Since this disclosure came to light during some unwanted newspaper coverage detailing a scandal involving Maxwell (who was eventually cleared), it was decided by all concerned, Maxwell among them, that a quick and unceremonious exit was in everyone's best interests.

As profiled in the *New Yorker* in 1932, Gene Buck was held in the highest regard by the songwriting community. "Few men command the trust and loyalty he does. Stage people and music people have been bringing their troubles to Buck since his early *Follies* days. He has been confidante and counselor, oracle and guide to thousands. Today he is the village padre of Times Square."

Buck had gone to work for Flo Ziegfeld in 1912, breaking in with "Daddy Has a Sweetheart and Mother Is Her Name," written for the actress Lillian Lorraine. Until Ziegfeld's second marriage, to Billie Burke in 1914, Buck roomed with Flo and, in addition to writing lyrics for the *Midnight Frolic* on the roof of the New Amsterdam Theater, served as his right-hand man and main talent scout. In this capacity he brought into the Ziegfeld camp such artistic types as the stage designer Joseph Urban, the comic monologist Will Rogers, and comedians Ed Wynn and W. C. Fields. Buck continued to write for the *Follies* until 1926, at which point he'd already been the unpaid president of ASCAP for two years.

Not that he was hurting for money. According to the *New Yorker* profile, he lived with his wife and two sons on a three-acre estate in Great Neck, designed by Joseph Urban, that had its "own orchard, truck garden and vineyard." It was a neighborhood that included the writer Ring Lardner, Ed Wynn, Broadway's own George M. Cohan, the actress Lillian Russell, the droll comedian Groucho Marx, Oscar Hammerstein II, the dancer Marilyn Miller, the pie-eyed crooner Eddie Cantor, and the newspaperman Herbert Bayard Swope, whose fabulous weekend parties were said to have inspired scenes in F. Scott Fitzgerald's *The Great Gatsby*.

Located on East Shore Road in Great Neck, Swope's place was the Jazz Age incarnate, a weekend retreat for the wits of the legendary Algonquin Round Table, among them rabid poker and croquet players like Irving Berlin biographer Alexander Woollcott, *New Yorker* editor Harold Ross, playwright George S. Kaufman, and Groucho's silent brother, Harpo Marx. According to Alfred Allan Lewis in his biography of Swope, *Man of the World,*

> In the summers the house in Great Neck had a permanent sleep-in population of 16 family members and servants. There would be about 10 more in residence every weekend. As many as 40 more would drive out from the city or from other parts of Long Island for Sunday lunch and remain for dinner. Originally, Sunday dinners were buffets. People would get plates of food and wander off to find seats on the porch or in the living room. Fitzgerald, followed by a crowd of admirers, would wander far afield to the gazebo, where the group would ensconce themselves with a couple of bottles of Swope's excellent bootleg whiskey. The revelers never brought their dishes back. Sometimes they would not even bring themselves back but would curl up in the gazebo or in the garden and go to sleep. Fitzgerald was famous for having slept on every lawn from Great Neck to Port Washington.

Among Buck's major challenges of the 1920s was the arrival of the talking pictures. Ever since the evening of October 6, 1927, when the first feature-length talking picture, *The Jazz Singer,* opened at the Warner Theater on 51st Street starring Al Jolson, the relationship between ASCAP songwriters and the silver screen has been a resounding home run. Al sang four pop songs in the movie—all of which became hit singles again in 1928—as well as "Blue Skies," Irving Berlin's hot new number from the show *Betsy*, which collected six covers in 1927, including the number one version by Ben Selvin. A year later, *The Singing Fool* premiered at the significantly bigger Winter Garden, containing the two-sided number one smash "There's a Rainbow 'Round My Shoulder," written by Billy Rose and Dave Dreyer, and "Sonny Boy," written by Buddy De Sylva, Lew Brown, and Ray Henderson (both titles also credit Al Jolson as a cowriter). "Sonny Boy" was the first American million-selling record, spending a whopping 19 weeks on the charts, including 12 at number one, both longevity records for Jolson. In the first published survey of ASCAP writers' performances, put out in November of 1928, these were the top two songs, garnering 396 and 352 performances, respectively.

On the other hand, ASCAP's early relationship with the men who ran the movies and especially the movie theaters was more of a two-base error.

"The Alley had had a long relationship with the movies, beginning, in a sense, with the song slides of the '90s—transparencies illustrating a song that were projected during vaudeville performances," Ben Yagoda wrote in *American Heritage* magazine in 1983. "With the popularity of silent films there were theme songs that accompanied pictures and were repeated so often that audiences presumably developed an addiction and bought the sheet music immediately on leaving the theater."

As far back as 1922, the Motion Picture Theater Owners Association had tried to form its own licensing group to compete against ASCAP, but they could never get it off the ground. An action brought to restrain ASCAP on the grounds that it was a monopoly was resolved in ASCAP's favor in 1924, enabling ASCAP's field force to start collecting fees from every movie theater in America that wanted to use ASCAP music behind its silent screen.

The advent of the "talkies," like any emerging new delivery system, created as many problems for ASCAP as opportunities. One of the first blows to the bank accounts of ASCAP songwriters came when Nathan Burkan, among the world's leading authorities on copyright, determined that the performance of a song in a movie constituted a "grand right" and thus was not within the scope of the ASCAP charter, which only covered what the Copyright Act referred to as the "small rights." Traditionally, "grand rights" related to dramatic performances of a song on the Broadway stage or in an operatic work, and were negotiated between the individual songwriter, the song's publisher, and the show's producer. In a similar fashion, songs placed into movies were also one-time deals between the principals. As far as future performance royalties went, ASCAP writers and publishers could collect only from the owners of the movie theaters in which the film containing their song or songs was shown.

"In the past ten years of sound pictures," Hubbell wrote in the late 1930s, "you have listened to a whole pile of songs and as long as the theaters in which they were publicly performed had an ASCAP license, the rest of it was none of the Society's business."

Soon this situation would dramatically change, but not before a lot of ASCAP songwriters enjoyed a virtual Hollywood gold rush.

It started in 1933, when a piece of material arrived in the office of Warner Brothers producer Darryl Zanuck that would change everything. The ASCAP writing team of Harry Warren and Al Dubin were handed a set of galley proofs of a book called *42nd Street*. "Dubin and I sat down and wrote the score practically from the galleys," Harry Warren told Max Wilk in the book *They're Playing Our Song*. Including the number one hit "You're Getting to Be a Habit with Me," the film broke box office records and rescued Warner Brothers from bankruptcy. Soon many other ASCAP songwriters on Depression-struck Broadway started heading out west in their merry Oldsmobiles.

From 1934 through 1937, songs from Hollywood dominated the radio, written by some of ASCAP's greatest songwriting teams, including Mack Gordon and Harry Revel, Dorothy Fields and Jimmy McHugh, and George and Ira Gershwin. Cole Porter hit the top with the title tune from *Rosalie*. Irving Berlin certainly wasn't going to miss out on the action, scoring with "Cheek to Cheek" from *Top Hat*, "This Year's Kisses" from *On the Avenue*, and "I'm Putting All My Eggs in One Basket" from *Follow the Fleet*. In 1938, Johnny Mercer teamed up with Harry Warren for "You Must Have Been a Beautiful Baby" from *Hard to Get* and "Jeepers Creepers" from *Going Places*, and Frank Loesser and Hoagy Carmichael collaborated on "Two Sleepy People" from *Thanks for the Memory*. In 1939 Harold Arlen and Yip Harburg won the Oscar for "Over the Rainbow" from *The Wizard of Oz*. Of the 201 songs that hit the number one spot on the charts during the 1930s, nearly a third of them (65) originated in a Hollywood film. And all of them belonged to ASCAP. Not surprisingly, a small minority of publishing companies, many of them owned by movie studios, accounted for a vast majority of those hits. "It was a great period," Harold Arlen told Max Wilk.

> Maybe it was the accident of all of us working there because of the Depression. It was a sensational period. I went to the studio when I damned well pleased, or when they called *me*. Got my check every week. And we were pouring it out. Oh sure, we all wrote for pictures that were bad. But people were having flops

on Broadway too, weren't they? I wrote at home. I could write at midnight, or at five in the afternoon—it made no difference. As long as I came up with something the producers liked. And believe me, when it came to matters of quality, their guess was as good as mine.

It would not be the first time the public's perception of what was popular and what was good in music was altered, if not fixed, by powers unseen and out of their control. Or the last.

"The publishing houses were acquired primarily in an effort to avoid paying excessive prices for the use of music in films and to protect producers' interests in songs popularized in their films," wrote Lucia S. Schultz in an essay for *Notes*, the journal of the Music Library Association. "Once the venture had proved to be a profitable one, however, most of the companies expanded their operations. By 1935, these companies together controlled over half the music licensed by ASCAP."

Warner Brothers bought out the great Witmark imprint, which also housed T. B. Harms and New World Music, among others, giving them the catalogues of ASCAP greats like Victor Herbert, along with Cole Porter, Jerome Kern, Oscar Hammerstein II, Rodgers & Hart, and the Gershwins. Metro-Goldwyn-Mayer shelled out for Leo Feist, home of "Over the Rainbow," and Robbins Music ("Singin' in the Rain"). Paramount ("Thanks for the Memory") took over Famous ("That Old Black Magic"). In return for a hefty loan, Bourne Music, at the time co-owned by Saul Bornstein and Irving Berlin, got the rights to the first three Disney movies, including all the music from *Snow White* and *Pinocchio*.

With that onslaught, "Hollywood brought Tin Pan Alley to its knees," Ben Yagoda wrote. "The songwriter's gold rush was the publisher's downfall. After the initial burst of demand for Alley music, the movie companies eclipsed the publishers in importance and power."

Not surprisingly, Warner Brothers, for one, began to think of itself as a superstar publisher, deciding in 1936, under the leadership of vice president of music operations Herman Starr, that its ASCAP royalty classification wasn't high enough and withdrawing its 36,000 copyrights to start its own rival music licensing arm. But ASCAP was big enough to withstand the blow; radio, not wanting to antagonize what was still the major source of its music, simply stopped playing Warner Brothers' tunes. Nobody in the listening audience cared, except the Brothers Warner, who saw their movie profits dip when there was no radio airplay for the songs that plugged their movies. Similarly miffed were the ASCAP songwriters signed to Warner Brothers. The boycott lasted eight months, at which point Warner Brothers reluctantly re-upped with ASCAP. But the whole episode, especially its resolution, was a precursor of major troubles ahead.

Two years before the ill-advised Warner Brothers defection, the Justice Department, at the suggestion of the broadcasting industry, had begun a suit against ASCAP, claiming they operated in violation of the Sherman Antitrust Act. In June of 1935, the government portrayed ASCAP as "a gigantic music trust, unreasonably suppressing free competition in interstate commerce." But the case went nowhere. As reported in *Time Magazine*, July 1, 1935, the government's witnesses "wavered so under cross-examination that it was glad to adjourn to bolster up its case." ASCAP's lead lawyer here was, of course, the legendary Nathan Burkan, who rebutted the government's argument that "music is a commodity which is transmitted from state to state" by saying that music was "intangible and incorporeal." ASCAP also had Thomas Day Thacher, solicitor general under Herbert Hoover, working the case. He "pooh poohed the idea that the organization was potent enough to dominate an industry which includes such major interests as American Telephone & Telegraph Co., General Electric, Westinghouse, and the Radio Corporation of America."

Also in 1935, Senator Ryan Duffy brought a decidedly anti-ASCAP attitude to a bill he was trying to pass, recommending that the United States join the Berne Convention, which, according to Hazel Meyer in *The Gold in Tin Pan Alley*, "would have had the effect of nullifying the Supreme Court decision of 1917, by permitting local courts to decide on infringement cases without reference to the mandatory decree of the constitution." After his defeat, Duffy was on the record as saying ASCAP was "arrogant, unjust, uncouth, and should be put in its place."

The government suit was stalled in 1936, complicated by Warner Brothers' departure, which undermined the notion of monopoly. But throughout the remainder of the decade, ASCAP's right to exist was constantly challenged, if not by the federal government, then by the states. Starting in Montana and moving on to Washington, anti-ASCAP laws were proposed in thirty states, passed in nine, and went into effect in seven, including Florida, Tennessee, Nebraska, Kansas, and North Dakota. They all eventually failed on appeal. In Michigan, governor Frank Murphy vetoed the bill outright, stating, "The act is clearly invalid because it is an unconstitutional attempt to destroy the exclusive right of copyright owners, guaranteed to them by the United States Constitution and the federal copyright law."

Having avoided doing any business in Montana since 1937, Gene Buck tried to reinitiate collections in 1939 but was prohibited from doing so by a judge. When ASCAP filed suit, the judge put out a warrant for Buck's arrest on charges of extortion. Buck was captured in Phoenix, Arizona, on Washington's birthday, with bail set at $10,000. He was finally released from jail when the governor of Montana refused to issue extradition papers on the ASCAP president and the governor of Arizona said he wouldn't honor them even if he did.

Buck's eventual successor as ASCAP president, the generally mild-mannered classical musician and essayist Deems Taylor, described the situation this way in a 1939 note to the membership: "If you have been an observer of current events during the past half a dozen years, you could have enjoyed the grotesque spectacle of a national government, which grants copyrights, trying to destroy, via a monopoly suit, the only effective mechanism that copyright owners have devised for protecting those copyrights."

In 1942, the movie house owners of America were back in court, when 164 owners of independent movie theaters challenged ASCAP's right to collect performance fees in their theaters, claiming it was in violation of the Sherman Antitrust Act. Going back to the 1920s, movie theaters had been required to take out an ASCAP blanket license in order to show films with music in them. Since its membership agreement with its songwriters and publishers gave ASCAP the exclusive right to collect their performance royalties, any theater owners not licensed by ASCAP were effectively shut out of making separate deals with individual ASCAP writers, film producers, or distributors. Not only did this prevent them from showing most current movies unless they took out an ASCAP license, but it also gave ASCAP the ability, should it choose to do so, to raise the prices of such licenses indiscriminately.

In the suit entitled *Alden-Rochelle, Inc. v. ASCAP*, a decision was handed down that was emphatically in favor of the theater owners by the United States District Court for the Southern District of New York in 1948. "The allegation was that ASCAP and its members had conspired to essentially 'fix' the price of the music in the movies," said Richard Reimer, ASCAP's senior vice president of legal services.

> That was accomplished by the fact that the motion picture studios also controlled the music, and had their own music publishing companies, and so the theater companies were forced to deal with ASCAP. Thereafter, ASCAP and the Department of Justice entered into negotiations that resulted in a revised consent decree in 1950. So that's the reason why since then, in this country alone, there is no public performing rights license issued to the theater operator for movie music or the music in the films. We license movie theaters for their use of music before the film starts. You can have music playing when you walk into a theater in the lobby or you sit down and there's a slide show of community ads with music behind it, or the music playing over the speakers before a concert starts. But that's all ASCAP can license.

Nancy Knutsen, for years a senior vice president of film and TV at ASCAP and now a consultant, is also well versed in the unpleasant history of *Alden-Rochelle*. "After that, we could no longer get paid for music heard in movie theaters in the United States," she said. "So when their films are played anywhere else in the world, including Canada, our composers get paid, but not in their own country. That means when foreign composers' music is played in the United States, they don't get paid, but we expect our composers to be paid in their countries, so that can be tricky."

Writing music for films has been "tricky" to say the least ever since the medium began. "In most cases the studio or production company will require at least a portion of the publishing, because they feel the need to own the copyright," said Richard Bellis, who has for years run ASCAP's prestigious film scoring workshop.

The system was first challenged in the 1930s by the Screen Composers Association, a union founded by the legendary composer Bernard Herrmann. Said Bellis,

> They bargained with the studios for a number of years, until at one point they sued the studios because they wanted to retain their publishing rights. The composers who were negotiating with the studios at that time contended that the studios were publishers in name only, that actual music publishers would be exploiting their work in other marketplaces and the studios didn't do that. Over a period of seven years, the studios outlasted the composers. And then, after the composers went back and said they were ready to negotiate again, the studios said, "You've presented a bunch of witnesses who have testified to the fact that you're really independent contractors, so I don't think we're going to negotiate with you." So for all intents and purposes they busted the union.

By the early '40s, Gene Buck's tenure as president was over. But it was not the battle with the film studios and the movie theater operators that did him in. It was ASCAP's contentious relationship with the barons of the radio broadcasting industry, which had become the organization's largest source of performance income, that led to his eventual ouster. "Today, from radio alone," wrote Herman Greenberg in 1937 in the *ASCAP Journal*, "over my desk pass payments from approximately 600 stations, totaling in excess of $300,000 per month."

Toward the end of the decade and into 1940, ASCAP's pitched battle with radio captivated the media as much as it consumed Buck. In a 1940 article in *Harper's Magazine* entitled "The Battle of Tin Pan Alley," Leonard Allen quoted a weary Buck as saying, "This year will either see lasting peace or else ASCAP may become entangled in the greatest commercial conflict in the history of the American music business."

Was this any way to end a Golden Age?

CHAPTER **3**

RADIO WAVES

To fully understand how the thirty-year Golden Age of ASCAP came to an end, to be followed by the twenty-year Golden Age of its upstart rival, Broadcast Music Incorporated (BMI), it's necessary to go back to the beginning of ASCAP's tumultuous relationship with its number one client since the 1920s, the radio broadcasters of America. From the earliest days of radio's inception, when the broadcasters tried to convince the government that their business was not based on a public performance of music for profit—since their broadcasts didn't take place in front of an audience, they weren't making a profit, and, to top it off, it wasn't really music they were broadcasting, just beams of electrical energy—ASCAP knew it was facing a cagey and resilient opponent, not just for the short haul of five- and ten-year licenses, but, in the truest sense of a marriage, till death do them part.

At first, ASCAP let the young medium slide until it gained some traction in the marketplace. But as soon as it did, and ASCAP started coming up with an appropriate pay scale, the fledgling broadcasters' position was that rather than pay, they'd let the courts decide. In the 1923 case brought by M. Witmark & Sons against Bamberger's department store (owners of radio station WOR), the judgment came in ASCAP's favor. In 1924, the National Association of Broadcasters (NAB) was formed, expressly for the purpose of urging Senator Clarence Dill from the state of Washington to pass a bill that would effectively reverse the

Supreme Court ruling of 1917 in *Herbert v. Shanley* by declaring that music was presented on the air as a public service to listeners. For those greedy New York City songwriters and publishers to demand payment was a slap in the face to all the working stiffs of middle America who depended upon the solace radio provided. Instead, the NAB suggested, composers owed the radio gods their gratitude for deigning to promote their lowly songs.

Even before the Dill bill died a merciful death in Congress, the broadcasters were back in court. Highlighting the uphill quest ASCAP would face for decades to come, in 1924 the case of *Jerome H. Remick & Co. v. American Automobile Accessories*, where many of the earliest arguments were once more floated, was decided by an Ohio judge named Smith Hickenlooper in radio's favor. It was left to the Sixth Circuit Court of Appeals in Cincinnati to overturn it on appeal in 1925, the decision in part reading:

> A performance, in our judgment, is no less public because the listeners are unable to communicate with one another, or are not assembled within an inclosure, or gathered together in some open stadium or park or other public place. Nor can a performance, in our judgment, be deemed private because each listener may enjoy it alone in the privacy of his home. Radio broadcasting is intended to, and in fact does, reach a very much larger number of the public at the moment of the rendition than any other medium of performance. The artist is consciously addressing a great, though unseen and widely scattered, audience, and is therefore participating in a public performance.

Fifty years later, the Supreme Court made reference to this decision when adjudicating *Twentieth Century Music Corp. v. Aiken*, in which the owner of George Aiken's Chicken in Pittsburgh, Pennsylvania, was sued for infringement by the publishers of "The More I See You" and "Me and My Shadow" after the songs were heard over the radio in his establishment (which did not have a license from ASCAP). Although deciding in favor of Mr. Aiken, Justice Potter Stewart reached back to the past with one hand and well into the future with the other.

When this statutory provision was enacted in 1909, its purpose was to prohibit unauthorized performances of copyrighted musical compositions in such public places as concert halls, theaters, restaurants, and cabarets. . . . In short, it was soon established in the federal courts that the broadcast of a copyrighted musical composition by a commercial radio station was a public performance of that composition for profit—and thus an infringement of the copyright if not licensed.

In one of the earliest cases so holding, the Court of Appeals for the Sixth Circuit said: "While the fact that the radio was not developed at the time the Copyright Act . . . was enacted may raise some question as to whether it properly comes within the purview of the statute, it is not, by that fact alone, excluded from the statute. In other words, the statute may be applied to new situations not anticipated by Congress, if, fairly construed, such situations come within its intent and meaning."

To ASCAP's membership, radio came as a decidedly mixed blessing. After years of honing their promotional methods, publishers were loath to submit to the new technology. Where a song had once been allowed to gather its slow and steady momentum strictly through the applied efforts of publishers, radio had the power to instantly make or break a number, spinning it from obscurity to overexposure in the course of a few weeks. The publishing community held that sheet music sales, dependent on a song's exclusivity, would dry up if the song was too available. And they were right.

Writing in his syndicated column called "The Brighter Side" in 1938, famed Broadway chronicler Damon Runyon eloquently espoused the publishers' cause in terms that remain relevant today.

In the time of "Tin Pan Alley," a song that sold no more than 500,000 copies [of sheet music] was not deemed such-a-much by the trade. A real hit song sold into the millions. Today a sheet music sale of 250,000 is tremendous. The reason is the radio. It has knocked the sheet music sales cockeyed, as well as shortened the life of the song to just a few good long breaths. It has made the songwriting profession a mighty precarious one, though there are more songwriters today than ever before, and more songs are being written.

Despite early misgivings about the new medium, ASCAP licensed radio stations left and right in the early 1920s. In 1926, the NBC radio network was founded. In 1927, Columbia bought the United Independent Broadcasters network and CBS was born. In 1929, the trade paper *Variety* weighed in: "Burlesque, the beer garden, the music hall singer, the illustrated slide vocalist, the vaudeville headliner, the Broadway revue, cabarets, picture house presentations, public ballrooms. Nothing remains but the radio."

Nevertheless, in a desperate attempt to control radio's withering effect on the integrity of their music, many famous songwriters, mostly of the Broadway persuasion, tried their best to control how often radio stations aired certain of their songs, usually those contained within the score of their current Broadway show. This they did by demanding their publishers get special permission from them to allow a radio station to play a "restricted" composition—which permission would be granted at a much higher royalty rate. Soon the phrase "by special permission of the copyright holder" that radio announcers had to use to introduce such songs became so ubiquitous that it turned into a running joke with broadcasters.

ASCAP's new general manager, E. Claude Mills, addressed the embarrassing issue in a letter to the broadcasting community.

There has recently been a rather noticeable inclination on the part of announcers and masters of ceremonies to make a joke of or a facetious comment upon the announcement required to be made in connection with the rendition of restricted numbers—"By special permission of the copyright owner." It is requested that very definite instructions be issued that these practices not be indulged in. The purpose of the copyright owners in restricting the broadcasting of certain compositions is one of self-protection against excessive renditions. Restricted compositions are not included in the repertoire of the Society and we go to a great deal of expense and inconvenience in our endeavors to comply with the requests of broadcasters for "special permissions."

This directive apparently didn't go over very well. A few months later, Mills wrote to the 24 members of the ASCAP board of directors: "The public clamor against [the directive] has reached such a point that even newspaper columnists and the comedy magazines are beginning to poke fun at the announcement. It is bringing more ill-will than can possibly be justified by any remote benefit now received from the making of the announcement."

In this pressing matter, the 12 publisher members and 12 writer members comprising the board showed uncommon unity, leading to Mills' letter to broadcasters several weeks later.

With a view of conveniencing the operations of our licensees, our board of directors has authorized discontinuance of the requirement that the above announcement be broadcast at the time of a performing a restricted composition. The discontinuance of the announcement does not, however, in any way affect the continuance of the restricted list, which still remains imperatively necessary to safeguard certain works from excessive broadcasting and the complete destruction of their value as a part of musical comedies, etc.

If Broadway writers and their publishers were determined to keep some of their best tunes off the air, the band leaders who dominated the live nightly network broadcasts of the '20s and '30s, from Tommy Dorsey and Benny Goodman to Teddy Powell and Richard Himber, were all too eager to accept "cut-ins" from publishers, a piece of the action, in return for favoring a given tune on their programs. Most publishers loudly denigrated their peers for indulging in what they viewed as "payola" while proclaiming innocence themselves. As a not entirely disinterested third party, the authorities at ASCAP jumped into the fray with both feet. A lengthy letter written by Gene Buck on April 20, 1931, underlined their stance. Referencing discussions held at the most recent annual meeting of the Society, Buck's letter attempted to nip the "cut in" practice in the bud by banning one-time under-the-table payments, royalty cut-ins, or any other nefarious attempt by publishers to persuade artists to perform their songs.

Buck then quoted at length Article XIV, Section 4, in the Articles of Association of the Society, providing ASCAP's complaint committee the right to expel a member who violated the letter and the law set forth in the membership agreement, specifically: "To abolish abuses and unfair practices and methods in connection with the reproduction of musical works."

Buck concluded on an ominous yet forthright note: "All members are duty bound to notify the Society in writing of any instance where [royalty] regulations are violated. We feel certain that such of our members as have the future welfare of the Society at heart will cooperate with us to eradicate this serious evil which threatens the future of our industry."

E. Claude Mills brought another issue to the attention of the publishing community when he suggested that the ban on "restricted compositions" was often used as a bargaining chip in these illicit dealings with band leaders. On May 19, 1932, he wrote to the membership:

> The practice of publishers' representatives promising orchestra leaders blanket releases on restricted compositions as a consideration for favors to be extended in reference to unrestricted numbers is growing. This practice is nothing more or less than the equivalent of a bribe or a cut in, and the Society cannot be made a party to it. Members place the Society in an extremely embarrassing position when they grant these blanket releases, which amount to serious discrimination in favor of certain persons and against others. Please instruct your representatives that such blanket permissions are under no circumstances to be granted to orchestra leaders.

Although new on the job, Mills was a vociferous and impassioned defender of ASCAP's noble cause. He summed up the organization's mission and its plight in a 1932 essay entitled "What Is ASCAP?"

> Endeavors upon the part of the commercial users of music in public performances to so amend the Copyright Law, as to

whittle away the rights vested in composers and authors, is constant and never ending. These users do not want to pay, and the composers, in justice and good morals, must be paid. The Society is the sole hope and refuge of the indigent, aged, or ailing composer and author in our country. It is dedicated to the principle that no man or woman in the United States who writes successful music, or anyone dependent upon them, shall ever want. The butcher, the baker, the candlestick maker cannot be paid with honors and glory. They demand money. Our Society seeks the most equitable means of making it possible for them to live—by protecting them in their lawful rights and collecting for them their infinitesimal portion of the enormous profits made by commercial users of their products, which but for the availability of music, could not be successfully operated.

In 1932, a year in which record sales declined to six million from a peak of 110 million just ten years before, not only publishers and song-writers (as well as the musicians' union under the leadership of James Petrillo) were objecting to radio's drastic remodeling of the business. Some record labels had taken to affixing the warning "not licensed for radio broadcast" on their discs, another worrisome practice that soon enough had broadcasters seeking redress from E. Claude Mills.

Mills dutifully forwarded the broadcasters' concerns to Columbia Records, which drew a response from one of their directors, Arthur E. Garmaize. If radio's wanton repetitions served to devalue music, it was the intention of Columbia Records' Garmaize to remind them of

the labor and skill developed and employed over a period of many years at great cost in searching out and properly combining the constituents forming our physical records, the labor and skill very costly in time and money developed in impressing upon our records with an accuracy recognized by the public all over the world, the high priced and famous artists and orchestras, the expert orchestrations utilized and the famous and high priced artists and orchestras themselves in many cases representing a continuing expense through royalty payments, all combine to make our records a valuable property right.

As the decade neared its end, broadcasters' bickering with ASCAP, songwriters, and record labels had escalated to such an extent that drastic measures were being considered. These would take the form, espoused in the February 18 issue of the NAB bulletin, of "the establishment of an independent source of music supply." While the NAB was busy signing up stations to form their own rival performance rights organization to ASCAP, to be called Broadcast Music Incorporated, ASCAP went ahead and doubled the rates it was planning to charge radio, for the first time asking networks like NBC and CBS (two of BMI's major players) to pony up their share for their next contract, slated to begin on January 1, 1941. (BMI was not the first ASCAP competitor to emerge in the United States. A small, privately owned performing rights organization known as SESAC—the letters originally stood for Society of European Stage Authors and Composers—was founded in New York in 1930. SESAC is currently based in Nashville.)

The new rates were fair, said ASCAP, considering how much radio had grown since the last rate hike, and how much music it depended upon daily. The radio mavens replied, in effect, that they'd rather banish ASCAP music from the airways of America than submit to the proposed rate increase. At that point in time ASCAP music was the only music America was accustomed to hearing, ten out of ten on the hit parade, 100 out of 100 on the all-time list of evergreens. But if ASCAP had the lock on the greatest songs and songwriters of all time, the broadcasters could explain why: because of ASCAP's blanket licensing policies, whereby a station had to pay a certain fee no matter how much or how little ASCAP music they used, stations just couldn't afford to play anything else.

BMI knew, or at least hoped, there was other music worth playing—and any of its early executives who were single and desirous of a nightlife would have known for sure. According to Mark Coleman in his 2003 book, *Playback*, while radio limited its repertoire to ASCAP music, the jukebox had become the hidden arbiter of the underground culture. "Since jukeboxes were often situated in bars and restaurants, the repeal of Prohibition in 1933 greatly enhanced their appeal," he wrote. "Loud music for dancing fared best on the new machines. The rise of hillbilly and race records in the '20s continued apace in jukeboxes of the '30s: the hillbilly market tripled during 1930–32 alone. Half of all records produced in 1936 were destined for jukeboxes, and half of these jukeboxes were in the South. By 1939, 225,000 jukeboxes consumed 13 million discs per year."

Since jukebox plays were unaccountably excluded as public performances by the Copyright Act of 1909, ASCAP's early efforts to license them were fruitless. It was only after years of pitched battles in Washington, DC, that the Society succeeded in gaining but a pittance of the compensation its members felt they deserved, none of it retroactive.

An unlikely ASCAP ally against the radio industry (and, tangentially, the jukebox industry) was the American Federation of Musicians, led by the megalomaniacal and defiant James Petrillo—whose middle name was Caesar. As far back as 1927 Petrillo, then the president of the musicians' union in Chicago, had gone on the record as despising records and radio's predisposition to play them at all hours, claiming such "canned music" deprived live musicians of a living wage. To supplement their declining income, in 1929 he initiated the practice of installing a union musician or two at every radio station, just to flip platters and identify recording artists—the first deejays! And then suing the stations who refused to use them.

So the battle lines of 1940 were well defined, with the once plucky defender of the common man, ASCAP, now cast in the role of the old fat cat establishment, and the true fat cat titans of the broadcasting industry shedding their wolf's clothing in favor of lambskin, i.e., the vulnerable mien of the hungry, downtrodden young fingerpickers who made up much of BMI's rootsy repertoire. However, BMI was far from noble in matters of the music business. In fact, in the early days of BMI, according to author and professor Dave Sanjek, son of longtime BMI employee and historian Russ Sanjek, only publishers were members. "There was the implicit assumption from the people at BMI, to some degree with their hands over their eyes, that the publisher would then be distributing the performance money to the writers," he said. "It was a number of years before the writers themselves were formally and properly affiliated."

Even then, early songwriters were at the mercy of their labels and management to educate them on the niceties of music publishing, to say nothing of performance rights. "The company I was with, King Records, said there's no such thing," said Hank Ballard, author of "The Twist," along with a host of classic R&B hits. "On my early tunes I didn't have a BMI contract. I got it later, but they didn't even tell me I had to apply for it. They'd tell me, 'You've got to write 100 songs before you can get a BMI contract.' I found out later all you had to do is write one song. I didn't know there was so much money involved in publishing."

In the austere boardroom of ASCAP, high atop its new location at the RCA Building in Radio City, where most of the members had been secure in their positions for over a decade, including such regal eminences as Jerome Kern, Otto Harbach, Gene Buck, Max Dreyfus, Gustav Schirmer, and Will Von Tilzer, no one could accept that the Golden Age forty floors below would soon end.

So they responded to the threat by doing what they did best. They started planning a grand extravaganza of American music, to celebrate their upcoming 25th anniversary. The World's Fair was in New York City that year, but with the war in Europe casting a pall over the populace, the mood at the Fair was foul. That's when New York's nightlife mayor, Fiorello LaGuardia, and ASCAP's Broadway president, Gene Buck, put together a series of free concerts, the finale being two all-day events just coincidentally featuring nearly every big name on the ASCAP honor roll. ASCAP also planned a similar concert for the Golden Gate International Exposition on Treasure Island in San Francisco. Both events were scheduled to be broadcast and recorded.

Buck wrote an introduction for the program.

The American Society of Composers, Authors and Publishers, celebrating its 25th Anniversary, and honoring especially all American creative artists, presents with its compliments and deep gratitude to the whole American people, a week of music by native composers. The songs and serious works you will hear are all the products of the genius of our own free country. They were created by our own people—some of but a few years' residence—others whose ancestors helped to found the country. Serious and frivolous, sacred and secular, songs of the soil or works for the symphony—these compositions all speak a universal language to understanding hearts.

We are—thank God and the founding fathers—a free people, privileged under just laws to develop our talents unrestricted and unhampered by any form of political over-lordship. Let us miss no opportunity to recognize and praise—when deserved—the creations of our own people.

The event in San Francisco went off as planned on September 24, 1940, and it was by several accounts one of the greatest concerts in American musical history. The evening show was moved indoors to the 10,000-seat California Coliseum at the request of opera star John Charles Thomas (another 10,000 people crammed into the nearby Festival Hall to hear it over loudspeakers). In his autobiography, one of the night's spotlight performers, W. C. Handy, called it "a program that never before nor can ever again be duplicated this side of kingdom come."

Due to the ongoing battles with the radio broadcasters and the looming threat of their ASCAP boycott, the equally successful New York concert was never broadcast and never recorded. However, the San Francisco concerts survived, with a 78 of the proceedings turning up at auction 65 years later. A four-CD set was put on the market by the Music & Arts label in 1997, containing nearly 110 tracks, some of them the fevered introductions delivered by Deems Taylor for the afternoon program of classical music, and by Gene Buck in front of the evening's festivities. In sum, the concerts were a history of Tin Pan Alley, featuring performances by the writers of all-time classics like "Take Me Out to the Ball Game" (Jack Norworth and Albert Von Tilzer), "Love in Bloom" (Leo Robin and Ralph Rainger), "My Blue Heaven" (Walter Donaldson), "My Melancholy Baby" (Ernie Burnett), and "Sweet Adeline" (Harry Armstrong). Judy Garland, fresh from filming *The Wizard of Oz*, sang "Over the Rainbow," with Harold Arlen accompanying her on piano. Hoagy Carmichael played "Stardust," Jerome Kern played "Smoke Gets in Your Eyes" and "All the Things You Are." There were tributes to George Gershwin and Victor Herbert. W. C. Handy performed "St. Louis Blues," complete with a cornet solo. Peter DeRose performed "Deep Purple" with the San Francisco Symphony. Jimmy McHugh revealed that his song "I Can't Give You Anything But Love" was inspired by overhearing a guy talking to his girl outside of the famed New York City jewelry store Tiffany's.

Nodding to the somberness of world events, the concert rose to yet another peak with the appearance of the Broadway legend George

M. Cohan, who performed a medley of his biggest patriotic hits: "I'm a Yankee Doodle Dandy," "You're a Grand Old Flag," and "Over There." He was followed to the stage by Irving Berlin.

"As Berlin launched into a creaky version of 'God Bless America,' the audience stood up and joined him in singing it," a reviewer for the Web site Music Reports wrote about the 1997 release. "Berlin hadn't thought much of the song when he wrote it toward the end of World War I and stuffed the music in a trunk. In 1939, when singer Kate Smith asked him for a patriotic song, it now seemed to fit the times. Smith's radio rendition of it became the high point of her career. Now, as the shy and diminutive Berlin concluded the song, the applause rose like a tidal wave, and the concert ended."

It was as if ASCAP were throwing this historic night across the bow at the radio broadcasters of America. Take all of this amazing music off the air? You have to be kidding. The American public wouldn't stand for it. Yet that's exactly what they did. And not only did the American public stand for it, they hardly seemed to notice when, starting on January 1, 1941, the broadcasting industry eliminated ASCAP music from the radio waves of America on all but a few independent stations.

The government, however, did notice. As the radio wars were heating up through 1940, the Justice Department revived its antitrust suit against ASCAP, hoping for a quick settlement. But ASCAP resisted. Late in December, confounding the industry, the government then brought criminal charges under the Sherman Antitrust Act against not only ASCAP, but the nascent BMI, as well as NBC and CBS. In January 1941 BMI signed a consent decree and the government dropped its charges against NBC and CBS. In February, in front of U.S. District Judge Henry W. Goddard, sitting in New York, ASCAP finally accepted a consent decree as well, enabling the government to write the rules by which it would have to run its business in the future. The major changes were to ASCAP's membership criteria. Now, for songwriters a single published song, and for publishers a year in business, was all that was required to join the Society. The method of selecting the board of directors was also changed to make the process a bit more democratic.

"The logic of ASCAP's operations, particularly the logic of the blanket license, is the logic of monopoly; only by gathering all copyrighted compositions into its repertory could ASCAP give users a blanket license that would enable them to perform any musical composition without fear of a lawsuit," wrote Paul Goldstein in *Copyright's Highway: From Gutenberg to the Celestial Jukebox.*

But monopoly breeds discontent—and not only in the U.S. Congress and among the antitrust enforcers in the Justice Department. Many of ASCAP's newer members chafed under a royalty distribution calculus that they believed the founding members had weighted against them. But with no competing organization to join, they had to make do with the system devised by ASCAP's older members. It took a new technology, radio, to ignite this discontent and radically transform ASCAP's way of doing business.

ASCAP finally submitted to radio's demands in October of 1941, accepting a new deal that gave members about a third of the radio performance royalties they had been looking for when the negotiations started. Within a couple of years of ASCAP's return to the airwaves, however, income for the Society and its membership would return to and exceed former levels. Perhaps the main casualty of the Tin Pan Alley wars was Gene Buck. In April 1942, at ASCAP's annual meeting, he was asked to relinquish the position he'd held since 1924.

One of the first orders of business facing ASCAP's new president, Deems Taylor, was to restore collegial relationships with the organization's two most vociferous opponents, who were also the two entities most vital to its ability to operate successfully: the broadcasting community and the US government. At ASCAP's annual dinner, staged at the Astor Hotel in the fall of 1942, Taylor made sure the room was filled with all the important names from the world of radio, including the chairman of the Federal Communications Commission. Instead of the usual arguing, they invoked what would become an ASCAP tradition when facing necessary antagonists: they all broke into song.

Luckily, James Petrillo of the AFM wasn't in attendance; otherwise he might have shut the proceedings down. That July, under his command, musicians had gone on strike against the recording industry (because Petrillo believed that they were conspiring with radio broadcasters to put musicians out of work), with reverberations felt not only in songwriting, publishing, and radio, but in the creation of national musical trends. Now, just as deejays had made do with roots music, foreign titles, and public domain classics when radio forced ASCAP off the air, the labels made do with their stockpile of previously recorded sides, which radio stations were more than happy to play. As the strike continued through 1943 and '44, and this source of music dried up, former big band vocalists like Frank Sinatra and Perry Como (who had apparently received a bye from Petrillo) stepped into the breach to much acclaim, accompanied only by choruses. By the time the strike was settled, at the end of 1944, with several labels contributing to a fund that would provide backup musicians and sidemen with royalties for playing on records, the vocalists had supplanted the big bands as the favored music of the new postwar generation.

Although ASCAP lost a few members to BMI, the '40s started out somewhat quietly for the new performing rights organization. Future Louisiana governor Jimmie Davis wrote "You Are My Sunshine," sung by Tex Ritter in the film *Take Me Back to Oklahoma*, and used it as the theme song for his run to the statehouse. That song was part of pioneering country music publisher Ralph Peer I's huge Peer Music catalogue, which gave BMI most of its international hits in the early part of the decade, including "Maria Elena," "Perfidia," "Brazil," and "Besame Mucho," as well as an incredible stockpile of country music gems by A. P. Carter, Roy Acuff, and Bill Monroe, among others. ASCAP renegade E. B. Marks came over to BMI, bringing with him "Amapola," "The Breeze and I," and three songs made famous by Billie Holiday: "Strange Fruit," written by Lewis Allan; "Fine and Mellow," written by Holiday herself; and "God Bless the Child," cowritten in 1941 by Holiday and Arthur Herzog Jr.

BMI started gaining momentum in 1943, with Al Dexter's "Pistol Packin' Mama," the first country song to top the pop charts, but it wasn't until 1947 that it began focusing on country music and rhythm and blues, establishing a name and sound distinctly apart from what ASCAP was offering. Over a two-year period, not only did BMI corner the market on the biggest songs in these two emerging genres of American roots music, but because of its corporate ties, it was able to perform the even more amazing feat of getting them significant radio airplay. As epitomized by BMI songs like "That's All Right" by Arthur

"Big Boy" Crudup, "Good Rockin' Tonight" by Roy Brown, and "All She Wants to Do Is Rock" by Wynonie Harris, rock 'n' roll was right around the corner.

While the ASCAP board didn't see rock 'n' roll coming, they hardly sat out the '40s, although this story told by Duke Ellington's lyricist Billy Strayhorn illuminates some of the difficulties the radio ban created. As he told Stanley Dance in *The World of Duke Ellington*, "When we opened at the Casa Mañana in January 1941, we had air time every night, but could not play our library. We had to play non-ASCAP material. Duke was an ASCAP member, but I wasn't. So we had to write a new library and 'Take the A Train' was one of those numbers." Strayhorn eventually joined ASCAP and teamed with Duke on "Just A-Sittin' and A-Rockin'" and "Something to Live For." Nat "King" Cole kicked off his hit-making career in 1944 with "Straighten Up and Fly Right" and sent it into high gear in 1946 with "(Get Your Kicks on) Route 66," written by Bobby Troup. Lyricist Andy Razaf ("The Joint Is Jumpin'") and "I'm Gonna Move to the Outskirts of Town") was a major contributor. While Walter Bishop ("Jack, You're Dead") and Wilmoth Houdini ("Stone Cold Dead in the Market") kept the beat going, Dizzy Gillespie turned it around with the beginnings of bebop ("Salt Peanuts," "A Night in Tunisia")—although the earliest bebop performances, by Gillespie and Charlie Parker, were never recorded due to the musicians' strike. ASCAP writers and publishers also provided some future blues standards, among them "Going to Chicago Blues" by Jimmy Rushing and Count Basie, "Stormy Monday Blues" by Earl Hines, Billy Eckstine, and Bob Crowder, and "Back o' Town Blues," by Louis Armstrong. Several of R&B titan Louis Jordan's early works were ASCAP, like "Is You Is or Is You Ain't My Baby" and "Choo Choo Ch' Boogie," cowritten with Milt Gabler. Early rocker "The Honeydripper" by Joe Liggins belonged to ASCAP. By far their biggest success was spurred by the rhythmic twists of boogie-woogie, with ASCAP's Don Raye being particularly prolific in the genre, authoring such enduring titles as "Beat Me Daddy, Eight to the Bar," "Boogie Woogie Bugle Boy," "Cow Cow Boogie," "Down the Road a Piece," "Mister Five by Five," and "The House of Blue Lights." In the last two, with Freddie Slack, boogie-woogie met country music to form Western swing, a genre pioneered by ASCAP member Bob Wills in "San Antonio Rose," recorded in 1938 and a hit in 1941.

Still smarting from their battles with radio and their loss of movie theater revenue as a result of the *Alden-Rochelle* decision, the leaders of ASCAP could be forgiven for taking their eye off the approaching rock 'n' roll ball. Perhaps they were further distracted by the comforting glow of a new source of performances and revenue that they were convinced would restore the Golden Age. It was called television. On the revenue aspect, they were correct. As far as the Golden Age, they were dead wrong.

CHAPTER 4

TV VS. ROCK 'N' ROLL

The battles with radio and BMI would define the 1950s and much of the '60s for ASCAP. In 1953, for example, incoming ASCAP president Stanley Adams, in his capacity on the board of the Songwriters of America, inaugurated a $150 million lawsuit against BMI, alleging "un fair treatment by publishers, record company domination of the song business, payola, artist favoritism, moving picture company power in the music industry, and the closing of avenues for the display and performance of a song."

Such dramatic conflicts may have convinced ASCAP's membership that the Society's triumphal era was still in full flower, stalled only temporarily by forces outside its control. Once they were properly vanquished, normalcy in the form of the types of popular songs in which ASCAP writers specialized would return. Rock 'n' roll was merely a passing fad, totally the product of BMI's manipulation of the marketplace (to the delight of its ownership, the radio broadcasters of America). But the arrival of television, with its mission to provide family entertainment, seemed to promise a stylish, lavish, even spectacular alternative to radio, filled with regular performances of the kind of vintage ASCAP songs treasured by TV's older, more sophisticated audience.

With their inroads into television established as far back as the late '30s, it was no wonder ASCAP was banking on the new medium to swamp radio. According to *The Complete Directory to Prime Time*

Network TV Shows, 1946–Present, by Tim Brooks and Earle Marsh, a pioneering one-hour show called *The Wednesday Night Program*, broadcast in New York City in 1939, contained among its regular features songs by the Three Smoothies, whose members (Arlene Johnson, Charlie Ryan, and Little Ryan) had sung with bandleader Hal Kemp on the hits "Three Little Fishies," "Love for Sale," and "The Little Red Fox"—just the kind of mildly swinging music ASCAP assumed well-heeled, mature TV family audiences craved. Other shows were to follow in the '40s, populated by pleasant music of the ASCAP brand. Especially after the war, when R&B and country music were evolving into rock 'n' roll on the radio, television offered a comfortable respite from the din.

The first network variety show, *Hour Glass*, was broadcast over NBC on Thursday nights in 1946 and 1947 and featured Evelyn Knight, who benefited with two number one songs in 1948: "A Little Bird Told Me," written by ASCAP's Harvey O. Brooks, and "Powder Your Face with Sunshine," written by Carmen Lombardo and Stanley Rochinski. Homespun radio star and ukulele player Arthur Godfrey had two shows on the air in the late 1940s: *Arthur Godfrey and His Friends* and *Arthur Godfrey's Talent Scouts*. Among the easy-listening talent they shared were the Chordettes, Julius La Rosa, the McGuire Sisters, and Pat Boone. The bandleader was Archie Bleyer, who was running Cadence Records, home of BMI artists, the Everly Brothers.

The first of Ed Sullivan's Sunday night programs, known as *Toast of the Town*, aired in 1948, with a guest appearance by Richard Rodgers and Oscar Hammerstein II. (In 1968, Ed devoted a special 90-minute program to the music of Irving Berlin, who appeared at the finale, singing "God Bless America.") Comedian Jack Benny transitioned from the radio, bringing his ASCAP theme song, "Love in Bloom." Comedian Milton Berle transitioned from vaudeville, bringing his ASCAP theme song, "Near You." The highly influential *Your Show of Shows* was famous for the comedy of Sid Caesar and Imogene Coca, but also featured opera and ballet. In 1950, *Broadway Open House* showcased Eileen Barton, whose "If I Knew You Were Comin' I'd've Baked a Cake," written by ASCAP's Al Hoffman, Bob Merrill, and Clem Watts, spent ten weeks at number one that year. *Saturday Night Revue*, airing in 1953–54, was hosted by ASCAP vet Hoagy Carmichael.

In 1961, revenues from TV constituted ASCAP's single largest source of income.

Thus, while ASCAP's legal team, prodded and supported by the board, spent most of the decade in court attempting to squash BMI, deep in their hearts they must have believed, no matter what the outcome of the various anti-payola, anti-BMI proceedings, that the craze for roots music singles from dozens of pesky, hole-in-the-wall, fly-by-night labels and publishers was bound to wear itself out. Which is probably why ASCAP either rejected for membership or passed on such future legendary publishing outfits as Acuff-Rose (Hank Williams), Arc Music (Chuck Berry), Progressive Music (Ray Charles), Tiger Music (Leiber & Stoller), Pearl Music (Berry Gordy Jr.), Travis Music (Fats Domino), Lois Music (James Brown), Ludlow Music (Pete Seeger), Nor Va Jak Music (Buddy Holly), and Venice Music (Little Richard), while waiting for TV to restore the traditional balance.

Meanwhile, ASCAP cherry-picked what publishers, songs, and writers it felt might measure up to its standards. Always cognizant of the bigger picture, Elvis Presley, by way of his manager, Colonel Tom Parker, was savvy enough to establish an ASCAP publishing company, named after his mother, Gladys, to go along with his BMI company. Among the hits belonging to Gladys, and thus to ASCAP, were "It's Now or Never," "Good Luck Charm," "Can't Help Falling in Love," and "Stuck on You." The first successful collaboration between ASCAP's Burt Bacharach and Hal David would result in "The Story of My Life," a country hit for Marty Robbins in 1957. Eminent theater writer Charles Strouse had a lilting pop rock smash with "Born Too Late" for the Poni-Tails. Buck Ram, who wrote for and produced the Platters, established Panther Music in 1955 with "The Great Pretender." Slightly less exalted an operation, Ross Bagdasarian's Monarch Music ("The Chipmunk Song," "Witch Doctor") also belonged to ASCAP. Dion & the Belmonts' first hit, "I Wonder Why," written by Ricardo Weeks and Melvin Anderson, was published by ASCAP's Schwartz Music, introducing Dion DiMucci to an eventual long-term relationship with ASCAP. Bill Haley, who sang rock 'n' roll's first number one hit, "(We're Gonna) Rock Around the Clock," written by ASCAP's Max Freedman and Jimmy De Knight, opened his own ASCAP publishing company for "Skinny Minnie," which he cowrote. Two more slick ASCAP teams that would have much success in the '60s, Slay and Crewe ("Tallahassee Lassie," by Freddy Cannon) and Pockriss and Vance ("Catch a Falling Star," by Perry Como), broke through at the end of the '50s.

But the song of the most interest to the forward-thinking parties at ASCAP in 1959 may have been the Top Five trifle "Kookie, Kookie (Lend Me Your Comb)," written by Irving Taylor, sung by Edd "Kookie" Byrnes and Connie Stevens, and published by M. Witmark & Sons (which also published the year's most massive hit, "Theme from *A Summer Place*," by Max Steiner). Emanating from the popular TV series *77 Sunset Strip*, "Kookie" was just a small glimpse into the future of television as a hit-making machine in which even ASCAP writers could capture the elusive youth market seemingly owned by BMI.

Meanwhile, anticipating the continued prominence of sophisticated songs on TV and in the movies, ASCAP pinned its future on writers like Arthur Hamilton, author of "Cry Me a River." Although the song was eventually made famous by Julie London, Hamilton had originally written it for Ella Fitzgerald to sing in the film *Pete Kelly's Blues*, produced by Jack Webb, to whom Hamilton was under contract. "One day Jack came to me and said, 'A lot of people don't think Ella Fitzgerald would be believable singing the word *plebeian*,'" said Hamilton. "So I spent the next four days writing new bridges for the song so I could avoid that word. But I wasn't happy with any of them because they spoiled the song. So that's what I told Jack and he cut it out of the picture." Not only that, but since Hamilton's three-year contract was ending, Webb refused to renew it for another year. So at the time Julie London made the song a hit, Hamilton was collecting $57 a week in unemployment insurance. Said Hamilton, "The funny part is that four months later, after the song was a success, I went into a club on Hollywood Boulevard where Ella Fitzgerald was playing, and she was singing it. That's how I met her. I sent my name backstage and she came out to say hello to me, and I said, 'Did you know I wrote that song for you?' And she said, 'Nobody ever played it for me.'"

Adding a deliciously ironic twist to the story, Julie London just happened to be Jack Webb's ex-wife.

Far and away Hamilton's biggest hit, "Cry Me a River" made the Top 10 in 1955, just as the phenomenon known as Elvis Presley was cresting. Instead of representing the next wave of pop music, Hamilton was part of a vanishing ASCAP breed of TV / Broadway / Hollywood / Tin Pan Alley songsmiths being swept away with the tide. Of rock 'n' roll, he echoed the vast ASCAP ranks when he said,

> It was a language I didn't speak. I just simply disregarded it and wrote the stuff I knew how to write. The things that made me a writer were the songs that I considered, and still do, the best-written songs of that whole century, songs written by the Gershwins, Johnny Mercer and Harold Arlen, Rodgers and Hart, Rodgers and Hammerstein, Cole Porter. Those were wonderfully crafted songs and those are the songs that taught me how to write songs.

In 1969, when he joined the board of ASCAP, Hamilton sat next to the luminaries he idolized, like Harold Arlen, Cy Coleman, Morton Gould, Richard Rodgers, and Arthur Schwartz. One of his biggest personal crusades was to extract a payment from the jukebox owners of America. "I recall going to Washington a dozen times or more to discuss those issues and having special meetings with groups of jukebox owners," he said. "The jukebox owners kept saying, 'Well, we're putting your music in the boxes, people come in and they put quarters in there, and they play your music and it's making your music more popular. So why should we have to pay you?'"

This was an argument ASCAP had no choice but to go along with, since by dint of coincidence, collusion, or just plain oversight, jukebox performances had been specifically exempted from the Copyright Act of 1909. Yet since 1926 ASCAP had been introducing bills in Congress to eliminate what became known as the jukebox exemption. By the mid-'50s the fight with the jukebox industry had reached the same historic dimension of futility epitomized by the Brooklyn Dodgers, with ASCAP's scrappy, determined forces chanting, "Wait 'til next year" with undimmed fervor each time another bill, usually sponsored by New York Congressman Emanuel Celler, chairman of the House Judiciary Committee, withered on the vine.

In 1956, Celler was preoccupied by the ASCAP–BMI vendetta, as part of his ongoing investigation of the radio and television industries.

Testifying before the Judiciary Committee as reported in the *New York Times*, outgoing ASCAP president Stanley Adams said that BMI's collection methods, which did not assign songwriters any performance fees from broadcasting, had cost songwriters $75 million in lost revenues: "This is what the broadcasters, through BMI, have saved by depreciating the value of performance rights."

Appearing with Adams on behalf of the Songwriters of America, Jack Lawrence, Otto Harbach, Alan Jay Lerner, Arthur Schwartz, Oscar Hammerstein II, and others gave Celler a preview of the pending lawsuit against BMI (which also included the three networks, and Columbia and RCA Records), alleging that BMI's alliance with radio broadcasters led to a virtual blacklist of ASCAP songs on the air. As reported in the *New York Herald Tribune*, Adams said, "Now the criterion is not the merit of the music, but whether it is controlled by the broadcasters." Jack Lawrence's comments, noted in *Broadcasting-Telecasting Magazine*, were particularly dire: "Mr. Lawrence said that when ASCAP's contract with the networks expires next year, 'We fear a repetition of the 1941 blackout.' If such a blackout occurred, he said, he believes broadcasters could keep ASCAP off the air indefinitely."

Although ASCAP had been making similar arguments against BMI since it was formed in 1940, the stakes were rising as the new era of rock 'n' roll started surging. In *Big Beat Heat*, his biography of pioneering rock 'n' roll deejay Alan Freed, John Jackson quoted Freed's brother as saying that Alan's major claim to fame was "his impact in popularizing BMI-licensed rhythm and blues, which was probably the most vital factor in the bust-up of ASCAP domination."

In 1955, ASCAP started prohibiting its writers from collaborating with anyone affiliated with BMI. Between 1955 and 1956 ASCAP's performance income dropped 23 percent.

In the words of Cliff Doerksen, writing on popular music history for the *Chicago Reader* in 2002, "As profits slid, the old guard groped vainly for effective countermeasures." One of the most eloquent of early rock 'n' roll antagonists was Frank Sinatra, who called it "the most brutal, ugly, degenerate, vicious form of expression it has been my misfortune to hear, the rancid aphrodisiac of every sideburned delinquent on the face of the earth."

Emanuel Celler was not exactly an impartial observer, either, declaring the music "violative of all that I know to be of good taste" before
instigating a separate Justice Department investigation into BMI's practices in 1957. One prize ASCAP witness, the author Vance Packard, got
into trouble with the entire state of Tennessee when he cited country
music as being part of "the gross degradation in the quality of music
supplied to the public over the airwaves through BMI."

In *American Popular Music Business in the 20th Century*, Russ
Sanjek wrote that the then governor of Tennessee, Frank Clement, was
reported to have wired Celler that the case was "part of a scheme of a
small group in New York and California to gain complete control of
the music business." It was the same people "who for so many years had
prevented free enterprise in the American music industry."

Celler's 1957 bill died in committee. Early in 1958, the five-year-
old suit by the Songwriters of America was dismissed with a statement
that "Because the songwriter plaintiffs neither published nor licensed
their music themselves they were not directly engaged in any activity
that could be injured by an alleged conspiracy." But then, according to
Doerksen, "In their darkest hour, the anti-rock interests received a gift
from the gods: the quiz show scandals of 1958."

Led by Representative Oren Harris of Arkansas, the investigation
produced revelations that the handsome Ivy League professor Charles
Van Doren, who was one of the biggest winners of the popular program
Twenty-One, had been given the answers. After cleaning up the quiz
show genre, Harris was eager to prolong his time in the spotlight. In
1959 he segued into an investigation of payola in the music business,
in which deejay Alan Freed wound up taking the fall for an entire industry if not the entire history of gift, bribe, and bonus giving in the
music business since it began. Overlooked in the process, according
to Sanjek's book, was the widespread practice of "videola," in which
producers were illegally induced to play certain songs on TV. Two of
the prime perpetrators of "videola" were the same Jack Barry and Dan
Enright who produced *Twenty-One*.

Writing about Barry and Enright in *Variety*, Herm Schoenfeld reported that "they saw the gravy potential in TV music and set up their
own publishing company, Melody Music, which one year earned 100K

from ASCAP." From Sanjek: "Commercial bribery had become a prime factor in determining what was played on many network TV programs. Income from public performances allowed producers to ask for money before they selected music. In one case, reported in *Variety*, a TV producer asked for $5000 before he gave a publisher all rights to a theme song he'd written."

John Jackson wrote: "While the payola hearings did not directly inhibit the development of rock 'n' roll, they ultimately altered the sound of the music that the public heard on radio and television," such that rock 'n' roll became "almost as bland as the average legislator no doubt believed it should be."

Harris finally folded up his tent, but payola as an entrenched part of the hit-making process hardly followed suit. Quoted by Cliff Doerksen in the *Chicago Reader*, Robert W. McChesney, professor of communications at the University of Illinois at Urbana-Champaign, said, "You can't really believe the music you're listening to is there because some of it actually is good music. The idea that there's someone listening to the music who really knows music and cares about it has been corrupted."

As far as payola's place in the history of music, Doerksen admirably summed it up: "Nobody can distinguish by ear the payola-tainted tunes on the hit parade from the pure ones, because none of them is pure. Anyone who regards associating with payola as proof of aesthetic bankruptcy would be well-advised to leave the entire American popular songbook alone."

"To be honest, it did look like an antitrust thing," John Jackson elaborated on the validity of ASCAP's case against BMI.

> RCA and CBS were part owners of BMI, and they also owned RCA Victor Records and Columbia Records, so on the surface of it, it seemed like it was collusion. I can see ASCAP's point. These guys who owned the radio stations also owned the record companies that were making the music.
>
> ASCAP was basically older white men, and even in general society, all of the adults hated rock 'n' roll. So, with the members of ASCAP, not only were they older and they hated rock 'n' roll, but here is rock 'n' roll picking their pockets, so it was a two-pronged sword jabbing them. You can see that in

the payola hearings from 1959. Those guys really did hate the music and they really believed that it was only played because of payola. But Dick Clark proved you can't make a hit with a bad record. If you look at some of the records he played on *American Bandstand* that he owned on his record labels, that didn't become hits with all kinds of airplay, it was not true that you could make a hit. But without a certain amount of exposure, you could kill one.

Although they made as little headway against BMI as they were making against the jukebox owners, ASCAP kept the lawsuits flowing. "They were the biggest optimists," said Jackson.

After being hit on the head for 20 years they still kept pursuing the same thing, instead of saying, "Let's forget about trying to bring down BMI and use our resources and get a share of this pie." Because in the '60s the money aspect of it really ballooned as far as the total pie goes. When you compare the money in the '60s to what was going on in the '50s it was laughable as far as what they were originally fighting against.

By 1964, BMI controlled 80 percent of the *Billboard* Top 100. This did not escape the attention of either ASCAP or the US government, which sued BMI over antitrust violations in December. BMI settled at the end of 1966, signing a new consent decree stripping them of their side businesses in publishing and records. Perhaps not coincidentally, 1966 was also the year ASCAP started changing its payment formulas to entice young (i.e., rock 'n' roll) writers.

According to the September 3, 1966, issue of *Cashbox Magazine*, "As part of the new procedure, ASCAP will now make advances to writers based on evidence of current activity, such as listings of songs in trade paper publishing charts." *Variety* reported, "Under ASCAP's new proposals, any writer will be permitted to elect to start out on a current performance basis." The Society also revamped its royalty reporting schedule to a method that "puts a new writer on the same footing with older members."

Billboard quoted ASCAP's returning president, Stanley Adams: "With these proposals, ASCAP hopes to accomplish three objectives: first, to give all possible aid, encouragement, and financial assistance to new talents who wish to enter the songwriting profession; second, to keep songwriting as a profession alive and independent; and third, to build an American musical repertory equal to the stature of our nation."

Most ASCAP writers had been enrolled in a program called the Four Funds, which was based on a formula that rewarded those with a long history of hits, at the expense of current performances. "It was a very complicated system," said Paul Adler, who was in charge of membership during the late '60s and early '70s.

> It was so complicated that I once spent months going back and forth about it with the songwriter who used to say he was the one who designed it. The way you tried to sell it to people was that in a business known for its ups and downs, it gave you some sense of continuity, so if you can't get arrested after having a couple of good years, you've still got money coming to you. It was a point of view that some people bought into, but that over time they were less and less interested in. Early on, when the organization was a much smaller one, there were reasons for doing it, tax reasons for deferring income—which disappeared over time. The younger generation of writers really wanted to have the money sooner rather than later.

"Finally, a few board members realized they needed to change the payment system in order to get the contemporary repertoire or ASCAP wouldn't have anything," said former longtime ASCAP membership VP Todd Brabec, who broke in working for Paul Adler.

Nevertheless, in 1967 BMI still claimed 78 percent of the Top 100 and 92 percent of the country charts, as well as 100 percent of the rhythm and blues charts. "When I started there in 1967, it was right around the time they started actively going after rock," said Paul Adler.

> For a long period of time when ASCAP and BMI were engaged in an open battle to sign and keep writers and publishers, if you needed to pay a substantial sum of money to sign

someone there was a committee you had to go to, chaired by Leon Brettler of Shapiro Bernstein. Leon devoted a lot of time to that. I remember talking to him on evenings and weekends. He understood that for ASCAP to have any kind of long-term usefulness in the industry, you had to have a catalogue that users want to use. So he was very much involved in the Society's outreach. He made friends everywhere he went.

Leon Brettler was on the board for 40 years. "He was one of the great old-time salesmen," said his son Michael, who now runs Shapiro Bernstein, one of ASCAP's original founding publishers.

ASCAP was a fundamental part of his life. He loved ASCAP. He said he ran "the green army," whose purpose was to make money for songwriters and publishers. He'd go to the board meetings in a full combat uniform as Generalissimo Snowflake. I think he took out a trademark on the name. He was a go-getter. He disarmed people with his charm and then he'd go get them with his brains. He really understood the issues and how to get things done. He always saw the big picture, that things had to be right on a macro level for this company to survive. If you get some bad legislation out there, it could be devastating.

One of Brettler's biggest priorities was to awaken the ASCAP board to country music. "My father loved country music," said Michael Brettler. "He understood that country music was viable; it wasn't just a bunch of hillbillies. He was a big mover and shaker in getting ASCAP to open a Nashville office and go into competition with BMI—because BMI was dominating the market at the time."

In the rock arena, ASCAP's long climb back to contemporary viability through the '60s was indirectly helped by a character even more unlikely than Giacomo Puccini in 1910 or Leon Brettler in 1960: one Bob Dylan, who signed with Lou Levy in 1961.

Lou Levy, top man of Leeds Music Publishing company, took me up in a taxi to the Pythian Temple on West 70th Street to show me the pocket-sized recording studio where Bill Haley

& His Comets had recorded "Rock Around the Clock"—then down to Jack Dempsey's restaurant on 50th and Broadway, where we sat down in a red leather upholstered booth facing the front window.

This is the first sentence of Bob Dylan's autobiography, *Chronicles*. On page two, Dylan explained, "I had just signed a contract with Leeds Music giving it the right to publish my songs, not that there was any great deal to hammer out. I hadn't written much yet. Lou had advanced me $100 against future royalties to sign the paper and that was fine with me. John Hammond, who had brought me to Columbia Records, had taken me over to see Lou.

"'John's got high hopes for you,' Lou said."

"I once asked my father, how did you know enough to sign Bob Dylan?" said his son, Leeds Levy, now a publisher himself. "His story is that Dylan had been sent over by John Hammond, a guy who everybody respected, so he had that going for him. My father said that he was intrigued with [Dylan's] performance of 'House of the Rising Sun,' and he said on that basis he signed him. And I thought, well, my father was a compulsive gambler, so that was very possible."

After Dylan's first album, Albert Grossman and his partner Roy Silver started managing him. They brought him to Artie Mogull, who was operating out of Witmark Music at the time. "Blowin' in the Wind" had been written but not yet released. Dylan's mentor at Columbia Records, John Hammond, described what happened next in his book, *John Hammond on Record*.

Dylan sang "Blowin' in the Wind" one night in a Greenwich Village joint before his record was out. Peter, Paul and Mary happened to hear it, liked it, and took it to their manager, Albert Grossman, to arrange for recording it in their next album for Warner Brothers records. Their songs were being published by Artie Mogull, and when he heard "Wind" he wanted it. Of course, Dylan told him that Lou Levy had already signed him for all his songs. Mogull said he thought he could take care of that. "How much advance did they give you?" he asked. "Five hundred," Bob said. Mogull handed him $1000. "Why don't you go find out if you can buy your contract back?"

Leeds Levy elaborated: "The irony of course is when my dad was out of the office, his number two couldn't stand the way Dylan looked. When presented with Mogull's offer, he said, 'Let me get this straight. I get the money back that Lou Levy blew on you, which is a complete waste of time, no one is going to cut these songs, and I make a profit? Great!'"

Mogull's company, M. Witmark & Sons, was one of ASCAP's esteemed charter members. With Peter, Paul and Mary's version of "Blowin' in the Wind" becoming a giant hit, according to Hammond, "the venerable American Society of Composers, Authors and Publishers was suddenly plunged into the marketplace of rock and folk songs."

With Dylan as a drawing card, ASCAP set out to capture the nascent folk music genre, which in 1961, despite its rootsy forbears, was now showing signs of appealing to a well-scrubbed collegiate demographic. Thus, along with Paul Stookey and Peter Yarrow, ASCAP soon gained signatures from Ian Tyson and Sylvia Fricker, of Ian & Sylvia (Tyson wrote "Four Strong Winds," Fricker wrote "You Were on My Mind"), Tom Paxton ("The Marvelous Toy"), Malvina Reynolds ("Little Boxes"), Gordon Lightfoot ("Early Morning Rain," "For Lovin' Me"), and Richard Fariña ("Hard Lovin' Loser"). By the end of the decade, Woody Guthrie's son Arlo ("Alice's Restaurant") would join, along with close Dylan associate Robbie Robertson of The Band ("The Weight").

In 1965, however, in one of the great moments of recent music history, Dylan became a rock star with the release of "Like a Rolling Stone," thereby enabling ASCAP to get a toe in the door of that domain. Among the highlights of the late '60s were the signing of the Doors, Bob Seger, and Janis Joplin and the luring over from BMI of Jimmy Webb, as well as Felix Cavaliere and Eddie Brigati of the Rascals.

"By the late '60s, the kind of longstanding Tin Pan Alley animosity that could fuel a narrative that identifies BMI with rock 'n' roll was frankly over," said Dave Sanjek. "But I remember as a kid my dad talking about early meetings of the Songwriters Hall of Fame, which was entirely composed of old school Tin Pan Alley interests, and him saying we should induct Chuck Berry. Chuck Berry? That shyster! I mean, old-line Tin Pan Alley writers couldn't get behind that stuff."

Neither could most ASCAP board members and vets, among them famed lyricist Yip Harburg ("Brother, Can You Spare a Dime?," "Over the Rainbow"). Speaking to Max Wilk in 1973, in his book *They're Playing Our Song*, Harburg tried to explain his feelings about the music all around him. "No more Rodgers, no more Gershwin, no more Arlen or Kern. Most of what I hear is written very naively and crudely, without real form, real taste. Here and there are glimmers of some kind of really good talent, but it's usually lost in the noise. I can't distinguish one song from another."

While the changes to ASCAP's membership and advance paying policies that allowed more young songwriters to consider entering the fold would presage a much greater piece of the action in the decade ahead, the Society would first have to weather yet another onslaught of legal debates over their blanket licensing practice, brought on by their old friends at the Columbia Broadcasting System. As reported by Jack Gould in the *New York Times* of December 22, 1969, CBS had told ASCAP, "The network will pay only for music it uses on television, ending a 35-year practice of giving the music licensing organizations percentages of its gross broadcasting business."

Since the lawsuit also involved BMI, the threat of a huge music strike loomed. "The CBS move is perhaps the most significant event in broadcasting's use of music since ASCAP withdrew its catalogue and set off the music strike of the late '30s," the article concluded.

In fact, it would take an entire decade for the case to wend its way through the legal system, all the way up to the Supreme Court, which decided against CBS. As reported in the *New York Times* of April 18, 1979, "Justice Byron White said, 'In the face of available alternatives, the blanket license has provided an acceptable mechanism for at least a large part of the market for the performance rights to copyrighted musical compositions. We cannot agree that it should automatically be declared illegal.'"

But, writing in the same issue of the *Times*, music critic John Rockwell commented, "Yesterday's Supreme Court decision concerning the licensing of music used on network television involves one of the knottiest issues in the whole field of broadcast law. It is so knotty, in fact, that the case the Supreme Court decided yesterday has been in the courts since 1969 and a CBS spokesman said yesterday that his side would 'definitely' pursue the matter further."

Thus, for an organization whose charter was effectively created "at the discretion of Congress" there would be no lasting peace, either for the short haul or in the long run.

But if anxiety was part of ASCAP's daily DNA, so was survival.

"Organizations that rely on an enforced consensus are constantly faced with the possibility that a decision will be reversed, that the law will somehow be reinterpreted, or that it will lose the support of the existing agency," John Ryan wrote in his prescient 1985 book, *The Production of Culture in the Music Industry: The ASCAP-BMI Controversy.* "ASCAP was in a sense created by the legal system," he wrote, "and it was the legal system in the form of the Justice Department that tried to put an end to ASCAP." Ryan was speaking of the government's role in the rise of BMI in 1940—but he had nevertheless identified a thread that runs through ASCAP's 100-year history.

CHAPTER 5

THE
COMEBACK

I f the immediate result of the Bob Dylan effect could mainly be seen in ASCAP's swelling ranks of folk singers in the early '60s, the first whiff of a comeback to commercial parity with BMI began to be felt in the springtime air of Nashville by 1962, when Leon Brettler's venerable Shapiro Bernstein & Company provided ASCAP with several country hits. Merle Kilgore collaborated with Claude King on the massive "Wolverton Mountain," a number one country song that crossed over to number six on the pop charts. In 1963 Kilgore would cowrite another number one country crossover, "Ring of Fire," with June Carter. Among other promising signs, Shapiro Bernstein, as old-school Tin Pan Alley as anyone, opened up a small office in Nashville, and soon ASCAP followed suit, installing a woman named Juanita Jones in a two-room suite in the RCA Building. Before the ASCAP building went up in 1968, Ed Shea took over.

"In the '50s and early '60s, if you wanted to join ASCAP you would have had to go to New York," said one of Shea's early hires, Connie Bradley. "BMI was on 16th Avenue in Nashville and you could pull up, get out of your car, walk in, and join. In order to join ASCAP you had to either call New York, write to New York, or go to New York. It wasn't convenient. They didn't have anybody here who could tell you what a performing right was."

In essence, Nashville was a one-PRO town, presided over by a benevolent sheriff named Frances Preston, who eventually rose to the position of BMI president and CEO and was inducted into the Country Music Association Hall of Fame. "Frances Preston developed a strong relationship with the writers and the publishers, with the producers, and with the record labels," said Connie Bradley, "so everybody in Nashville automatically thought of Frances. She signed Willie Nelson, Dolly Parton, Porter Wagoner, Waylon Jennings—almost everybody." Though some legendary country writers like Jimmie Rodgers and Hank Williams had some ASCAP titles in the repertory early in their careers, Rodgers didn't become an ASCAP member until 1933, the year he died, and Williams never wound up joining ASCAP at all. Eventual ASCAP board member Fred Rose, cofounder of the legendary Acuff-Rose publishing company, originally joined BMI when ASCAP refused to grant him membership. As Gene Autry is famously quoted as saying, "It was easier for me to get into the White House than it was to get into ASCAP."

As much as she was Bradley's rival, Preston was also a family friend, especially close to Connie's father-in-law, country music pioneer and BMI writer Owen Bradley. "Owen and Frances socialized together, so I knew and liked and respected her," Connie Bradley said. "She was a mentor of mine, because it seemed like everything she did turned to gold. Not to watch her and not to emulate some of the things she did would have been stupid. She formed very strong friendships, and those kinds of relationships will last a long time."

In country music as in rock, ASCAP gained slow momentum through the '60s. Ed Shea signed Buzz Cason ("Everlasting Love"), Bobby Russell ("Little Green Apples"), and Billy Edd Wheeler ("Coward of the County"), among maybe a dozen others. But this was small potatoes compared to BMI. Even into the early '70s, courting a country songwriter, let alone signing one, could be as dangerous for an ASCAP rep (to say nothing of said writer) as attempting to collect a license fee from a speakeasy in the 1920s and early '30s. "Frankly, when I started, the writers down in Nashville were afraid to be seen with ASCAP people," said then membership director Paul Adler. "God knows what Frances Preston would do to them."

"You want to talk about being a pariah in town," observed veteran music publisher Nicholas Firth.

Remember the ads about the guy who sells the washing machines, how he's the loneliest guy in town? That was what it was like to be in ASCAP in those days. Juanita had run the ASCAP office down there for years. People liked her but nobody signed with her. I think Ed Shea had been the mayor, and he was a terrific glad hander, but I don't think he knew what the hell he was doing. Connie Bradley, if I remember correctly, was our secretary at Chappell in Nashville, who had once been married to one of our managers, Henry Hurt. She got a job at ASCAP and then she married Jerry Bradley, Owen Bradley's son, who was at RCA. Connie was a fantastic hire.

When Bradley arrived at ASCAP in 1976, she was one of the first female membership representatives hired there.

I knew as a woman I couldn't go to clubs and hang out all night and run with the boys, so I took another approach. My approach was to help them with their career, but more importantly, to do whatever I said I was going to do. A lot of people would give you lip service and you wouldn't see them again for a week or a month. If I told someone I was going to do something, they could count on it. I'll help you pitch your songs, put together a financial plan. The ones who were good enough, we'd try to set them up with cowriters. Part of my daily job was to sign new and up-and-coming writers and/or writer-artists.

Connie's family ties to the Bradley clan resulted in Ronnie Milsap joining ASCAP, but that didn't sway the reigning country superstars, Alabama. "I talked to Randy Owen about switching over once, because he was their big writer," said Connie, "but BMI had advanced him so much money and Frances was there for everything he needed. If he needed a tour bus, or whatever he needed, she was there. She did help him build his career, so he was loyal and I respected that."

Bradley's earliest triumphs were with soon-to-be legendary country writers Wayland Holyfield and Bob McDill.

I think the year before we signed Bob McDill he was BMI songwriter of the year. I went to his publisher at the time, which was Bill Hall at Welk Music, and I said, "I'd like to do a performance run for your writers, just do an exercise." I didn't know if we paid more or less than BMI, because I didn't know what BMI paid. But I could tell him what ASCAP would have paid. So we went through it, and I showed him title by title what we would have paid, and it was considerably more at that time, so it was profitable for them to make the switch. Because any time you switch performance rights organizations it's a big ordeal. Not only in the United States, but people all over the world are paying performance royalties to either ASCAP or BMI. So you've got to change world records. And songwriters feel close to wherever they are, so it's almost like a divorce when you leave one and go to another. So they had to think long and hard. Although some writers just flip-flop back and forth to whoever's paying the most that year. And by the time all the paperwork's done, they sometimes find out they would have been better off staying where they were.

The getting and keeping, as well as the losing of members, both journeyman and superstar, was always an issue for the membership department, primarily during the final quarter of each year. Because of the way ASCAP's agreements were drawn up at the time, any member could resign at the end of any year upon giving three months' notice. But if resigning was relatively easy, which, if any, songs a writer could remove from the ASCAP repertory was a much more complicated matter, dependent on the status of his or her cowriters' contracts, their various publishing companies, and the licensing agreements in place at the time of the proposed resignation. Some writers, discovering they were unable to move certain songs due to contractual licenses with radio or TV, often decided it wasn't worth the effort to move—while others jumped every few years in the hopes of gaining a few extra dollars.

When Wayland Holyfield switched in 1980, his publishing was represented by future ASCAP board member Dean Kay. It was, according to Holyfield, a relatively painless process. "It can be punitive if you switch and leave your catalogue because of their bonus system and they kind of hold it over your head a little bit," he said of BMI. "But Dean was able to work it out so we were able to switch the catalogue to ASCAP with the previous songs. Connie Bradley and Hal David had a lot to do with that."

But transferring from BMI to ASCAP, especially in those days, had less to do with money and the opposing philosophies of the organizations than it did with personal loyalty to BMI's Frances Preston. "She was a great friend of the songwriter and a great friend of mine," Holyfield said. "After I switched, later on we became civil again, but she took it personally. I was a pretty hot writer and it was helpful to ASCAP locally to say, 'Holyfield and Bob McDill and some of these other people have switched, so hey, maybe it's okay to be at ASCAP.'"

Although she didn't drink with the boys, Connie Bradley was a regular presence at the Grand Ole Opry and Tootsie's Orchid Lounge. "Every songwriter in country music used to hang out at Tootsie's," Bradley said. "Lots of songwriters and publishers slept on Tootsie's couch when they were down on their luck; she took care of a lot of them—Kris Kristofferson, Willie Nelson. There were other clubs in town, but none of them had any notoriety until the Bluebird Café came along."

By then it was the '80s, and ASCAP was on an equal footing with BMI in Nashville, largely due to Bradley's efforts. But she was quick to pay homage to her roots: "We wouldn't have jobs here today if not for country music pioneers like Ralph Peer I and Owen Bradley." In turn, it was ASCAP executives like Hal David, Connie Bradley, and Merlin Littlefield, and writers like Bob McDill and Wayland Holyfield, who helped open doors for the next generation of hit-makers.

One of these hit-makers was Don Schlitz, just off the bus from Durham, North Carolina, who was directed by songwriter Buzz Rabin to a publishing house looking for material.

So I go over to this place and this guy with curly hair and glasses comes out. The lady in front, the gatekeeper, says, "Is anybody listening today?" And he says, "Oh, I'm listening." I go in and I play four or five songs. I've got a harmonica on a rack like everybody had in those days. And I'm thinking, "I'm this guy's big break. I'm this guy's big break!" Right then and there he says, "You know what? Can we just go and produce some little demos on them?" He goes in the next room and says, "I want to show you what I'm doing. This guy's a friend of mine. This is a B side." So he puts the needle on it. The label was JMI, the artist was Don Williams. The song was "Amanda," and that man was Bob McDill, who for the first few years in Nashville was the only person who would listen to my songs. He turned out to be a big inspiration. What better teacher as far as learning about process?

Not too long after that first meeting, Schlitz was stuck for the ending of a particular song. In the manner of most folks in Nashville, he confided his problem to a fellow Nashville songwriter, Jimmy Rushing. "I said, 'I've got this one I can't finish. I think it's gonna take five more verses.' I played him what I had of the song; it was everything except the last eight lines. He said, 'You ought to finish that one.' It took about six more weeks to write. It took 20 minutes to write everything but the end . . . and then it took two years to get it cut."

The song was "The Gambler," and everybody in Nashville passed on it, including J. J. Cale, who did a demo of it. "It was a lot of words for Cale, too," said Schlitz. Eventually Schlitz put out his own version of it and it was covered by Hugh Moffatt. Neither version made it out of the country Bottom 40.

Merlin Littlefield was Don Schlitz's contact at ASCAP. At the time he signed, BMI had offered him a $50 advance. "You know what's funny; I could have used the money," said Schlitz.

I remember Merlin saying, "I'm not going to insult you by offering you money. This is who owns ASCAP. It's owned by the songwriters." I listened to him. He said, "I'll work with you; I'll do my best." So I signed with ASCAP after "The Gambler" came and went, and he kept pitching it to people. He pitched it to his friend, the producer Larry Butler. I got a call one morning at 10:00 after coming home from work. He says, "Larry Butler cut your song on Johnny Cash's album." The next day I get another phone call at 10:00 in the morning. "Larry Butler cut your song with Kenny Rogers." This is a good way to be awakened in the morning. So I remember going into Merlin's office and he had Kenny's record and said, "It's going to be the album title. It's going to be the first single." It was all Merlin.

While they were shoring up the Nashville front, as of 1972, ASCAP's share of the pop charts was down as low as 12 percent. "That's when they knew they had to change," said longtime publishing veteran Irwin Z. Robinson, who joined the board that year. "There were still people on the board who were living in the ancient days and who were upset by the way the rules for distribution were changing so that some of them lost their seniority."

"If you look at the charts at the end of the '60s it was really a strange mix, where rock 'n' roll was coming in but you had the *Hit Parade*–type stuff still in existence," said former ASCAP membership executive Todd Brabec. "And then at the start of the '70s, I think Neil Diamond and Hal David and Burt Bacharach were the only ones on the chart. The rest of it was rock 'n' roll, and R&B. I've got to be honest with you, when I first joined in 1971, because I went to all the board meetings as soon as I got there, some of these older writers were vehement against contemporary music."

But there were also forces on the board with the vision to know ASCAP needed to begin courting new writers. Its ability to pay advances that could match or better those offered by BMI was a major factor in the new gold rush. "There was a progress committee of the board that would deal with advances every month, led by Leon Brettler, and he really helped turn ASCAP around," Brabec said.

I had to present all the proposed advances to them, and we got an awful lot of people to switch based on financial inducements. Another thing ASCAP had going for them was that their contracts were shorter. At ASCAP there were year-to-year contracts. BMI's contracts were two years for a writer and five years for a publisher, so there was a big difference in how long you had to stay at a place. But ASCAP had no programs for newer writers. Finally, the board figured out that if they didn't have this new repertoire, ASCAP would go out of business. BMI had the bulk of the radio stuff. Then they raided ASCAP

in the '60s for TV and film composers. John Williams and a lot
of others went over based on these huge advances.

Breaking entirely new ground in terms of both genre and perception, Motown president Berry Gordy's decision to switch his massive
Jobete publishing empire from BMI to ASCAP in 1971 was a huge
milestone in the Comeback.

Gordy was concerned that other publishers were getting better deals
than he was at BMI. At ASCAP he was assured that under the ASCAP
payment system, scientifically designed, objective surveys of public performances guaranteed that all members were being paid on the same
basis. Once he was satisfied that ASCAP's radio surveys covered the
stations that most played the Motown catalogue, the deal was signed.

The Great Motown Switch was one of the first things Todd Brabec
worked on. "That really changed ASCAP's life completely," he said.
One of the things that changed because of a Berry Gordy demand was
that ASCAP writers gained the ability to collaborate with BMI writers,
overturning a ban of many years. "That was unbelievable," said Brabec.

Once they changed that, which was at the start of '71, it allowed ASCAP writers to cowrite with BMI writers and get paid
by ASCAP. With the Motown thing, we did a comparison for
Jobete's lawyer showing what ASCAP would have paid for all
of these great compositions. And these comparisons showed
that ASCAP would have outpaid BMI. It was a long negotiation, and probably in late '71, they moved over as much of their
catalogue as they could, which included Marvin Gaye, Stevie
Wonder, Smokey Robinson, Berry Gordy, and quite a few others. Some big writers stayed at BMI, but most of them switched
to ASCAP. And because of that, ASCAP's percentage in the
charts went from I think 15 percent to 25 percent overnight.

But many of the old-timers were still rooted in their Tin Pan Alley
suspicions. "At the very beginning there were songwriters on the board
who called me a BMI spy," said Irwin Z. Robinson, who at the time
was vice president and general manager of Screen Gems-EMI Music,
"because my catalogue was much heavier on the BMI side." He has

since helmed such major international companies as Chappell & Co., Paramount Music, Famous Music, and EMI Publishing.

Casting a pall over every otherwise optimistic reading of the record charts was the shadow of the big CBS lawsuit, in the form of similar cases that threatened ASCAP for two decades after the network sued in 1969.

"I started at ASCAP right after I graduated from law school in 1971," said Richard Reimer, who is senior vice president of legal services.

> Fairly shortly after I started I was asked to work on discovery in what was then a pending antitrust action. ASCAP had been sued in 1969 by the CBS Television Network. One of the allegations in the lawsuit was that the ASCAP blanket license offered to the television network was an unreasonable restraint of trade in violation of the federal antitrust laws. ASCAP had been accused as well of conspiring with its members to monopolize the ASCAP share of the performing rights market.

BMI was a codefendant at the trial of CBS' antitrust case, which was held in the Federal Court, Southern District of New York, before Judge Morris E. Lasker. Previously, the Court of Appeals for the Ninth Circuit had supported ASCAP, ruling in a case involving a radio station that the 1950 ASCAP consent decree effectively precluded the station's antitrust charges against ASCAP. In its brief to the Supreme Court in that case, the Department of Justice agreed with the result reached by the Ninth Circuit, bowing to the reality that songwriters needed "some kind of central licensing agency by which copyright holders may offer their works in a common pool to all who wish to use them." Citing the Justice Department's earlier brief, Justice Byron "Whizzer" White's 1979 opinion for the Supreme Court in the CBS case confirmed what had essentially been ASCAP's operating credo from the start.

> The extraordinary number of users spread across the land, the ease with which a performance may be broadcast, the sheer volume of copyrighted compositions, the enormous quantity of separate performances each year, the impracticability of negotiating individual licenses for each composition, and the

ephemeral nature of each performance—all combine to create unique market conditions for performance rights to recorded music. . . . the blanket licenses issued by ASCAP to individual radio stations were neither a per se violation of the Sherman Act nor an unreasonable restraint of trade.

In addition to antitrust issues that had plagued ASCAP for decades, the early ASCAP cases involving copyright infringements dealt with "public performances for profit" as the underlying principle for licensing in restaurants, movie theaters, and radio broadcasts. In 1976, Congress amended the Copyright Act for the first time since 1909. Among its other provisions, the wording of the act eliminated the phrase "for profit" from its performance requirement, replacing it with a number of exemptions that would ensure ASCAP's presence in court for many years to come, advocating to protect the rights of its members in proceedings with religious broadcasters, veterans and fraternal organizations, colleges and universities, jukebox operators, public radio and television stations, wired music, home taping, and record and video rental establishments, over who should rightfully be exempted from an ASCAP license.

As recently as the late '80s, the job of collecting fees for the use of music directly or indirectly in obscure bars and restaurants, pizza places, and grocery stores all across the country was still a daunting, complicated, and often dangerous job. Milwaukee-based publisher Keith Mardak got a call from ASCAP's then managing director, Gloria Messinger, one night shortly after he joined the board in 1989.

She said, "We have a serious problem in Milwaukee. Our licensing person is in jail. Do you have a good local lawyer we could use to get him out?" It turns out the guy was calling on some bars and one bar took exception and called some police friends. The cops arrested him and roughed him up, put him in jail, and he got roughed up again in jail by the prisoners. We got him out the next morning, but it was very traumatic and he quit.

This was nothing new. As far back as the 1920s and '30s, the job of collecting the ten- and twenty-dollar payments from the reluctant bar, nightclub, and tavern owners of America was not one for the faint of heart. Writing in the *ASCAP Journal*, Zelma Wooten, of the Salt Lake City, Utah, office, told of her travels with a friend through the Nevada desert in those early Wild West days, in 1937. "Pulling up at a service station next to what looked like an abandoned outhouse, we bought some gasoline and inquired about the dance which was advertised for that night. 'Well, if either one of you girls can play the piano, it won't take me long to drum up a dance,' the gas station attendant responded. 'If you want to stay here all night I have an extra bed in the shanty and me and the dog are the only ones around.'" She dutifully marked her file card "use of music inconsequential."

Most of the places Wooten and her friend visited were "very crude beer parlors and it often takes courage to enter them. So far we have been able to make our own exit, but time will tell." In Reno, they found a couple of clubs already licensed by ASCAP. But the third venue was suspicious.

> The management of this particular place had changed about six times within a few months, so we were anxious to find out what had gone wrong. About two miles from the city we were directed down a dark, narrow lane. There it was. It looked like an old barn, but a few cars were parked around it, so we went in. A few men were very busy with large glasses of beer. There were two small gambling tables operated by women, a lounge directly in front of the orchestra stand, and a small dance floor with a half dozen tables. The lounge consisted of three worn-out divans and two broken overstuffed chairs. A threadbare carpet was on the floor.

The atmosphere was so creepy, the ASCAP rep and her friend departed without questioning the owner. "As we left the place, the few that were there seemed to follow us out. We were almost afraid to get in our car for fear there would be some criminal hiding in the back seat. But we turned on the ignition and got away as fast as we could."

By the end of the '70s and into the '80s, probably the best job to have at ASCAP was in the membership department, which had grown from two or three paper pushers into a vibrant, nightlife-loving crew of approximately 40, some of them operating out of offices in Los Angeles,

Nashville, Chicago, Atlanta, and even Puerto Rico. In contrast to the staid, corporate atmosphere of the past, now music could be heard wafting through the corridors as staffers loudly sampled the latest releases of current and prospective members.

Debbie Rose joined the A&R team in the '80s. "There were no musical boundaries," she said. "I was able to work with every genre of music from hip-hop to punk rock to singer/songwriters." Among the people she brought to ASCAP were Shawn Colvin, Arturo Sandoval, and Sir Mix-a-Lot. "I was out every night looking for new talent, but it was never about signing everybody. It was about signing quality. We were on the very front lines, helping people get record deals and publishing deals and find lawyers."

Even in the newly vital atmosphere, there was palpable fear in every office that one chilling court case looming on the horizon could drastically affect ASCAP's income and way of doing business in the future. In *Buffalo Broadcasting Co. v. ASCAP*, "five plaintiffs who owned and operated one or more local television stations represented a class of all owners of local television stations in the United States who obtain music performing rights pursuant to license agreements with ASCAP and/ or BMI." At the time, these amounted to approximately 450 owners of approximately 750 local stations. These local station owners believed that because individually they lacked the power of CBS, the blanket licenses that ASCAP and BMI were offering them violated the antitrust laws insofar as the stations were required to obtain licenses for music in their syndicated programs.

Having just survived the network TV onslaught against the blanket license brought about by CBS, some might have thought a deep breath of relief was in order. However, in 1982, after a bench trial in the District Court for the Southern District of New York, Judge Lee P. Gagliardi held in favor of the plaintiffs, based on his conclusion that ASCAP and BMI blanket licenses were unreasonable restraints of trade because they required local TV stations to license music in all of their programs, even though they had not chosen the music for the syndicated programs. The decision barred ASCAP (and BMI) from "licensing to local television stations nondramatic music performing rights for any syndicated program"—once again bringing ASCAP to the breach and to the brink. In one swoop of a foul judgment, all royalty payments for writers of TV theme, background, and feature music played on 750 local stations were stopped in the mail and put into abeyance until such time as ASCAP could marshal its legal forces to the appropriate battlefield to take up arms against a decision that ran completely counter to the recently revised Copyright Act.

In outlining the Second Circuit Court of Appeals' decision on the appeal, which was argued on November 1, 1983, and decided on September 18, 1984, Judge Jon O. Newman offered a short course for the novice on the history of ASCAP's exhausting, lifelong battle to secure performance rights income for its membership.

"Perhaps encouraged by our 1977 ruling in favor of CBS, the local stations began this litigation in 1978," wrote the judge.

A four-week bench trial occurred in 1981 before Judge Gagliardi, resulting in the decision now on appeal. That decision holds that the blanket licensing of music performing rights to local television stations unreasonably restrains trade and enjoins ASCAP and BMI from granting to local television stations music performing rights in any syndicated programs. With respect to syndicated programs, the injunction thus bars ASCAP and BMI from offering either blanket or program licenses and also prohibits them from conveying performing rights to such programs on any basis at all.

If Judge Gagliardi's decision stood, an entire class of composer looked to be wiped out overnight. The decision hinged on "whether the plaintiff had proved that it lacked a realistic opportunity to obtain performance rights from individual copyright holders." Submitted in evidence were letters from various station owners attempting to shift the responsibility of determining the price of licensing music onto the program suppliers. In reply, one of these suppliers "made the entirely valid point that since syndication licensing without music performing rights had been the industry practice for years, it was Metromedia's responsibility to advise us in what manner you would like to change the current arrangements."

This evasive tactic cut little ice with Judge Newman, who said, in reversing Gagliardi, "Notably absent from all the correspondence tendered by the plaintiffs is the customary indicator of a buyer's seriousness in attempting to make a purchase—an offer of a sum of money."

With the shadow of CBS thus removed from ASCAP's rearview mirror at last, it was time for the Society to launch itself into a new Golden Age, this one increasingly based on service to its growing songwriting community.

CHAPTER **6**

SEEDING THE GARDEN OF CREATIVITY

One side effect of the favorable *Buffalo* decision was that after it both BMI and ASCAP agreed to stop paying advances. Far from hindering its operations, this decision served to kick the creativity of ASCAP's staffers into a higher gear. The ultimate result: with writers like John Mayer, Diane Warren, Elliot Goldenthal, Lin-Manuel Miranda—and some notable others—all getting a leg up from ASCAP and ASCAP Foundation initiatives, word got around that for an artist looking to be discovered, ASCAP was the place to be.

"That's when we started rolling out tons and tons of programming to help songwriters," said Debbie Rose of the membership department.

We created a lot of programs that had never existed before. Some are still going on. Some have been completely revamped and expanded. We had the theater writing workshop, six-week songwriting workshops twice a year, networking events so the songwriters could meet publishers, lawyers, and managers. We started a really successful showcase series where we put on bands and invited the creative community to come out. There were collaborator workshops where we set writers up with each other to create new songs and meet new writers. We put together the first Rhythm & Soul Music Awards, to recognize the growth in rap and hip-hop. We helped the dance music community try to figure out things, because they weren't getting the same kind of financial recognition because their music was only being played in clubs and not on the radio or on TV.

The ASCAP Foundation Musical Theatre Workshop was started in the late '70s by Charles Strouse, composer of such American classics as *Bye Bye Birdie*, *Annie*, and *Applause*. Over at rival BMI, Lehman Engel had been conducting a theater workshop since 1961. "I went to the board and I said, 'BMI, which is basically an organization that represents country writers and pop writers, strangely enough is doing a theater workshop,'" Strouse said. "So I pleaded the case that ASCAP ought to have one. After all, we were once an organization of theater writers."

The Strouse workshop took a different direction from BMI's approach. "What BMI does is more like a prescribed lesson plan of what needs to be part of a musical," said Ted Chapin, a veteran theatrical publisher, who is now president and executive director of the Rodgers and Hammerstein Organization. "ASCAP is more wide-ranging."

"Unlike what Lehman Engel was doing at BMI, my path was not to instruct them so much, but rather to play their works in front of choreographers and producers and critics and people of that ilk, producers particularly," said Strouse.

There was usually a panel of six to nine people, so aesthetic criticism crept into it, certainly from me. When Lee [longtime collaborator Adams] and I began to write shows, we found that the most instructive thing in the long haul was to keep playing the show for agents and producers, and the reception of it kind of sharpened our instincts. So I thought that process was better than telling somebody how to write the songs. Because of ASCAP, I was always able to get the very best people in the theater to come to our panels, so it was a wonderful lesson for the people writing.

Among the newer talents to emerge from the workshop was the late Jonathan Larson, who wrote the music and lyrics for *Rent*. Strouse doesn't recall being overly impressed by Larson at first, although one of the writers he persuaded to join the panel that season, Stephen

Sondheim, certainly was. Larson even referenced a phone call he received from Sondheim in his autobiographical musical *tick . . . tick . . . BOOM!* "I remember him having what I thought was an innocent use of rock," said Strouse. "But that so-called innocent use of rock stunned Broadway."

Once upon a time, during the Golden Age, Broadway songs and popular songs were one and the same. These days they are a breed apart. "They're usually two very distinct types of writing," Stephen Schwartz agreed. Perhaps the last pure theater writer to achieve a hit on the pop charts (with "Day by Day" from *Godspell* and "Corner of the Sky" from *Pippin*, which peaked in the Top 20 in 1972), Schwartz (who also wrote *Wicked*) took over the workshop when Strouse stepped down in 1992.

Where a hundred years ago songwriters like Irving Berlin emerged from poverty as teenagers to learn their craft on the street or at the feet of Florenz Ziegfeld, today's Broadway writers emerge from prestigious music programs at NYU or the Berklee College of Music and hope to get a job working for Walt Disney, whose productions of *Beauty and the Beast* (1994) and *The Lion King* (1997) helped transform Broadway. Stephen Schwartz commented,

> When I first started, people got their experience and training in other ways for theater. Now I think there are so many programs that have been set up for aspiring musical theater writers that a lot of people do come out of them. Another thing that has helped give opportunities to new writers is the arrival of movie studios, like Disney and DreamWorks. So, let's say one of those studios decides they want to turn their movie *Elf* into a musical. They won't necessarily go to Stephen Sondheim or John Kander or myself. They will give a chance to younger writers, and sometimes those things work out very well.

The preponderance of outlets for new work is something of a mixed blessing for Ted Chapin. "It's not that they don't have value," he said. "It's just if you're going to do a festival of 30 new musicals over two weeks, how many good ones can actually emerge?"

Schwartz would disagree with that assessment. "In general," he said, "I think it's a good deal easier for new musical theater writers to be heard and to be given a chance than it was back in the '80s. Part of that is because of the success of musicals like *In the Heights* or *Spring Awakening*, because it shows that a young talented first-time writer can have both a critical and a commercial success."

The team behind *Elf—The Musical*, lyricist Chad Beguelin and composer Matthew Sklar, met in 1993, when Chad was just gradu- ating from the NYU dramatic writing department and Matt was still an NYU undergrad with a part-time job as a pit pianist for *Les Misérables*. In addition to *Elf—The Musical*, they've collaborated on *The Wedding Singer*, *The Rhythm Club*, *Judas and Me*, and *Wicked City*. They are also past winners of the Jonathan Larson Performing Arts Foundation Award. Beguelin has written the book for the stage ver- sion of Disney's *Aladdin*. Much like their forebears, they were given a major boost by ASCAP via the ASCAP Foundation Musical Theatre Workshop in 1998.

"We sent in two shows," said Sklar. "One was fully realized and the other we'd only written part of, and we were accepted for the one we hadn't written yet. So that forced us to get moving on it." That show turned out to be *The Rhythm Club*.

"After we did the workshop, we got interest from commercial pro- ducers and got a production at the Signature," said Beguelin. "We have ASCAP to thank for that."

ASCAP's assistant vice president of musical theater and cabaret, Michael Kerker, has been involved with the workshop's selection pro- cess for over 20 years. "I would say we get about 200 musicals for New York and about 200 musicals for LA," he said. Schwartz has also held special workshops in Chicago and Miami, as well as one in 2010 at the University of Tasmania. He described the program's structure and its premise:

> It's basically two presentations, the first of which is about half an hour, and then there's usually a couple of weeks in between for them to do revisions, and then the second presentation is somewhere between 50 minutes and an hour. The only require- ment we have is that whatever section they present, it needs to be consecutive. One thing I learned from Charles is that people would come in and do their greatest hits, and it wasn't really

Top: An early 20th century view of Tin Pan Alley (West 28th Street in Manhattan), home to the sheet music publishers at the heart of the era's popular music industry.

Right: Irish-born composer Victor Herbert, a driving force behind the founding of ASCAP, served as the Society's vice president from 1914 to his death in 1924. Herbert's musical legacy includes many classic operettas, including *Naughty Marietta, Sweethearts,* and *Babes in Toyland.*

Justice Oliver Wendell Holmes Jr., who wrote the 1917 U.S. Supreme Court opinion in *Herbert v. Shanley*, which provided ASCAP with the legal backing to pursue licensing of music users. (Photo by Harris & Ewing)

Nathan Burkan (1878–1936), ASCAP's founding general counsel, who led ASCAP's legal efforts until his sudden passing at the age of 57.

(GENERAL)

MEMORANDUM OF AGREEMENT between AMERICAN SOCIETY OF COMPOSERS, AUTHORS AND PUBLISHERS (hereinafter styled "Society"), and

JOHN MATTER, operating MATTER'S BALLROOM

(hereinafter styled "Licensee"), as follows:

1. Society grants and licensee accepts for a period of **ONE YEAR** commencing **OCTOBER 13, 1936,** a license to publicly perform at **DECORAH, IOWA** , and not elsewhere, non-dramatic renditions of the separate musical compositions copyrighted by members of the Society.

2. This license is not assignable nor transferable by operation of law, devolution or otherwise, and is limited strictly to the Licensee and to the premises above named. The license fee herein provided to be paid is based upon the performance of such non-dramatic renditions for the entertainment solely of such persons as may be physically present on or in the premises described, and does not authorize the broadcasting by radio-telephone, transmission by wire or otherwise, of such performances or renditions to persons outside of such premises, and the same is hereby strictly prohibited unless consent of the society in writing first be had.

3. This license shall not extend to or be deemed to include:

   (a) Oratorios, choral, operatic or dramatico-musical works (including plays with music, revues and ballets) in their entirety, or songs or other excerpts from operas or musical plays accompanied either by words, pantomime, dance, or visual representation of the work from which the music is taken; but fragments or instrumental selections from such works may be instrumentally rendered without words, dialogue, costume, accompanying dramatic action or scenic accessory, and unaccompanied by any stage action or visual representation (by motion picture or otherwise) of the work of which such music forms a part.

   (b) Any work (or part thereof) whereof the stage presentation and singing rights are reserved.

4. Society reserves the right at any time to withdraw from its repertory and from operation of this license, any musical work, and upon any such withdrawal Licensee may immediately cancel this agreement. Either party to this agreement may, at any time, upon giving to the other party thirty days' prior notice in writing, by registered United States mail, terminate this agreement. Upon the termination of this agreement pursuant to any provision of this article "4", there shall be made to the Licensee a pro rata refund of any unearned license fees.

5. Licensee agrees, upon demand in writing of the Society, upon forms supplied by Society, whenever requested, to furnish a list of all music rendered at the premises hereby licensed, showing the title of each composition, and the publisher thereof.

6. Upon any breach or default of any term or condition herein contained Society may, upon notice in writing, cancel this license, and in event of such cancellation shall refund to Licensee any unearned fees paid in advance.

7. The parties hereto hereby agree that this agreement shall be deemed to be, and the same shall be, extended and renewed from year to year, unless either party, on or before thirty days next preceding the termination of any year, shall give notice in writing to the other by registered United States mail of the desire to terminate the same at the conclusion of such year.

8. Licensee agrees to pay Society for the license herein the sum of **THIRTY FIVE & NO/100** . . . . Dollars ($ **35.00**) annually, payable in advance at Des Moines, Iowa.

IN WITNESS WHEREOF, this agreement has been duly subscribed and sealed by Society and Licensee this **13th** day of **OCTOBER** , 19 **36**

AMERICAN SOCIETY OF COMPOSERS, AUTHORS AND PUBLISHERS

By......

In the 1930s, ASCAP's licensing of establishments using copyrighted music became a nationwide effort with the formation of district licensing offices. Pictured here is an ASCAP license agreement with a Des Moines, Iowa, ballroom from 1936.

"Rock Around the Clock," written by ASCAP members James E. Myers (Jimmy De Knight) and Max C. Freedman, was recorded by Bill Haley & His Comets in 1954. After it was used under the opening credits of the film *Blackboard Jungle* in 1955, it became one of the best-selling singles of all time.

The success of the novelty song "Kookie, Kookie (Lend Me Your Comb)," a tie-in to the hit detective show *77 Sunset Strip*, proved TV's power to sell music. The song, by ASCAP songwriter Irving Taylor, shot to number four o *Billboard*'s Hot 100 in 1959. Pictured are Taylor (*left*) and Edd "Kookie" Byrnes on the set of *77 Sunset Strip*. (Photo courtesy of the family of Irving Taylor)

ASCAP showed its deep commitment to Nashville when it opened a new building on the city's Music Row in 1969 (shown here). The building was replaced by a larger ASCAP structure in 1992. (Photo by Don Putnam)

On the next eight pages are some of the best-known ASCAP lyricists and composers who helped make the period between 1914 and 1945 a Golden Age of popular songwriting.

Duke Ellington (1899–1974) was one of many jazz greats to join ASCAP, along with Louis Armstrong, Count Basie, Benny Goodman, Benny Carter, Dizzy Gillespie, Ornette Coleman, and Wynton Marsalis. Ellington's original songs include "Mood Indigo" and "It Don't Mean a Thing If It Ain't Got That Swing."

Thomas "Fats" Waller (1904–1943). Original songs include "Ain't Misbehavin'" and "Honeysuckle Rose."

George Gershwin (1898–1937, *left*) and Ira Gershwin (1896–1983). Original songs written together include "I Got Rhythm" and "Embraceable You."

Oscar Hammerstein II (1895–1960, *left*) and Jerome Kern (1885–1945). Original songs written together include "Ol' Man River" and "All the Things You Are."

Top: Harry Warren (1893–1981). Original songs include "At Last" and "I Only Have Eyes for You."

Right: Hoagy Carmichael (1899–1981). Original songs include "Stardust" and "Lazybones."

Irving Berlin (1888–1989). Original songs include "Blue Skies" and "God Bless America."

Jimmy McHugh (1894–1969) and Dorothy Fields (1905–1974). Original songs written together include "On the Sunny Side of the Street" and "I'm in the Mood for Love."

Johnny Mercer (1909–1976). Original songs include "Skylark" and "One for My Baby (and One More for the Road)."

Jule Styne (1905–1994, *left*) and Sammy Cahn (1913–1993). Original songs written together include "Let It Snow! Let It Snow! Let It Snow!" and "Three Coins in the Fountain."

Cole Porter (1891–1964). Original songs include "I Get a Kick out of You" and "Night and Day."

Frank Loesser (1910–1969). Original songs include "Baby, It's Cold Outside" and "Luck Be a Lady."

Irving Kahal (1903–1942, *left*) and Sammy Fain (1902–1989). Original songs written together include "I'll Be Seeing You" and "Let a Smile Be Your Umbrella."

Jimmy Van Heusen (1913–1990, *left*) and Johnny Burke (1908–1964). Original songs written together include "Swinging on a Star" and "Imagination."

Richard Rodgers (1902–1979, *left*) and Lorenz Hart (1895–1943). Original songs written together include "Blue Moon" and "My Funny Valentine."

E. Y. "Yip" Harburg (1896–1981, *left*) and Harold Arlen (1905–1986). Original songs written together include "Over the Rainbow" and "Last Night When We Were Young."

helpful either to them or to the people attending. If you present a consecutive half hour, the problems are going to show up. If there are storytelling problems, if there are character development problems, if there are issues about how songs are being used, they are all going to show up.

Schwartz fills each panel with two or three other prominent members of the theatrical community: writers, directors, or similar experts, who can evaluate what they've heard and offer apt suggestions. However,

> I caution students, when you hear something that sounds smart and persuasive it can deflect you from your path. I tell them it doesn't matter from whom you are receiving criticism. It doesn't matter if it's the person you most admire in all the business; if what he or she is saying does not in some way resonate with you, and strike you as something you kind of knew already but just haven't done, or doesn't come as sort of a revelation, where you say, "Oh, of course, that makes perfect sense," then ignore that advice. Of course, when you have someone who is as respected and revered as Stephen Sondheim, one tends to take everything he says as gospel, but you have to remember that it's just his opinion.

The final performances are witnessed not only by the panel, but also by other writers. "Most of them are people who submitted and didn't get accepted or writers who did not submit but are writing musicals," said ASCAP's Kerker.

> One of Stephen's great gifts is that after the panel has spoken and after he has spoken, he'll make general comments on issues that writers need to think about—plus he skillfully distills all the suggestions from the other panelists—so that all the writers in the room will learn enough about their own pieces just by listening to the comments. Stephen is so good about knowing which musicals to use as teaching tools. He's just a brilliant teacher.

For aspiring film composers, the challenges are even more daunt-ing, but the dream is always the same: to write the score for an Oscar-winning film. Most composers, however, are way at the other end of the spectrum. "You work for IMDb credit," said Richard Bellis, who has run the ASCAP Television & Film Scoring Workshop for the past 17 years.

> You'll be on the Internet Movie Database. That's what they're offering. Some find out the hard way that if you wash cars for a buck then you're going to have to have them lined up around the corner to make a living. Some of the films they get are de-cent and others are just garbage, but they start off by taking a film without even looking at it. If you're doing it for free you should at least have the right to see the film.

It is in the hope of reaching the highest plateau, or at least leaving ground zero, that several hundred would-be composers submit their reels to the film scoring workshop each year, even though, as Bellis explained, "There is just not enough work to go around, because we have more people now wanting to be film composers than we ever have before in my lifetime."

This is more than confirmed by Nancy Knutsen, formerly the head of the film and television music department in ASCAP's Los Angeles office, now a consultant. "The biggest challenge is the fact that there are new generations of composers coming up through the ranks but the veterans aren't calling it a day yet, so you have composers in their 80s who are still working, and the people who are just starting have to compete with four or five generations of composers."

When Knutsen started at ASCAP in 1988, the film and TV depart-ment consisted of one other woman. "We shared an assistant and that was it," Knutsen said. "I developed it into a department of 12." She added,

> Ironically, when the idea of working at ASCAP was first sug-gested to me [by composer John Williams, her previous em-ployer], I kind of wrinkled my nose, because I thought it was only about royalty distribution. I certainly knew the history; I knew what it did as a copyright protection organization, but it

wasn't until I got the job that I saw there would be an opportunity to work with composers and produce events and things
like that. I think through the competition with BMI, in order
to attract new composers and songwriters and retain them,
there had to be something more than just handing out a check.
That's when the idea of career development, celebrating career
achievement, and doing outreach and networking on behalf of
our members started.

Another challenge facing film composers is that they are required
by the copyright law to sign work for hire agreements, thus giving up
ownership of anything they write, unlike independent songwriters,
who license individual songs to specific films. As Richard Bellis put it,

Basically, there are two categories of worker in the United
States: employees who receive pension and health benefits but
relinquish ownership in most cases because they work for an
employer who gets the ownership, and independent contractors
who don't get health and pension but who retain ownership
and that becomes their bargaining chip. Film composers have
the worst of both worlds, where we are considered independent
contractors, not getting health and pension, but are deprived
of ownership as well through a work made for hire agreement
mandated by the copyright law. Songwriters get mechanical
royalties depending on their contract with the film or television production. All we get are performance royalties.

Banned by the result of the *Alden-Rochelle* decision in 1948 from
collecting performance royalties from movie theaters in the U.S., composers can only earn royalties when the films in which their music is
heard are played overseas, or on TV, or on the rare occasion when the
movie's theme becomes a hit single. For its part, ASCAP tries very hard
to keep them informed on this complex subject.

"The distribution rules for TV play are carefully calibrated for
maximum fairness and objectivity," said Knutsen. "For instance, prime
time pays more than the afternoon, the afternoon pays more than the

morning, and the morning pays more than the overnight. ABC, CBS, NBC, and FOX pay the most, and all the other entities are on a sliding scale depending on how much they pay ASCAP."

Every film and every episode of a TV program has a cue sheet, on which every snippet of music, from the opening theme to the closing credits, is listed, and each pays the songwriter or composer differently, depending on how the music is used and its duration. Said Knutsen,

> When a composer says, "I'm writing music for a TV show, how much am I going to make?" I always ask, "What time is it going to be on?" and "What channel is it going to be on?" It depends on how many minutes of music they use and how often it's aired and what time of day it's aired. So if it's on at 4:00 A.M. and it has 10 minutes of music, then the writer is not getting much, but if it's a movie that's on at 9:00 P.M. and the score has 100 minutes of music, then they might do okay.

Though budgets for music in both film and TV have been shrinking over the last decade, one route to riches remains constant. "When James Newton Howard had the theme to *ER* it was on the air for 11 or 12 years," Nancy Knutsen said. "You just have to write it once and you can get paid 52 weeks a year. It's the luck of the draw."

Dan Foliart has made his living since 1978 writing music for television. Among his credits are the themes for *Roseanne* and *Home Improvement*.

> When I first started, we had ABC, NBC, CBS. I don't think Fox was there yet. Now we have hundreds of channels, so the need for music is huge right now, but of course, the real challenge is getting compensated. A smaller cable channel such as the Learning Channel (TLC) is not going to pay as much as a huge broadcaster, so some composers are finding themselves on some of these more fringe networks, trying to get compensated in a fashion that they're used to from working on these big networks.
>
> When I started back in 1978, there were probably 60 composers working in the field. Today I would say there are

thousands of composers working in the field. There are more opportunities, but the competition has gotten more intense. Also, I worked over at Paramount for almost ten years on shows, and almost any show I was doing had 30 musicians working in it. Right now I'm working with five musicians, and that is more than a lot of people, because so many people are doing music in their own home studios and not employing the great musicians that we have around the country. I still go to Capitol Studios once every week and a half to record my show with the greatest musicians in town, and unfortunately I'm in the minority. Another problem is that our creative fee, the amount that we are given to create the music for the show, has not gone up over the years, so that's the reason ASCAP has become even more critical to our livelihood.

Nancy Knutsen was more specific.

I used to say when I first got here that the ASCAP royalties were the icing on the cake. Now sometimes it's the whole cake. There are very well-known composers who are working for 25 percent of what they made 10 or 15 years ago because of the competition and because all the fees have gone down. But even though fees are going down, composers are asked to do more for the same fee.

This means composers are no longer just writing the music; they're budgeting for it.

Nevertheless, ASCAP payments in this area have been improving. As the current head of ASCAP's film and TV/visual media department, Shawn LeMone, noted, "Historically, ASCAP has paid more for songs on television than themes and underscore. Over the years, we have been steadily increasing the rate paid for theme and underscore to reflect the value that this music has in our negotiations with broadcasters. In fact, with every passing year, film and television repertory has become increasingly important to the overall growth of the organization."

With a look toward the future, as the use of music in video games continues to grow, ASCAP has also established a foothold in that industry. The addition of visual media to the name of the film and TV department reflects the expanded mission of LeMone and his colleagues. The department provides many other services to the composer community—by attending recording sessions and arranging for meetings with agents, attorneys, music supervisors, and studio executives. And the ASCAP film, TV, and visual media team works to make these opportunities widely accessible.

Knutsen pointed out: "There's a lot of mentorship that goes on in the film scoring world. Hans Zimmer, for instance, has helped many, many young composers make good careers for themselves. And Mark Snow, who did *The X-Files* and *Cagney and Lacey* and 30, 40 years worth of TV, does the same thing. He's hired a lot of young people, many from our workshops, who are now working composers in their own right."

Among those workshop graduates employed now by Zimmer are Jim Dooley, who received an Emmy Award for his work on the TV show *Pushing Daisies*, and Trevor Morris, whose prolific scoring assignments on *The Tudors*, *The Borgias*, and *The Pillars of the Earth* have won him two Emmys.

Like the theater workshop, the film scoring workshop has become an institution among young musicians trying to gain traction in the industry. Said ASCAP's senior director of film and television music, Mike Todd,

> We've built a reputation filtering talents and putting them out into the workforce by giving them the tools. It's a little different from the bubble of being in school, where everything is very academic. This is real life. So, what are all the tools you need? Well, you need to know who hires you. You need to know who your team is going to be. Who is your music editor? Who is your contractor for musicians? What stages are you going to record at? All these elements are critical, because you're competing with professionals who have teams in place, and they have a shorthand with that team, and they move at light speed. That's your competition. In order to arm composers with this, we pull from every element of the business and expose them to this each night.

For the lucky 12 selected each year for the ASCAP Foundation Film Scoring Workshop, the course extends over four weeks, four nights a week. "The thing we really stress on the first day is that everyone in the room is clearly talented, but there's a reason you're here," Todd said.

> You're building your career. So just as important as maintaining your skills and craft of composing is to realize it's a very social business, it's a team player business. In other words, you're not the decision maker in what music goes into each scene; the director is. So everyone is humbled by that and has to be reminded of that. If you think that a cue is perfect for a scene, and if the director doesn't think so, you have to let it go or they'll find someone else and you're out of a job. So a lot of it is facing the realities of the business.

Early in the program, the composers are each assigned a scene at random from one of four films. Then they get a week or so to score the scene for a 60-piece orchestra. As an added perk, when it comes time to get their scores recorded, the same top musicians used by the A-list directors perform their pieces. "These players do it at a demo rate, graciously," said Todd.

The workshop also hands out three ASCAP Foundation prizes at the end of the program: the Steve Kaplan TV & Film Studies Award, the David Rose Award, and the Harold Arlen Film & TV Award. The orchestra members also vote their favorite a $1500 credit toward a demo version.

Just as the home studio has largely replaced the working musician in the industry playing field, now the growing practice of filling up scores with pop songs has begun to marginalize the pure film composer. *Easy Rider* in 1969 is pointed to as one of the first films to make use of the literature of rock and folk in the soundtrack. On TV, Jan Hammer's work on *Miami Vice* in the mid-'80s is cited by Dan Foliart as a turning point.

> For example, when I first started, almost every moment within the body of a show was handled by composition or background music. Now, at times very artistically, and at other times, in

my opinion, not as artistically, songs have started taking up a lot more moments where underscore used to be prevalent. If it was a custom-crafted song, I was always in favor of it. But just to put a song in there because it's a popular song in my mind kind of undermines what we do as composers.

ASCAP's own history shows that pop songs in movies have always helped sell tickets, as well as records. Throughout the '80s almost every movie made came with its own soundtrack album. Responsible for selecting the songs, music supervisors became the new deejays, displaying their knowledge of arcane material interspersed with vintage hits, and selling tons of records in the bargain. But those days are over, says Jonathan McHugh, senior vice president of film, TV, and soundtracks at Def Jam.

You get your shades of hope, your *Juno* and your *Twilight*, but they're few and far between. For years soundtracks were America's compilations. For a long time record companies never let compilations in this country. The *Now That's What I Call Music* series was big in Europe, big in Australia, but wasn't allowed in America, because they felt it would cannibalize sales. So they held out. That means the only real compilations in America were soundtracks. If you saw the movie and heard something you liked, then you would buy the soundtrack. Today, kids don't care about an album; they'll just download the best songs off the album. All my company really talks about today is TV. All they care about is, can you get on *Glee* or *Gossip Girl* or *The Vampire Diaries*, because of the immediacy of it. You can see the next morning what happens. I watch TV with my daughter; she watches *Gossip Girl*; she's got the laptop out; she's got the phone; she's texting her friends. By the time the commercial hits, she's bought the song if she likes it. Whereas I did a film placement for a song by a new band. I have no idea when the thing is going to get out there. So I'm not even telling them about it. Once a *Tonight Show* appearance used to be the be all and end all, and now it's like, "I'd rather have my song on *Gossip Girl*."

As an example of how television has supplanted film in creating a buzz for an artist or a song, consider the case of Jason Mraz, whose "Geek in the Pink," from a previous album, *Mr. A-Z*, was revived by Chris Richardson on an episode of *American Idol*. "In fact, that album had probably been gone for two or three years when he came out and sang the song one week and he ruled," Mraz said. "It's really kind of like a hip-hop/R&B song and I never could embrace all the energy that a song like that could afford, and this guy just killed it. And then I noticed the very next day the song showed up on the iTunes Top 50 out of nowhere and I was really tickled by that."

In the pursuit of similar exposure and its potential for career-changing rewards, many songwriters are willing to submit their material for the diminishing rates being offered by today's TV producers. It is a situation that Barry Coburn, ASCAP board member and president of Ten Ten Publishing, finds intolerable.

> If you look at what television and film pay now compared to what they paid five years ago, it's all because of independent artists who would rather give their material away for free, believing there's going to be some payoff. It's absolute bull. There is no payoff. But they have basically stopped all of their fellow artists from getting any payment because now you've got television networks that believe they should be getting the music free. I had a CBS television executive say recently, "We're not going to pay anything for music in this coming series." And I said, "Then I'm not giving you a song," and I stood up and walked out. We have to push back, and that's what ASCAP does. ASCAP has invested millions and millions of dollars to fight for the rights of creators. We're dealing with the bloody cavalry on the other side, because you've got Verizon and AT&T saying, "We're going to resist for as long as possible paying for it; we have in-house counsel who can do this," while ASCAP is spending part of its income to try and ensure that we get paid.

Longtime ASCAP songwriter Earl Rose, who started out writing for the soaps before graduating to film and TV scoring, is not of the generation who believes that free should be part of the new business model. "When you're asked to give away your music, you're really giving away yourself," he said. "You're showing no pride in what you do. You're saying your music is worthless. It's one thing to donate a song to a charity; that's a beautiful thing. But to just give it away? To me, it shows you have no self-esteem. If it's good enough for somebody to want to listen to it, it's good enough for somebody to want to pay for it."

For his part, Dan Foliart remains optimistic. "The positive sign is the proliferation of music. It's never been more appreciated. Our role in ASCAP is to make sure we can monetize that, so our great creative talents can continue to do it."

Which explains the popularity of the theater writing workshop and the film scoring workshop, as well as the country songwriting and pop songwriting workshops, and their increasing importance in ASCAP's efforts to seed the fields of the future. One recent winner of the ASCAP Foundation Leon Brettler Award, named in honor of the venerable ASCAP board member and publisher who helped ASCAP set up shop in Nashville in the early '60s, country rocker Jenn Bostic, found value in both workshops. A graduate of the Berklee College of Music in Boston, Bostic recalled an early mentor at ASCAP, Robert Ellis Orrall, a famous country writer who spoke at the country music workshop she attended.

> He listened to our music and we developed a little bit of a relationship with him. I ended up doing some demos for him after the workshop was over, and we talked a lot about the business. Jesse Willoughby at ASCAP helped me a lot, too. Twice a year you're allowed to go in and play a song for a publisher. I had heard about that from a friend and so I signed up. Afterwards you could have a personal meeting with Jesse and I did, and he really liked some of the songs and thought they were pitch-able, so he reached out to some other publishing companies. Although nothing happened with them, I felt like a relationship grew as far as feeling comfortable calling him. He was very, very helpful in connecting me to the right people and making sure I knew what I should be doing. Then a pop workshop came along and I applied for that and ended up going and I got to ask more questions.

Twenty-four-year ASCAP veteran Brendan Okrent, an assistant VP of creative services in the membership department in Los Angeles, has helmed the pop songwriting workshop there since 1989, apart from a several-year hiatus. Now known as the ASCAP Foundation Lester Sill Songwriters Workshop, after the prominent ASCAP board member and publisher, each year the workshop accepts 14 songwriters for a month-long program consisting of eight sessions. (The ASCAP Foundation Jerry Ragovoy Songwriters Workshop in New York is the East Coast version.)

Like the other marquee workshops, the mission is to offer a realistic picture of today's music business and to provide the tools to compete in it. Says Okrent,

> The kind of guests we bring in and the information we deliver has been structured around what's going on in the music business today. In 1989 the big get was a record deal with the majors or a publishing deal. Now there's only a small percentage who are going to have a career like that. In 1989, if you got an album cut, that could sustain you because there were mechanicals. We had a guy in one of the first workshops I did who had a song on the *Bodyguard* soundtrack, which sold 35 to 40 million records. You can live off that for a pretty long time. But that's not happening anymore, even if you get on an Adele record. Now, with being able to make a record in your bedroom and being able to get directly to your audience through your website, people have all different kinds of careers. So we try to encourage and enlighten them to do whatever it is they need to do to be songwriters or songwriter/artists. A lot of alums of this workshop have gone on to do completely different things. One of them wrote the score for the TV show *Modern Family*. He's still in a band, still writes songs, but now has a budding career as a composer.

Another notable ASCAP program that fosters musical creativity of a different sort—books, articles, and broadcasts about music—is the Deems Taylor Awards Competition, named for one-time ASCAP president Taylor, a distinguished composer, critic, author, and radio personality. Established in 1968, a year after Taylor's passing and presently funded by the Virgil Thomson Foundation, the Deems Taylor Awards are unique in that they annually honor the writers (with cash awards), publishers, and broadcasters of the best books, articles, liner notes, and radio and television programs on the subject of music. Panels of ASCAP members adjudicate the competition, which in recent years has also included websites and blogs.

Through the auspices of ASCAP and many ASCAP Foundation programs and industry networking events, there are moments when songwriters currently struggling for a piece of the pie, and anyone else within hearing distance, can be reminded through the power of music why they got into this business in the first place—and why ASCAP is so important to its future. Such moments occur with exhilarating regularity at ASCAP's annual "I Create Music" Expo, where in 2013 one powerful voice dominated the proceedings during a songwriters' swap session, mesmerizing the assemblage with her songs of jealousy, pain, and vengeance. By the time the first song was done, the harried conventioneers, jaded industry heavyweights, and assorted sleep-deprived visitors from the press were turning to each other, whispering *Who? Is? That?* At the showcase's conclusion, the room rose into a spontaneous standing ovation for the singer-songwriter, a rising Nashville talent named Brandy Clark, who had already cowritten Top Five hits for Miranda Lambert ("Mama's Broken Heart") and the Band Perry ("Better Dig Two").

Typifying the Society's commitment to its membership, the "I Create Music" Expo was literally born in the ashes of a 1994 restructuring, when a program called MOVE was implemented to develop future executive talent from within. Lauren Iossa, then a ten-year ASCAP veteran who'd previously headed the New York membership office, was teamed with several other people to focus on ways to service, satisfy, and thus increase the ASCAP membership base.

"We had done a lot of free educational programs for our members," said Iossa, who is now senior vice president of marketing. "We did workshops. We did showcases. We did different kinds of seminars scattered throughout the country, organized by different membership people. But we didn't have a single annual conference-type event."

Iossa's boss at the time, Phil Crosland, immediately bought into the idea. "I have to say that I could have been standing on a desktop out in the middle of the sixth floor and screaming about how great this was," he said, "but nothing would have happened without John LoFrumento recognizing the value in this, which he did." With LoFrumento wielding the hammer, the only remaining hurdle was also the biggest: getting the board of directors to sign off.

While the makeup of the board has always been a chief selling point for ASCAP in attracting new members—a place where creative folk can join hands with business folk to chart the destiny of the franchise together—in practice, the 12 publisher members and 12 songwriter and composer members of the board often approach new ideas from different perspectives. When Iossa's MOVE group first presented their program to the board, she said, the reaction was typically mixed.

> In general, the songwriters were more supportive than the publishers. I think the publishers had a business outlook and they saw risk, and the songwriters had a more intuitive response, knowing that the event would resonate with the creative community. The publishers wanted a little more research done, which was fine, so we presented them with a detailed business plan and then they signed off on it conceptually. And then John became a champion of the idea internally. He basically brought a lot of people together who would have to get involved in the program, and he said, "I want you to know this is a priority for me. It's a priority for ASCAP. We're gonna do this and you have to help make it work. At one point he said, "If you don't want to come to the party, then you don't have a place here."

Late in the summer of 2005 all the key executives flew to the Hollywood Renaissance Hotel, where the Expo was set to debut the following April, to map out the details and tap the membership database for panelists. "We took a cross-section of hip, young, veteran, and just amazingly great panelists," said Iossa. "And then I booked Tom Petty as our first keynote speaker, and that sealed it."

Since then, the list of panelists and performers, interviewees, critiquers, and master-class leaders who have donated their time to the Expo reads like a dream night at the Grammys, the Oscars, the Tonys, the Rock and Roll Hall of Fame, and the Country Music Awards combined, interspersed with a million-dollar Rolodex of behind-the-scenes publishers, lawyers, producers, and music supervisors, including Jackson Browne, Carly Simon, Wyclef Jean, Randy Newman, Jill Scott, Don Schlitz, Quincy Jones, John Mayer, Jon Bon Jovi, Ann and Nancy Wilson, Judy Collins, Steve Miller, Chaka Khan, Jeff Lynne, Marshall Crenshaw, Ludacris, Katy Perry, Stephen Schwartz, Jimmy Webb, Paul Williams, Desmond Child, Jermaine Dupri, Mary Chapin Carpenter, Mark Isham, Justin Timberlake, Jimmy Jam & Terry Lewis, Jackie DeShannon, Kenny Burrell, Loudon Wainwright, Wayland Holyfield, Jason Mraz, and Bill Withers.

"What does it say about ASCAP?" said Phil Crosland.

First of all, it says we are all about our members. It shows that when our members succeed, we succeed. And even our more successful members recognize that a new generation is coming up and if we can make them better, their catalogue is going to be worth more, because ASCAP is going to have more money to distribute. We don't pay anybody a cent for this. We might, on rare occasions, get some travel costs, maybe a limo in LA to pick them up and bring them over, but this is volunteer work.

"The Expo works on two levels," said John LoFrumento.

The first level is new members. Most of them are hardworking people who want to become songwriters, and this event engages them. They learn a lot and that's good. The other side is all of the accomplished members who come to give back to the community. I saw an urban writer on a panel say to a whole bunch of kids, "Here's the deal. Are you ready? I'm going to give you an address and you are going to send me one, not two, not three, but your best song, and I'm going to listen to it and get back to you." He was an extremely successful writer and performer and he just felt that he needed to give back. And I have to tell you, that was worth volumes to me, absolute volumes about the value of the Expo.

"It was also an opportunity for so many departments to come together," Lauren Iossa added. "There was such a good energy at the first Expo. Our writers appreciated it so much, and I think it was a wonderful bonding experience for ASCAP. It actually changed the corporate culture to one of more widespread cooperation and less working solo, just because of how busy it was."

Phil Crosland added, "It was a shared success, and as a result I think now the walls are broken down in terms of 'I'm in distribution so I don't need to talk to this other group.'"

"One of the things that we've been committed to is the mix," Iossa said.

We have veteran songwriters telling their stories, next to emerging songwriters. We have panels that are mixed genre, so if you have a producers panel, you have a country producer, a hip-hop producer, and a pop producer. Plus, you have within the genres different panels. Another thing that's always very popular is when we bring in a top professional songwriter to critique songs submitted by the audience. So it's a mix of creative programming versus business programming. The performance panels are always really popular. But the business panels are key to a new writer's success.

Expo, like the programs of The ASCAP Foundation, is but one of the many initiatives that help put ASCAP among the major forces in talent development in the music industry today. "Not one single unknown songwriter is going to be able to walk in the door of any major publishing company or any major record label and get beyond the receptionist telling them, 'We don't accept unsolicited material,'" then executive vice president of membership Randy Grimmett said.

But you can walk into ASCAP and get a meeting with someone who works here who will listen to your music and take some time to talk to you about the record industry, the publishing industry, and the world of performing rights. So that's a *huge* leap in development for writers right there, just the fact that we have an open door. More specifically, on both coasts and

in Nashville, we have songwriter workshops, composer workshops, and showcases. We do events at places like the Sundance
Film Festival, the CMJ Music Marathon, South by Southwest,
and you have individual reps here who take writers under their
wing on a regular basis and introduce them to publishers, other writers, people at record labels, lawyers, managers. At the
Expo we use all of our big writers—the Dr. Lukes of the world,
the John Mayers of the world, the Justin Timberlakes of the
world—to help educate younger writers about the music business and about the creative process and about how they got
their first creative breaks.

At the Lester Sill workshop, the basics predominate. One thing
that hasn't changed for the aspiring songwriter since the Top 40 began
(or since the days of Irving Berlin, for that matter) is the necessity of
learning how to write a hit song. "You have to be able to know how to
deliver songs that are competitive," said ASCAP's Okrent.

Not everybody wants to write singles, but that's the mentality of
the business. When people come to us and say, "I have all these
songs. I want to meet with publishers," I don't want to blow a
hole in anybody's dream, but I take out a copy of *Billboard* and I
say, "See this Hot 100? This is where people in publishing make
money. The people who work at these companies; this is how
they keep their jobs. By getting songs on this chart."

Whether or not the songwriters in the workshop are capable of
writing a hit song—or are even concerned with it—the thing that
Okrent finds admirable is their persistence.

What really astounds me is how the people in our workshops
find a way to have a career. Once they realize that diversifica-
tion is key, the amount of commitment and enthusiasm they
have is amazing. We're just trying to give them powerful information to help them sustain themselves, by having colleagues
and people around you on your team. Songwriting can be a
very solitary thing; we're trying to take them out of that by

bringing them into the family of ASCAP. Most of them are so appreciative of the care we take of them and how much they learn and how much they get from each other. There was one writer I knew and mentored who went on to cowrite a Mariah Carey cut, and it's the end title theme to *Oz the Great and Powerful*. People are now calling her. I don't take any credit for what she's done, except for cheering her on all these years. That's the unseen work we do at ASCAP. Our big job obviously is to get people paid, but the other job we do in membership is to inspire and educate songwriters and help them navigate their careers in any way we can.

CHAPTER 7

NEW BLOOD, NASHVILLE, AND CAPITOL HILL

Toni Winter worked as an executive assistant to four ASCAP presidents from 1956 to 1994: Stanley Adams, Paul Cunningham, Hal David, and Morton Gould. She was hired by Sylvia Rosenberg, who started at ASCAP in 1920 and worked for the Society's first six presidents: George Maxwell, Gene Buck, Deems Taylor, Fred Ahlert, Otto Harbach, and Stanley Adams. Winter took over as secretary to Stanley Adams when Rosenberg left in 1960. "When I came in, Stanley had been president and had been replaced by Paul Cunningham, because the term of president at that time was three years and you had to step down. And then the bylaws were changed and Mr. Adams could come back—and he stayed 21 more years."

Prior to Adams' first term, Otto Harbach, lyricist for dozens of Broadway shows, including *The Desert Song* and *Roberta* (from which came his most famous song, "Smoke Gets in Your Eyes"), served from 1950 to 1953. He succeeded composer Fred Ahlert ("Mean to Me," "Walkin' My Baby Back Home"), who held the position from 1948 to 1950. Between Adams' two separate terms, Cunningham, who coauthored the Gaylords' 1954 hit single "From the Vine Came the Grape," presided over ASCAP from 1956 to 1959, during which time he hosted the Victor Herbert 100th anniversary celebration, penned a tribute to W. C. Handy called "Eulogy to William C. Handy," and signed a major

TV rights agreement. "Paul Cunningham was in vaudeville with his wife," said Winter.

> Mr. Cunningham was a night person and he didn't get to the office till after 12:00. So when people were leaving at 5:00, they had to sneak out. When Mr. Adams became president the second time, he was already married and living in Great Neck, so he had a regular train schedule. That was easier. When Hal David became president, I think he had made up his mind he was going to settle in California, but they got an apartment not too far from the office and therefore Hal was available for longer hours.
>
> We were not allowed to play music. I remember when the ladies first got permission to wear slacks. That was during Stanley's reign. He was a very conservative person, so it took some talking to by the head of personnel, because the younger staff were sort of demanding this. So then he qualified it by saying, "Well, all right. They can wear slacks but not blue jeans." Hal David was basically a quiet man who didn't speak above a whisper, but he could be very tough with what he wanted or how he perceived things. Hal was not afraid of anybody.

Known primarily as Burt Bacharach's lyric-writing partner ("Do You Know the Way to San Jose," "Raindrops Keep Fallin' on My Head"), David was a former young Turk, part of a group of relatively youthful songwriters out to recast ASCAP in a more modern image. Unlike some of his contemporaries on the board in the '70s, he loved rock 'n' roll from the beginning.

> I used to listen to other writers who were very establishment-oriented who hated rock 'n' roll and thought it was a fad. I never could understand that kind of thinking. It was part of the environment, part of the young people. I have two sons, so I saw it happening before it became a big thing. I remember the first time I heard Elvis Presley. I happened to hear him because one of the songs he recorded at Sun Records was a song my brother wrote called "I Don't Care If the Sun Don't Shine." So I heard

that whole thing, and I will tell you, it was sensational. I eventually wrote a couple of songs for a movie he was in. I didn't see the movie, but I loved having him sing the songs.

This was back in 1961, when Mack David was still more successful than younger brother Hal. In fact, they shared the same collaborator, Sherman Edwards, on three songs for two Elvis movies: Mack wrote "I'm Not the Marrying Kind" for *Follow That Dream*, and Hal wrote "Home Is Where the Heart Is" and "A Whistling Tune" for *Kid Galahad*, the latter having been bumped from *Follow That Dream*. Hal also worked with Sherman Edwards on the hits "Johnny Get Angry" for Joanie Sommers and "Broken Hearted Melody" for Sarah Vaughan. Mack, who died in 1993, borrowed Burt Bacharach for the Shirelles' big hit "Baby It's You." Hal said of his brother,

In some ways his success was an intimidating thing to me, but I thought I was pretty good, too. I showed him my songs and he was encouraging, but he didn't encourage me to become a songwriter. All the way through school my interest was in writing stories, writing poems, writing for the school paper and the school magazine. My brother thought I'd be smart going into advertising. He didn't think songwriting was quite so legitimate for his kid brother.

Mack was certainly proud, however, to see his brother ascend to the helm of ASCAP, although Hal at first resisted the position. "They tried to get me to take the presidency for a few years and I was reluctant to do it," he said. "I wasn't sure I'd enjoy it."

During his six-year tenure, from 1980 to 1986, David concentrated on expanding the membership base in Los Angeles, Nashville, and London. "I took a big interest in Nashville," he said. "We went from a point where we were also-rans there, to being the top people in town."

Much of the credit for that also belongs to Connie Bradley, who signed a wide spectrum of country artists, from bluegrass instrumentalist/publisher Ricky Skaggs to a young unknown belter with a magic voice whom Bradley heard on the radio one day in 1982 as she was driving down the road in Denver, Colorado. "I'm going, 'I don't know who this girl is, but she's going to be a superstar,'" Bradley said. The girl was Reba McEntire, singing a song called "(You Lift Me) Up to Heaven," which would become her first Top 10 country single.

"There weren't cell phones back then," Bradley said. "So I pulled over on the side of the road and used a pay phone and called my cohort in Nashville, Merlin Littlefield, and I said, 'I just heard a girl on the radio and she is phenomenal. We've got to go get her and sign her now, because if we don't sign her now, by the time we get around to it, she's going to be a monster.'"

Bradley also recalls the early days of another of country's biggest names, Garth Brooks, who came to town a virtual unknown. "When Garth Brooks came along, an attorney in Texas told him to come to Nashville and see a guy named Merlin Littlefield and talk to him. And he did. He hung out in our lobby for 24 hours and he saw Merlin and he saw Bob McDill. He was playing little clubs that nobody had ever heard of."

A couple of years later, Garth was back in town, with a band. At ASCAP he met Bob Doyle, who was in the membership department. "His landlady called me and I said, 'Send me a tape and I'd be happy to listen to it,'" Doyle recalled.

> I listened to the tape and signed him up. Then he came by and played me four songs that were on the tape, and a few other things, and over the course of that interaction we tried to do what ASCAP typically does, which is to help people get placed with a publisher and get some activity going on. That went on for about six months without anything happening. At that point I'd been working at ASCAP for six years, and I made a decision to go on my own and try to get into the publishing business. I talked to Garth. I said, "In light of the fact that you don't have a deal, do you want to come with me and work together?" We went back and demoed this one song I had been really taken with at ASCAP, called "I'm Much Too Young to Feel This Damn Old," which eventually became his first single.

Bob shopped the demos, gaining covers by Crystal Gayle and Tanya Tucker, but there were no takers for Brooks as an artist. "Everybody passed," said Doyle, "including Capitol." Here ASCAP once again stepped into the breach, although this time accidentally.

There's an organization in Nashville called the Nashville Entertainment Association, which puts on publishing showcases. Through one of these showcases we were selected to present our material as a publisher, and Garth was the songwriter. An A&R guy at Capitol had come out to see another songwriter, Ralph Murphy, who is now an ASCAP membership guy. Ralph was late, so Garth went on early in Ralph's spot, so the A&R guy saw him more in a performance environment and less in an across-the-desk way. Afterwards he came up to me and said, "Get back to me." I wasn't going to tell him he'd already passed. The next day they made us an offer. "Much Too Young," the first single, had already been rejected by everybody; so had the third single, "If Tomorrow Never Comes," which was Garth's first number one.

Ricky Skaggs joined BMI when he first hit the country charts in 1981. "When it was time to renew in 1984 I went with ASCAP," he said.

And I've been there ever since. They really work hard for the songwriter, and I was a publisher as well, because I had a publishing deal with Welk Music. One of the smartest things I did when I came to town was to start a publishing company; we really had a machine going there for a while and ASCAP was great to me and helped me along. They even helped with things like awards, just kind of getting the word out and saying, "Ricky is up for this, that, and the other."

"Once we got hot, everybody wanted to be where the hot writers were, like Clint Black and Alan Jackson," Connie Bradley said. "BMI had all the people in the '60s and '70s, and then we got strong in the latter part of '80s and into the '90s." With such success behind her, it wasn't long before Bradley was named head of the Nashville office, joining such top-ranked female executives at ASCAP as Karen Sherry and Gloria Messinger.

Originally hired as the director of public relations when Stanley Adams was still president, the indefatigable Karen Sherry is now senior vice president of industry affairs. She had a very close working relationship with Adams' successor, Hal David.

> Before I knew it, Hal said to me, "I'd like you to be my assistant in addition to being head of public relations." So then I reported directly to him, which was very exciting. I would say Hal was one of my most influential mentors in terms of teaching me to write, how to write concisely, how to write in his voice. You might ask, why would Hal have me do that; he's the greatest at words that there is. But Hal was so busy he couldn't do everything, and so I would show him things and he would say, "This is great but cut this out, cut that out, this is hyperbolic . . ." He really taught me how to refine my writing, and pretty soon I got to the point where he said, "I don't have to change anything." And that made me feel great.
>
> Hal took me everywhere with him and I got to meet a lot of people. He was president for six years, and during that time I was gaining responsibilities and titles. I was director of public relations, assistant to the president, and also director of public affairs, because Hal revved up our legislative campaign and asked me to head that up.

It was David who appointed Gloria Messinger (who passed away in 2013) as ASCAP's first female managing director in 1981. "Hal David had a significant impact, no doubt about it," said Messinger.

> He was a smart man. He understood the competition. He didn't close his mind to what was going on on the other side of the world, namely BMI and the writers in Nashville. He was sympathetic to writers. Hal had been a dissident at one point in his career. He was somewhat challenging of ASCAP, so that gave him an insight, too. We didn't always see eye to eye, but I had a great respect for the man.

It wasn't only David's big-picture views, Messinger added, but his personal touch that made a memorable difference.

> My daughter went to Harvard, and one of her roommates was a black woman named Alice Randall, who was a very gifted writer, and she was also interested in writing lyrics. Hal spent some time with her and then she decided that she wanted to move to Nashville, of all places. And he saw to it that she was given opportunities to walk in doors in Nashville, which wasn't easy for a serious black woman from Harvard who wanted to write lyrics; and actually she did write some successful songs. And then she wrote the book *The Wind Done Gone*, which was a parody of *Gone with the Wind*. So I give Hal David high marks for recognizing her talent and helping her.

Gloria Messinger came to ASCAP as a graduate of Yale Law School in 1954, joining a staff of three other lawyers who were also Yale grads. "I like to refer to the ASCAP legal department as the Yale mafia," she said. "Yale was one of the few places that had a copyright class in those days; intellectual property, they now call it. Herman Finkelstein, then the general counsel, didn't have a problem hiring women, which was a real plus in those days."

One of Messinger's responsibilities in the ASCAP legal department in the late '50s and early '60s was to get involved with the Small Business Committee hearings held by Congressman James Roosevelt at the Department of Justice.

> There was a lot of rancor among a couple of very activist members who felt they were not getting their due and that all of the money was being skewed toward bigger publishers, and there were fights—not physical fights, but there were certainly long, difficult membership meetings in those days. They eventually got the ear of the Department of Justice, and the Roosevelt committee hearings were held, and changes were made in the ASCAP distribution system. I remember a man named Hans Lengsfelder, for example, who I haven't thought about in 50

years. I don't think he did any better in the new system, but he was that kind of activist, who got people together and said, "We have to change the way ASCAP is doing business." Eventually ASCAP did change the way it distributed members' money, more in the way of current performances.

As managing director, Messinger's major interest became the international arena. Because she was one of the first women to hold such a position in any performing rights society, she was viewed as an oddity.

Shortly after I was appointed managing director, one of our publishers went to Japan, and he came back and he told me this story. He said, "I went into JASRAC [Japanese Society for Rights of Authors, Composers and Publishers]," which is the Japanese performing rights organization, "and I was questioned heavily by executives and members of the board, and they wanted to know if it was true that there was a person named Gloria Messinger who was appointed managing director, and was it true that she is a woman." He answered yes. And then he said there was a long pause and one of the men said that if that happened at JASRAC, "We commit hara-kiri." That was the world even in 1980. I then became head of the international organization called CISAC [Confédération Internationale des Sociétés d'Auteurs et Compositeurs], and I was the first woman to occupy that position. So I had a lot of interesting times in Europe and South America and Asia.

One of the things they did that was totally outrageous was to put foreign lyric writers on compositions. Those lyrics were never performed, and yet they credited the foreign writers, so every time George Gershwin's work was performed, the lyric royalty was shared with a local writer. It was really a local game, and we never suspected it. So we got what was called the Amalfi Resolution, which was exponentially to the benefit of ASCAP's writer members.

It was current ASCAP senior vice president of international relations Roger Greenaway who brought the issue of foreign lyric writers claiming a share of American songs to Gloria Messinger's attention when he was chairman of PRS (Performing Right Society), the British performing rights organization. In 1988, the Greenaway-Cook composition "Something's Gotten Hold of My Heart," previously a hit in the '60s for Gene Pitney, soared to the top of the charts in Germany in a version by Marc Almond. Said Greenaway,

> A gentleman named Michael Koontz, who was on the board of GEMA, the German society, wrote the German lyric to it, and every time my version of it was played in Germany, he got 2/12 from my share. Clearly the number one version was the English version, and I wanted to be paid my full amount from Germany. I was chairman of PRS at the time, and I went to see Gloria Messinger in New York and I convinced her that the American composers were losing a lot more than we were at PRS because of this practice. She went to see the head of the German society and persuaded them to join a CISAC meeting in Amalfi to make a change, and hence the Amalfi rule came around and stopped the practice.

By the mid-'80s the bloody heyday of the competition between ASCAP and BMI had long since passed and parity reigned. On Hal David's watch ASCAP's chart totals of 1984 reached an impressive near–Golden Age level, controlling 73 percent of the year-end *Billboard* singles chart. From 1980 to 1985, total receipts rose from $154 million to $245 million. Using a given week of *Billboard*'s Hot 100 as a measuring stick, ASCAP's share went up from 45 percent in 1980 to 68 percent in 1986. On the R&B charts the trend was also upward, from 47 percent in 1980 to 65 percent in 1986. The growth in country music was similarly explosive, going from 33 percent in 1980 to 60 percent in 1986.

At the time of David's exit in 1986, however, there were toxic fumes of danger once again emanating from *Buffalo Broadcasting*, a case that had seemingly been resolved in 1984. Following their defeat in their efforts to have the courts declare the blanket license unlawful under the antitrust laws, the local television stations commenced a rate proceeding (a request to set a reasonable license fee made to the New York federal court) under the ASCAP consent decree and at the same time sought

legislative relief from Congress. In his farewell essay to the membership, published in the spring 1986 issue of *ASCAP in Action*, David referenced licensing bills H.R. 3521 and S. 1980:

> As you know, this is the *Buffalo Broadcasting* lawsuit revisited.
> What the broadcasters could not accomplish in the courts, they
> are now seeking to accomplish in Congress. These bills would
> amend the Copyright Law so that the music performed on syn-
> dicated local television programs would no longer be licensed
> through your performing rights society. Instead, these bills
> would totally alter the present system by shifting the payment
> for music performance from the broadcasters, to the program
> producers.

To the older members, this sounded quite familiar. For the newer
members, David spelled out what this would mean. "Composers would
have a virtual buyout forced upon them with a one-time payment made
for their music before its value is known. This would result in a loss to
writers and publishers of tens of millions of dollars annually; it would
destroy the music creator's most valuable right—the right of continuing payment for continuing use."

Summoning the strength of ASCAP's numbers, not for the first or
nearly the last time, David called for a grassroots effort,

> targeting the various members of the House and Senate ju-
> diciary subcommittees. This is important because these sub-
> committees have jurisdiction over the bills. Many of these
> congressmen and senators we have seen are now with us as a
> result of these meetings. But this still leaves so many out there
> who are uncommitted or who are opposed to our point of
> view. That's why we need each and every member of ASCAP
> and your families and your friends to get active and write to
> your representatives, urging them to oppose this legislation.

Although ASCAP's presence in Washington dates back to the days
of the Victor Herbert–Nathan Burkan–John Philip Sousa triumvirate,
the idea of establishing political action committees to lobby for ASCAP

interests in Washington on a regular basis was something that caused quite a bit of dissension on the board and in the membership at large in the early '80s. Eventually, whether reluctantly or not, ASCAP was forced to face the gift-giving realities. It was at this critical juncture that Hal David hired Ben Palumbo, an experienced Washington hand who had worked on Lloyd Bentsen's presidential campaign, to become ASCAP's new lobbyist/consultant. Palumbo was aware of the controversy surrounding his hiring.

That's not unusual in an organization that gets so involved in Washington. The syndrome is "Oh, well, that worked, so now we can close it down and everything's fine." And then all of a sudden they've got another problem and they have to create the whole thing all over again. Hal understood when I told him that an organization has to look at Washington as a community would look at having a fire department. The fire department may not have a fire for a day, a week, or a month, but it has to be ready for that fire. Therefore it has to have personnel, the necessary equipment, the necessary backing, so that when a challenge does occur, it can respond immediately and not have to lose vital time while it re-creates the tools and the organization.

It was Palumbo's suggestion that led to David making ASCAP board members and songwriters a regular presence in the halls of Congress. "There are two reasons members of Congress will decide on accepting an appointment," Palumbo said.

One is with a constituent. They don't like to turn constituents away. Two is with famous people. Songwriters are not necessarily famous; members of Congress may know the performers, but they don't necessarily know the songwriters. So if you asked for a meeting with a member of Congress for Hal David, they may not know who Hal David is, but they sure as hell know "Raindrops Keep Fallin' on My Head." Our concentration was on the Judiciary Committee and also other committee members on the Intellectual Property subcommittee.

One such senator, Palumbo said, is a songwriter and ASCAP member himself: Orrin Hatch, a Republican from Utah.

> I forget the issue, but we were having a battle in Congress and Strom Thurmond was on the other side. By this time Thurmond was getting really up there in years. Hatch was chairman of the Judiciary Committee at the time.
>
> The hearing was held and Thurmond was recognized to speak, and he started reading from this statement his staff had prepared for him, and he was droning on and on and on, and I noticed Hatch writing. Finally after about 20 minutes Hatch got very frustrated and turned to Thurmond and said something like "How long are you going to go on? I've already told you we're going to give you a vote on this." Thurmond said, "Okay, I'll just put the rest of my speech in the public record." So they had a vote and Hatch prevailed. After the hearing was over I congratulated Hatch on winning and told him how impressed I was that he'd been taking notes while Thurmond was speaking at such length. He said, "Notes? I just wrote three songs."

Through the concerted efforts of ASCAP members, the *"Buffalo Broadcasting"* bill died in committee. "Everything ASCAP achieved was due to the results of lawsuits," Gloria Messinger noted.

> Step by step, plugging through the courts, and in Congress. Because they were once a monopoly, they had to be extremely careful with how they operated. When ASCAP was originally given a consent decree, members were told that they had to offer their work to anybody who wanted to use it exclusive of ASCAP, and that could have been very dicey. But our legal department stepped up and made it clear what the obligations and responsibilities of members were.

Tracing her lineage from Nathan Burkan through Herman Finkelstein to Bernard Korman, her immediate boss before she became managing director, Messinger was proud of ASCAP's legal legacy in the realm of copyright, which is an ever-evolving field of endeavor.

"Now there is a whole world out there of professors who are teaching young lawyers how you have to do away with the whole notion of personal property, of property, period," she said.

> There are professors in important law schools who are all on the Internet bandwagon. It's like, "Music is free; you've got to run with freedom." From my point of view, you have to protect the creator. Every time there is a new vehicle for the delivery of music, ASCAP or BMI or SESAC is entitled to license it unless it is exempt from being licensed, and that is because of the lobbying issues that go on in Congress all the time.

Hot Nashville writer Robert Ellis Orrall was one of the songwriters who heeded Hal David's call in 1986. An ASCAP member since 1973, he was based in Boston when he got a chance to meet Ted Kennedy.

> I had a record deal that had come and gone and I was sort of out of the business, working construction, making music at night, and sending songs out to publishers. I got a call from someone at ASCAP. Since I was living in Massachusetts, and not many songwriters were available to do this, they asked me to go to Washington to speak with Ted Kennedy on behalf of songwriters' rights.
>
> It was a very heady experience. We went to a reception and Senators Ted Kennedy and John Glenn (the former astronaut) were there. Leiber and Stoller are sitting at the piano playing their hits in the corner, just as entertainment for this gathering. There are all these great, classic songwriters in the room. I still have a photograph of me and Henry Mancini and these two senators. It was a really exciting thing.

An essential part of ASCAP's Washington agenda in those days was to salute ASCAP greats on Capitol Hill before an enthusiastic audience of legislators. Karen Sherry, who produced all of those events, recalls: "We would reserve a room on Capitol Hill and since those areas were usually in use during the day, we had to pull together all of the logistics in short order. Many a time, we were just finishing the set-up and rehearsals as our guest legislators were entering the space. But the events we presented were among the most memorable for ASCAP and for those who attended."

Among those saluted in that venue were Lena Horne, Rosemary Clooney, Peggy Lee, Henry Mancini, Tony Bennett, Billy Joel, Garth Brooks, Billy Joel, and Stevie Wonder.

When ASCAP honored Stevie Wonder on Capitol Hill in 2007, he expressed his feelings about music and about ASCAP. "Music has played such a vital role in our existence," he said. "It has been the very thing that has allowed people who know nothing about America except for the music, to love America. We must consistently commit ourselves to securing the rights for the songwriters, unknown as well as known, because they are speaking about and writing about the very essence of our lives."

Hal David's farewell essay of 1986 was filled with sentiment. "I feel privileged and proud to have had the opportunity to lead this great organization," he wrote. "I would like to express my deepest gratitude to the ASCAP board of directors, to the ASCAP management and staff, and to you, our members—for your unfailing support these years, and for the confidence you've placed in me throughout my term in office."

He was justifiably proud of his accomplishments. "We established the annual ASCAP Pop Music Awards ceremonies, the PRS Awards for our British writers, and we'll be holding our first Film and TV Awards in Los Angeles," David wrote.

> The word on the street has never been better and our visibility has never been brighter. This constant presence, together with the continuous influx of new and prestigious members from every quarter of the music business, has given ASCAP the image of a society that is both current and traditional, a magnet for both the new writer and the more established, an organization that is forward-looking, yet still firmly grounded in its roots.

Entering this glowing picture as David's replacement in 1986, the classical composer Morton Gould couldn't have had any idea that the biggest challenge awaiting him would come not from any of ASCAP's former foes, but from within the organization itself.

CHAPTER 8

GRIDLOCK, GRANTS, AND GIGABYTES

Not since the beloved Deems Taylor had a classical composer led the organization. It was as ASCAP's president that Taylor, in 1943, arranged for the Hungarian composer Béla Bartók, who had escaped from the Germans and was living in the US, to stay at a private sanitarium in the Adirondacks. Fran Richard, ASCAP's former director of concert music, recalled, "I remember my father took me to meet Béla Bartók and I learned that ASCAP had taken care of him when he was sick. Bartók was poor. As many refugees did, he'd left everything behind when he ran away and had to start over again." In *Deems Taylor: A Biography*, James Pegolotti described how "later, ASCAP maintained a level of support for both medical and other living expenses, including two more summers at Saranac Lake, before Bartók died in 1945."

The assistance was appreciated. Richard continued,

> So all these years later I found a letter in the file from Peter Bartók to the president of ASCAP, thanking him for everything that was done for his father. I was so touched when I read the letter that I took it and framed it and put it in Morton Gould's office. I called Peter Bartók and told him I had found something, and when I read him the first sentence he started to cry. He said, "I know exactly what letter that is." He asked me if I would send him a copy, which I did.

Morton Gould must have found cold comfort in that framed letter, representing an era at ASCAP now unalterably passing him by. In a diary entry from early in his tenure, dated 1987, reprinted in *Morton Gould: American Salute*, he wrote, "There is all kinds of trouble at ASCAP. What can be done in one day can take a month. Bit by bit, I hope to get a more efficient apparatus going and to clean out a lot of old things that have been leftovers from different times."

Fred Koenigsberg, now counsel to the ASCAP board, spoke about the internal changes brewing. "The board became increasingly disenchanted with the way ASCAP's management was running the business," he said.

> It was very hidebound and old-fashioned. It was very structured, very stratified, very hierarchical. To give you an example, if a telephone inquiry comes in from a vendor to somebody at a lower level, rather than answer that question as asked, they're scared. "If I give an answer it could come back to bite me," because that's how the place was run. So they bump the question up to their supervisor, who bumps it up the line. The question would actually go up seven rungs to the director of membership. "The answer's no." Then it had to go down the seven rungs. Now it's four months later. "By the way, remember that question? Well, the answer is no." That's no way to run a railroad.

While many people both on and off the board at ASCAP may have thought the 73-year-old Gould would be a figurehead when he assumed the mantle of the presidency, too concerned with his ongoing career to want to deal with the myriad responsibilities of running the Society, the cultured and witty composer soon became immersed in perhaps the biggest internal battle in ASCAP's history. "There are conflicts with an entrenched general manager and entrenched general counsel who have delusions of grandeur and power," he wrote in his diary. "I have to fight them every inch to achieve what I think I should achieve. What they are doing is protecting their terrain."

"Management wanted to run the organization without the supervision of the board," Peter W. Goodman wrote in Gould's biography.

"But Morton was a working president and a working composer at the same time. As a musician he had always been intellectually and professionally interested in the latest ideas and techniques. He was never afraid of the future and he was determined to bring ASCAP fully in tune with the times."

The internal organizational battles he faced were in large part responsible for stifling whatever else Gould may have had in mind for the future. Ironically, when systemic changes were finally made, in the form of a reorganization nearly eight years later, it was the classical music area and its representation on the board that took a major hit. Where once classical composers and publishers had held six seats out of a total of 24, after the reorganization that total dwindled to two, with one writer and one publisher left to reflect the relatively minuscule income potential of the genre. Early in 1994, shortly after the changes were implemented, Gould resigned his position. He died in 1996.

Veteran publisher and board member Irwin Z. Robinson explained: "The shake-up came more from the board feeling like they were not being involved enough by the management of ASCAP. There was a disconnect between management and the board and that was why Booz Allen came in." The renowned consulting firm, specializing in business, engineering, and entertainment, did a top-to-bottom analysis of ASCAP's operations, lasting six months. "Not only were they looking at the organization, but they were looking at the board and how they conducted themselves and the role they played in terms of setting policy," Robinson said.

Seated outside the often closed door of the president, Gould's executive assistant, Toni Winter, was well aware of what was going on inside. "Morton Gould wanted to make changes," she said, "but some changes cannot be made overnight. It takes a very, very long time. Eventually they brought in these so-called geniuses who are now all over in all industries. They talked to some people, but you know, when you're a secretary, you don't have to answer to anybody but your boss."

"In essence Booz Allen's recommendation was 'You've got to get new management,'" Fred Koenigsberg said. "The board accepted that recommendation unanimously."

"From its very founding, ASCAP's board and management, of

necessity, relied heavily on the advice of attorneys," Gloria Messinger acknowledged years later, reflecting on her time as managing director.

> Our general counsel was right up there equal to me. And then in the '90s the board decided they'd had enough of these lawyers telling them what they couldn't do and they decided to clean house. Somebody told me that under the new regime the lawyers said, "We never tell the board no unless we absolutely think they're going to jail." Well, that was not quite the way ASCAP's lawyers had ever operated in the past. But they probably did take too much of a role in how board members functioned.

After the departure of Gloria Messinger, a search committee was formed to find a new ASCAP CEO from outside the organization, who would report to the board. Early in 1994, they tapped someone from the broadcasting industry, Dan Gold (previous head of Century Communications, Knight Ridder, and Comcast), whose tenure lasted only until December. Upon Gold's unceremonious exit, John LoFrumento was appointed acting CEO and then CEO in his place, a position he has held since then. Fred Koenigsberg credits the outgoing and upbeat LoFrumento with nothing less than "a cultural revolution. People got more responsibility, more training," he said.

"Before John LoFrumento came in, you had an ASCAP that was so compartmentalized that none of the departments knew what the other departments were doing, nor did they speak to each other," said Gould's successor as president and chairman of the board, Oscar-winning lyricist Marilyn Bergman. "John came in and changed all that."

"I came from a different world and in my world you got people involved," LoFrumento said.

> We brought our management people in the room in order to assess what we were doing, and why were we doing it. I needed my people at ASCAP to give me their input in order for us to build an improved ASCAP. And what we did was to energize the managers who today have become senior VP's. We said to them that what you have to say is important. You can't be trumped by the guy above you.

When there was a board meeting here in the old days, no employees were allowed to talk to the board with the exception of the senior managers, and there were four of us. Once I came in, the people reporting to me could talk to any board member.

One of the most painful of LoFrumento's early challenges was to reduce the staff. "Over the years our staff kept getting bigger and bigger," he said. "Every time something new came along we would hire more people to deal with the situation." By the time the dust cleared the 900 had gone down to 600. Many of those people, LoFrumento said, came from the field offices all around the country.

We had 300 people in 26 offices. They were the ones who would call up and say to a club owner, "Hey, I passed your bar and I noticed you were in as I was coming to work. You haven't paid us in four months. I'll come by tomorrow morning and I'll bring you a cup of coffee." So they became our telephone licensing managers in this new world and we eliminated about 215 positions. But we did it in a very humane way. Computers were just coming out in the early '90s and we gave them all computer training. We worked with them to help them find jobs.

Including everything from the music that is heard at shopping malls to that heard in large restaurants and at movie theaters before the movie starts, general licensing is overseen by Vincent Candilora, ASCAP's executive VP of licensing.

"I was hired by ASCAP in September of '95," Candilora said. It was a time for implementing new efficiencies.

We closed 25 of the 26 field offices. We were one of the early companies to adopt telecommuting. Our general licensing representatives worked out of their homes and out of their automobiles and they were connected by computer to our systems here at ASCAP. Since we represent the right to publicly perform music, there are no real tangibles. We don't have physical inventory. We exchange signatures on a piece of paper. One is a license, the other is a check. So to be able to continue to provide the best service we can for our members, reducing our cost is one of our missions each and every year.

One key mission for LoFrumento was to motivate the staff that remained after the Booz Allen posse rode off into the sunset. "By restructuring, I was asking, 'What are my core values and what do I need for the future for ASCAP to continue to succeed?'" he said.

> One of the things I need for the future is good young managers, people who have great experience in ASCAP. I said to them, "We have two choices. You can stand on the side and watch change happen. Or you can be part of the change and not even notice that it's changing. All you know is that you are building a new company, but it will be a part of you and you will be a part of it. When it's completed you'll be totally acclimated to it.

For Marilyn Bergman, who replaced Morton Gould to become ASCAP's first female president (serving from 1994 to 2009), there were far bigger issues to deal with than merely breaking the glass ceiling. "I was used to being the only woman in a room," she commented. "For years my husband Alan and I would go to meetings where whoever was on the other side of the desk would direct questions to Alan and not me. I never found that to be the case in the ASCAP boardroom."

The members had little time for such pettiness when the radical shifts in technology brought about by the Internet invaded their world. "I had to really do homework on the challenges to copyright caused by all the new technology," Bergman said.

> I was learning the whole time. The business was and still is so fluid. So we all had to keep up with what was happening at great speed. There were new rules being laid down, new ways of doing business, new challenges, constantly. We all became more savvy about these challenges as time went on and it became more and more clear that this is what the future would be. But the effect on ASCAP is still being felt.

Bergman's early tenure was consumed by the usual threats to ASCAP members' copyrights and the law, as it has been constantly reinterpreted by successive generations of music users hoping to gain access to vast stores of music without paying—and to the blanket license as ASCAP's chief means of preventing that. Long after having come to terms in 1917 with the club and restaurant owners of America, in the mid-1990s, ASCAP found small business owners (of clubs, restaurants, grocery stores, and any other establishments that had a single radio or television set playing through a set of speakers in the background) joining hands with religious broadcasters to essentially wage the same battle.

The run-up to H.R. 789, also known as the Fairness in Music Licensing Bill, was particularly vociferous, with Russ Hauth, the executive director of the National Religious Broadcasters Music License Committee, decrying ASCAP's ominous power to control the marketplace in favor of its songwriters and publishers. "In its 50-year history no broadcast group has successfully argued in rate court against ASCAP except the powerful independent television industry, which spent $15 million over 10 years to win a landmark case in 1994," he was quoted in the September 1996 issue of *Religious Broadcasting*. Hauth was referring to the local television stations' rate court proceeding, in which the court had established the rate for the stations' blanket licenses and a new formula for per-program licenses used primarily by stations affiliated with the major television networks. Also, by that time, the religious radio stations had launched their own antitrust suit against ASCAP.

In the same article, NRB president Brandt Gustavson chimed in. "ASCAP lobbyists are working overtime to create division between Christian songwriters and stations," he said. "We are encouraging stations to pray for success and to commit monetary gifts over the next year so the committee won't be left with a deficit."

On the other side of the aisle, Michael Kosser stated the case for songwriters in the September 1996 issue of *American Songwriter Magazine*: "What hypocrisy! Religious broadcasters banding together with bar owners to pass an anti-copyright bill. And some of the staunchest copyright destroyers are self-proclaimed conservatives who

122   A FRIEND IN THE MUSIC BUSINESS

cry out that government should keep its filthy hands out of private business, yet are using government power to destroy licensing procedures that have worked well for half a century."

"The licensing societies' recruitment of religious songwriters as stalking horses against my bill certainly cannot relate to the per programming period provisions of the Fairness in Music Licensing Act," said F. James Sensenbrenner Jr., a Republican representative in Congress from Wisconsin, in his remarks before the Judiciary Committee considering the bill.

> Religious and specialty broadcasters recognize their obligation to pay for licensed music and will still pay for performances of licensed material whether that material is of a religious nature or not. However, this payment ought to reflect the amount of licensed material included in a broadcast. This has been affirmed in the courts when television broadcasters challenged the societies. Now we are in the midst of a conceivably endless season of litigation so religious and specialty radio broadcasters might be treated fairly as well. As the licensing societies' coffers expand, I fear a portion of the licensing fees extracted from religious broadcast stations may surreptitiously end up in the royalty checks of such morally objectionable artists as Snoop Doggy Dogg and Marilyn Manson.

This comment actually refers to a weighting practice that has since been eliminated. ASCAP's Peter Boyle explained.

> It used to be all radio went to all radio, weighted based on their license fees. In the late '90s we made things explicit so that money from pop goes to pop, urban goes to urban, religious goes to religious. For live symphony and concert performances at Carnegie Hall and the New York Philharmonic we multiply the license fees by somewhere between three and four times from what they collect, for distribution purposes. That's the only area where there's subsidy like that, where the distribution is more than the fees collected. The additional money comes

from the membership across the board, with everybody contributing proportionally.

Speaking to the committee on behalf of the U.S. Copyright Office, Marybeth Peters said,

In the view of the Copyright Office, as a matter of general policy, the government should not interfere in the marketplace and place limitations on the contractual freedom of copyright owners and users to negotiate terms and conditions for the use of copyrighted works. Today, such governmental constraints have been imposed only in the context of antitrust law, through the operation of the consent decree under the jurisdiction of the federal court in New York. We also question the limitations on fee-setting, which, when combined with the mandatory nature of the per programming period license, appear to have the potential to greatly reduce the income generated for copyright owners under the current system, as well as the economic feasibility of a system that may require monitoring the broadcasts of every radio station in America. Both ASCAP and BMI operate under consent decrees. Thus, substantial safeguards already exist against abusive practices or unreasonable charges.

In spite of the heated objections of ASCAP and BMI, on October 8, 1998, Congress finally passed the Fairness in Music Licensing Act. The big winners were the small business owners, who gained a number of important exemptions from the ASCAP licensing process. The big losers, aside from ASCAP, were the religious broadcasters, although the second part of the act reiterated that they could always seek redress in rate court if they didn't like what ASCAP (or BMI) proposed. The act passed as a last-minute amendment to a piece of companion legislation called the Sonny Bono Copyright Term Extension Act, which increased the length of copyright by 20 years, to the life of the lyricist or composer plus 70 years (making it the same as it is in Europe). Since adding another 20 years to the life of a copyright was chiefly a financial matter, it passed through the House and Senate Judiciary Committees without a hitch. But Jim Sensenbrenner went to the Speaker of the House, Newt Gingrich, and asked him to hold up a vote until he could offer his restaurant and small business constituents their slice of the pie. ASCAP's man in Washington, Ben Palumbo, offered insight into that political process.

> Until this point the Intellectual Property subcommittee had almost always acted in a bipartisan way. But the restaurant owners and the Small Business Association were heavily supportive of the Republican party, which made it more of a partisan issue when we got to the floor of the House. Not so much in the Judiciary Committee, where we managed to fight them to a standstill. We had such a strong presence in the Judiciary Committees of both the House and the Senate that despite the fact that they had been massively supportive of the Republicans and Republicans controlled the committee, they couldn't get their bill reported out for action before the House. I knew if they ever did, they would prevail, because they were much stronger among Republican members generally than they were within the Judiciary Committee.

Now, Palumbo explained, the debt Gingrich and the Republicans felt they owed to the restaurant owners and the Small Business Association prompted them to agree to Sensenbrenner's request. He continued,

> The minute I knew the Fairness in Music Licensing Act was going to be offered as an amendment I knew we would lose. And, of course, it was offered as an amendment and it was approved and life plus 70 passed. But the Senate had reported life plus 70 without any such amendment. So they had to go to a conference, and leading the conference on the Senate side was Orrin Hatch. The conferees met in the office of the Senate majority leader, Trent Lott, from Mississippi, who had decided to support us after we brought up ten songwriters from Mississippi, who sat with him in his conference room. In a bravura performance, he asked their names and managed to find a connection with every one of them—oh, I knew your cousin Bill; I dated

a girl in the same sorority as your sister . . . and so on. So they made a strong case and he decided he was going to support Hatch. So there they sat, Hatch and Lott, and on other side, the speaker Gingrich and Jim Sensenbrenner, and they went tooth and nail for 35 minutes over the question of how many square feet should be exempt from needing a license to play music over speakers. With all of the important issues in the world that's what they were fighting over.

According to Palumbo, during an earlier negotiation with the Restaurant Association, ASCAP offered to increase the size of the exemption from 1000 to 3500 square feet. "There are hundreds of thousands of restaurants, and ASCAP and BMI don't have the money to hire enough manpower to go out and check every restaurant to see what they're doing," said Palumbo.

By virtue of agreeing to increase the size, essentially what ASCAP did was to recognize that since it didn't have enough manpower to check all the restaurants, with the extension, it was cutting out those establishments that never would have been checked anyway. But ASCAP was turned down. Now, after the conference, the final result was an exemption of 3750 feet. In other words, as a result of this fight they got an additional 250 square feet over what had been offered three years before.

The leeway the bill allowed for most of the restaurants and bars in the United States to use a radio or a TV on their premises without needing to take out an ASCAP (or BMI or SESAC) license was troubling. It also included similar exemptions for record stores, electronics stores, and other retail outlets that sell records and/or radios, TVs, CDs, etc.

Needless to say, ASCAP was not pleased by the results. Marilyn Bergman offered this statement.

In one sweeping legislative action, the House and Senate have passed music copyright term extension with one hand yet severely curtailed music copyright protection with the other. With this music licensing legislation, which seizes the private property of copyright owners, the United States government has severely penalized America's songwriters, composers, and publishers. Not only will our earnings be reduced, but so will the creative incentive for future generations of songwriters. It is important to let music creators everywhere know that we did everything humanly possible to combat this unconscionable legislation.

Frances Preston, Bergman's counterpart at BMI, was similarly outraged.

This is a sad day for all creators of music in America and intellectual property rights owners. This legislation challenges the spirit of the Constitution as it expropriates, without compensation, the intellectual property of our songwriters, composers, and music publishers. Even before this anti-music legislation was passed, music licensing costs constituted far less than 1 percent of the average restaurant gross sales. The earnings of songwriters, composers, and publishers have now been reduced by tens of millions of dollars annually.

From a purely public relations standpoint, it didn't help ASCAP generate much sympathy for the songwriter's plight that all this took place at about the same time the Society came under the national media microscope for a scuffle with no less sanctified an organization than the Girl Scouts of America. "We had negotiated an agreement with something called the American Camping Association for a significant discount off what the fee would have been for a single camp for all the members of the association," explained ASCAP's Richard Reimer, senior vice president of legal services. Now known as the American Camp Association, this nonprofit organization for camp professionals was founded in 1910. It now establishes health and safety standards for more than 2400 summer camps across the United States.

We said, "Give us a list of your members and we'll send out the license." And among the camps we sent the license to was apparently one that was operated by an individual, but it was essentially a Girl Scout camp. It was not the GSUSA operating the camp, but it was a camp for Girl Scouts. Somehow or other, the owner of the camp was interviewed by the *Wall Street Journal*, and that's when things got interesting. There was a great deal of negative publicity and suddenly we were on the network news.

On August 25, 1996, David Brinkley commented on it, just before signing off his weekly show on ABC-TV. With his typical tongue-in-cheek humor, he painted a picture of innocent Girl Scouts singing around a campfire while under siege from men in suits brandishing ASCAP licenses.

It took until August 29 before Charles Osgood set the record straight on his radio program broadcast over WCBS: "Did you read . . . that ASCAP is suing the Girl Scouts? . . . That would be terrible if it were true, but it's not true. They never intended to make the Girl Scouts buy licenses or to sue them. . . . In fact, ASCAP has paid millions of dollars to the Scouts over the years."

The monies earned not only from performances, but also from mechanicals and sheet music sales of "God Bless America" as well as "Oh! How I Hate to Get Up in the Morning" and several others, go directly to the God Bless America Foundation, set up by Irving Berlin in 1940 to benefit the youth of America, especially those in the Boy Scouts and Girl Scouts. To date the GBA Foundation has paid out more than $6 million to these two organizations.

"Ultimately the Girl Scouts were very nice to us," Richard Reimer said. "They took out an ad that ran in the *Washington Post* and *Roll Call*, the Congressional newspaper, that said that the Girl Scouts and ASCAP had always gotten along."

Far more gratifying for Marilyn Bergman in her presidency was her focus on "feeding the future and protecting the present" with education, primarily through The ASCAP Foundation. Established in 1975 by a bequest from Jack Norworth, cowriter of "Take Me Out to the Ballgame," the Foundation was "a sleeping giant" when Karen Sherry, ASCAP's vice president of communications, was given the task of awakening it in 1998. Today the Foundation offers about a million dollars a year in grants, cash awards, and scholarships. It supports a number of highly regarded songwriting workshops across many musical genres, and funds programs by other 501c3 organizations that complement its mission. For many years, its flagship program was a summer camp run in partnership with the New York City Department of Education and the Manhattan School of Music. The ASCAP Foundation provided the funding; the Manhattan School of Music provided the setting, the teachers, and the curriculum; and the city provided the transportation and the lunches. Underprivileged kids from all five boroughs auditioned for the limited spots. "The first years we underwrote this project with a grant of $100,000," Sherry said. "For ten years in a row we received a grant from the National Endowment for the Arts—a remarkable achievement—to help support this program."

"In the last 15 to 20 years the Foundation has grown enormously," Marilyn Bergman said. "It's a very important aspect of ASCAP." She takes special pride in the Creativity in the Classroom program. "It's a program that informs children that when they write a song or a poem or a story, they have created something they own, and if somebody else wants to use it or print it, they have to have permission," she said. "It has to start in the schools." She also spearheaded the Children Will Listen program, in honor of Stephen Sondheim, which brings the musical theater experience to inner city school kids.

In 2011, board member Valerie Simpson—who wrote and performed with her late husband, Nickolas Ashford, as Ashford & Simpson, co-authors of hits like "Ain't No Mountain High Enough," "Reach Out and Touch (Somebody's Hand)," and "I'm Every Woman"—started the "Reach Out and Touch" Award in her husband's name at The ASCAP Foundation.

It's for songwriters who are in the midst of a project but just don't have quite enough money to finish. So the first year I was able to give a young songwriter $5000 to finish up a project he was doing. By doing that I hope to shine a light on somebody who's not just beginning but who's in the middle of something and not quite there yet. The name of ASCAP has a lot of weight, and being able to say that I am a member of this board who cares about you means a lot to a struggling songwriter who's just at that place where you might give up or you might go forward. It's my way of encouraging them.

The "Reach Out and Touch" Award joins an honor roll of large and small grants handed out each year by The ASCAP Foundation to jazz and classical composers; musical theater writers; pop singer/songwriters; R&B, jazz, and country songwriters; film and TV composers; and aspiring music publishers. "We got involved in the Foundation to honor my father, who was a legendary music publisher," said Caroline Bienstock, whose father, Freddy, started out in the business at Hill and Range, pitching songs to Elvis Presley. He eventually headed his own company, Carlin Music, named after his daughter, and co-owned the Hudson Bay Music Company with Elvis' favorite songwriting team, Jerry Leiber and Mike Stoller.

For my father to be elected by his peers to the board of ASCAP was probably the proudest event of his career, an indication that he had arrived in the industry as someone who was a successful publisher. Because of his feelings about being on the ASCAP board, we felt that having a Foundation scholarship in his name would be something that would have made sense to him and to us. So we partnered with The ASCAP Foundation to create a paid internship for a business school student who wants to study music publishing, which would have been the kind of mentorship my father would have appreciated being able to do.

Bienstock noted that the many applicants for this coveted position must prepare to enter a different world from the one her father knew.

Young people don't realize what the challenges are in the industry, what the consequences of the Internet have been for the finances of the music business in general. They still think it's a glamorous and exciting business to get into. Since we give away an award, I've been to the last two ASCAP Foundation events and they're heartwarming. It's inspiring to see young people putting their faith in the future and imagining that it's going to be possible for them to make a living and live their lives being a musician or a composer. I believe it should be possible and I believe it will be.

One recent winner of the ASCAP Foundation Irving Berlin Summer Music Camp Scholarship was 16-year-old Sam Pennington, a student of the piano and clarinet, whose magnum opus at the time was "a choral work in the Dorian mode based on the *Dies Irae* text." Which placed him at about the furthest extreme on the musical spectrum from his benefactor, Irving Berlin himself, who mastered during his magnificent career only one key on the piano, the one with all the black keys, F-sharp. "For some reason it was a key that felt easy in his hands," said his eldest daughter, Mary Ellin Barrett. "I don't understand it. I think the key of C would be the best, with no black keys."

The coveted Foundation award named after the Oscar-winning songwriter and former ASCAP board member Sammy Cahn ("All the Way") was won in 2006 by John Mayer, now one of pop music's reigning heartthrobs. According to Karen Sherry, "He got $10,000 and he says he never forgot it. It was the first indication that somebody believed in him."

A Berklee dropout, Mayer attributed his discovery to ASCAP's Courtney Hard, who brought him to an ASCAP showcase at Stubb's Bar-B-Q in Austin, Texas, in 2002, held during the annual South by Southwest festivities. A massive industry networking event, South by Southwest is generally favored by indie bands of the alternative stripe. Mayer recalled,

> Either I wasn't big enough at the time or I wasn't South-by-Southwest-y enough, but I was invited to play at the ASCAP showcase, and I realized there was as much buzz about me there as there would have been for anyone else at South by Southwest. I remember at the end someone talked to my lawyer and asked, "Is he blind?" and my lawyer said, "No," and they said, "Oh, we thought so because he never opened his eyes the entire time."
>
> After that showcase, there was always something on the table. It was ASCAP that put into motion the concept of looking forward to tomorrow because the phone is going to ring. When

I got the Sammy Cahn Award, it was amazing. I never really thought I was going to create a body of work. I just wanted to write one more song, you know? It was such a gratifying experience. That's why ASCAP is one of the few places where, when people ask me to do something, I don't ask, "What do I get?"

Like many neophyte musicians, Mayer was fairly naive about performance rights when he got his first recording deal. "When I signed with ASCAP I didn't even know what a performance rights organization did," he said. "I had to learn that while I was in the office at Lincoln Center. And once I figured it out I went, 'Oh, okay, this is cool.' In some ways it's like a surrogate record company."

ASCAP Foundation composer board member Doug Wood is passionate about the work of the Foundation:

The ASCAP Foundation touches the lives of young composers in a way that is both unique and profound. Life can be lonely for young composers—they're toiling away for hours while their friends are out having fun. At times, I'm sure many of them wonder if they're on the right track—if their work is any good. How can they tell? And that's where the Foundation comes in.

I've had many Foundation award-winners tell me that the phone call from The ASCAP Foundation telling them they had been selected for an award was the single most exciting moment in their young careers. First of all, the award was from ASCAP—the most prestigious name in the music industry. And second, they were selected from among hundreds of their peers. An award from the Foundation is a pat on the back like no other, and an incredible incentive for a young composer to keep going, keep trying, keep writing. And sometimes, coming at the right moment, that validation can literally change the life of a young composer.

"My first introduction to ASCAP was with a lawyer in New York who was affiliated with Nina Simone," said Kenny Burrell, one of the greatest jazz guitarists of all time and a member of ASCAP since 1957.

In one of my conversations with him he suggested I join ASCAP, because I'd been a writer for many years, since I was a teenager, and I'm sure I expressed that to him, and he told me a few things that were encouraging enough for me to take that step. In all the time I've been a member of ASCAP, I've always felt well protected and that ASCAP was looking out for my interests, and they've never failed to serve me at the highest level.

With a career that encompasses nearly a hundred albums under his own name, innumerable sessions as a first-call guitarist for artists ranging from James Brown and B. B. King to Lena Horne and Tony Bennett, and tunes covered by the likes of John Coltrane, Stevie Ray Vaughan, June Christy, and Dee Dee Bridgewater, Burrell now teaches at UCLA, which cosponsors the ASCAP Foundation Louis Armstrong Jazz Scholarship Honoring Duke Ellington. "Jazz always has its problems, but all of music is having problems," he said. "But the point is, jazz continues to grow like a tree: always new things blooming on the tree."

If so, it will be in no small part due to the contribution of ASCAP to organizations that help spread the gospel. "We'd been sending out numerous requests for funding and getting declined for three years and then, much to my delight, The ASCAP Foundation came on board in 1996," said Hans Schuman, who runs an organization called JazzReach, dedicated to fostering new audiences for jazz throughout the country. "I guess something about our mission resonated with them and they gave us our first grant. It was an affirmation in many ways that our vision was a good one and the program was cohesive and well structured."

The much-recorded bassist Rufus Reid, who has worked with everyone from Dexter Gordon to Dizzy Gillespie and recorded with everyone from Thad Jones and Mel Lewis to Jack DeJohnette's *Special Edition* (which also featured Kenny Burrell), was a professor of jazz studies and performance at William Paterson University in Wayne, New Jersey, from 1979 to 1999. He often sits on the panel that judges The ASCAP Foundation's annual Herb Alpert Young Jazz Composer Awards program, the age limit of which is 30 years old. "Today's musicians are unbelievably more prepared and knowledgeable than when I was coming up," Reid said. "Jazz education has completely exploded. But one of the problems is, how does one sustain a career?" As opposed to similarly schooled classical musicians, who have much more defined and limited spots to compete for, jazz players always have the option of playing dives for pennies. But this is often the prelude to a long and merciless apprenticeship. "Many of the young players are so much more aware of marketing and getting management than in playing the hell out of their instrument," said Reid. "There's not that big a percentage of people who have the ability to persevere."

Obviously, perseverance, in whatever form of music, depends upon the promise of just rewards somewhere up the road. At ASCAP that promise has been kept to the nth degree, enabling an icon like Patti Smith to acknowledge as much in accepting her Founders Award in 2010.

> When I did *Horses*, I didn't know you got ASCAP checks. I just thought you did your record and that was it. When I got my first ASCAP check, I thought, "I've already been paid for this." When my husband passed away in November of 1994, I was a widow with two children. What helped bail me out and get me back on my feet were the ASCAP checks that I got from people covering "Because the Night." So I'm grateful to ASCAP in the good times, and I'm really grateful in the hard times.

CHAPTER 9

A COMMON CAUSE

From its inception in 1914, the 12 writer members and 12 publisher members of the ASCAP board of directors have been some of the greatest songwriters and most forward-thinking publishers in history. The first board featured Irving Berlin, Victor Herbert, and Raymond Hubbell; on the publishing side sat Max Dreyfus, Jay Witmark, Louis Bernstein, and George Maxwell, the Society's first president. In 1920, future presidents Gene Buck and Otto Harbach were seated. Jerome Kern served from 1924 to 1929 and again from 1932 to 1942. Richard Rodgers was on the board three times between 1929 and 1974. Deems Taylor was on the board for 32 years, Morton Gould for 37 years, and Stanley Adams for 50 years. Max Dreyfus was approaching 50 years on the board when he died in 1964, to be replaced by his brother, Louis. Publisher Wesley Rose came on the board in 1967, even when most of his business was handled by BMI. Irwin Z. Robinson was elected to the board in 1972 and is still going strong.

Every two years, board members must submit their statement of candidacy for reelection, which is then presented to the membership to vote on. ASCAP operates on a system of weighted votes, in which the more credits you have, the more your vote is worth, with any one vote being worth a maximum of 100. Every two years established and emerging candidates for the board submit their briefs gladly. Because serving on the ASCAP board is not just a job; it's a crusade.

And the crusade is the protection of intellectual property—which, in the Internet era, is under siege as it has never been before in ASCAP's history.

As the compiler of the daily newsletter *The Dean's List*, board member Dean Kay, the president and CEO of Lichelle Music and the author of "That's Life," is more immersed in the intricacies of the digital world than most. "We are going through the most drastic change we've ever been through in my entire history in ASCAP, which started in 1958," he said.

> There have been changes in the business through the years. As long as I've been on the board, there have been changes in how things operate. But today we're taking a look at a whole new world that hasn't existed before and trying to figure out how to deal with it. Take this newsletter I put out every day. I thought I would start it just to get our board up to speed. I thought, "As soon as they have a feeling for what's going on, then I won't do this anymore." But I haven't been able to stop, because every morning I get up and review the news stories available and there is a drastic change in what's going on. Everybody understands it now. The only reason I can't say that everybody is up to speed is that it's impossible. It's just impossible.
>
> Usually, when something's coming down the pike like cable you have ten years to get yourself in gear, go through a bunch of court actions, figure it out, but we don't have that time. We can't get through the court system fast enough to get anything settled before the next big thing is already up and operating. In many cases it is up and operating by people who don't care about copyright.
>
> On my end I'm certainly seeing less and less income. There are tons of users, but they make tiny payments. ASCAP's basis is if you get a performance on radio in Los Angeles you are likely to touch a million listeners, and on the Internet it is usually a one-to-one thing, so the payments are minuscule. Thousands and thousands of performances add up to no money. I had pages upon pages of uses of my writers' material in various Internet outlets that wouldn't add up to a dollar.

Nicholas Firth was the head of publishing at BMG when the company went into negotiations to buy the rogue free downloading site Napster. "There is no question the record companies got it wrong from the beginning," he said. "As opposed to embracing it and figuring out how we could get involved, their attitude was 'Let's build a chastity belt so you can't steal our music.' In a similar sort of way, the societies took a very aggressive position to try and license and collect from the Internet and ended up collecting pennies.""

ASCAP publisher vice chair Irwin Z. Robinson was on the board when the great white shark of the Internet first appeared in the mid-'90s. "When the word *digital* was first heard most of the people who were running record companies and perhaps still are today were old veterans like me," he said.

> I had conversations with them in those days and they said, "It's a novelty. It'll only be here for a while. We still think people like to go into stores and look at album covers and listen." So they paid very little attention to digital uses. They were almost forced into hiring somebody on their staff to supposedly deal with it, but they gave it short shrift and because of that they were late to get into the game. Finally, when they saw it was taking hold from a piracy point of view, they tried to set up their own Web site for legally downloading songs. But they just didn't know how to get it together. They were still in the brick-and-mortar world. They were still thinking it was a passing fancy, until finally their distribution was taken away from them. They lost control. They still put money into a product, they went into the studio, they signed the artist, but they lost control over what happened with it.
>
> You can have a number one record today selling very few copies, and that's because of two things. All of the major chains are now closed. You've got hardly any music retail stores open anymore, except for maybe some small shops, where people can go in and buy hard goods. And to the extent that digital is now the predominant way people are buying music, from a numbers point of view, they're buying singles, they're not buying albums. So when you sign an artist today, you can no longer do what we

did ten years ago and predict what the artist's album would sell. And if you had all ten or 11 songs, you were able to put your finger in the wind and say, "Okay, I'm willing to pay such and such an advance based on so many sales." But you can hardly do that today. And so as that piece of the pie has diminished there's been pressure on the remaining pieces to make up for lost income. The hope or expectation was that the performing rights piece would continue to grow. What that means is that ASCAP's job has become more rigorous in terms of having to license more Web sites; but will the dollars be the same? That certainly doesn't seem to be the case.

Recently, we went to a conference in Washington, and an important writer got up and said, "I don't care if my songs are free on the Internet. I want as many people to hear and use my works as possible." That was really the beginning of a sea change, not so much on the creative side, because I haven't heard many other writers echo what that writer said at that meeting, but certainly where you have whole groups of people who are convincing people of this, slowly but surely, and we have to fight them at every turn of the road. Every time something comes out in print telling people that these things should be free, we have to counter it. That's the gravest danger we have, the fact that people are going around saying that songwriters shouldn't make a living.

Former board member Jay Morgenstern, who was for many years the executive vice president of Warner Brothers Publications, the print music division of Warner Music, commented on the difficulty of tracking emerging artists whose work is shared predominantly online: "You don't even know what a number one single is because *Billboard* has so many charts. Is it sales or is it plays or is it downloads? ASCAP has to administrate all that. They have to keep updating their system. BMI as well. They have to keep putting money into it. They can't just sit back and dream of the way it used to be."

Warner Brothers Records is now run by Cameron Strang, a board newcomer at two years. He is also the chairman and CEO of the esteemed publishing company Warner/Chappell Music. Naturally enough, Strang is bullish about the future of the songwriting profession. "Somehow, year after year, songwriters keep writing these incredible songs," he said. "It's easy to lose sight of it, but one of the great things about having a career in music is you get to be part of that." Strang's unique corporate position enables him to keep tabs on a pair of historically antagonistic industries: music publishing and the record business.

On the highest level sometimes record companies and publishers are at odds with each other, but the age-old record-label-versus-publisher rivalry has diminished as we've moved into a digital world. We have to work together to figure out how to promote new services, new ways of distribution, new ways of people listening to music. We've had to figure out what are the business models around that; how do creators and copyright holders and content people get paid, how do record labels and publishers get paid, how do the distributors get paid and how much does it cost consumers and how are they going to pay for that?

The reality is, we've got new partners. Songwriters have always had artists as partners and they've always had record labels as partners; now we've got other people as partners and we have to figure out how we're going to deal with them. Some of them are out to get us and want to erode our rights. Some want to work with us. There's a whole new group of executives and artists and people in the business who want to face those challenges in new ways and come up with positive solutions. At ASCAP the board is all pretty much on the same page. Paul Williams and John LoFrumento are great leaders, who bring people into alignment with what we're doing. It's such a dynamic business with so many new players. I think it's a matter of keeping up with that.

Film/TV composer Bruce Broughton has been on the board for eight years.

After my first day on the ASCAP board, I remember thinking two things. The first was that this was a board that dealt with big issues. The second was that there was a lot of significant firepower in the room. Since that initial meeting, some of the issues have changed, but they have not become any easier. If anything, they've become more difficult. But my opinion of the board has not changed. It would be fair to say that one is never entirely prepared for what might be brought up at the next meeting of the ASCAP board. Although I've heard dismissive or critical comments about ASCAP being "a songwriters' organization" or that "the board is run by publishers," neither has been my experience. In my view, both sides are necessary to the other, and each side provides what the other cannot. In contrast to the writers, the publishers, whether representing large or small companies, all work in similar fashion. They are business people on the forefront of music licensing and copyright, dealing with the often-mercurial demands and needs of the music consumer. They understand the world of licensing. The writers, on the other hand, are essentially creative people, not business people, who often do not work similarly to each other. They, however, understand the world of the music creator. The 12 writers are a mixture of composers and lyricists, some of whom write songs, some of whom write audio-visual scores, and some of whom write concert music. But the issues of copyright protection and equitable licensing are the same for all of them, as they are for all of the members of the ASCAP board. I have seen writers *and* publishers equally challenge, question, or offer alternatives that address the organization's maximum efficiency in how it does its work.

One of ASCAP's slogans is "We Create Music." We work at protecting it as well. I can't say board members are always in agreement as to how that protection will happen, but as I said at the start, there's a lot of firepower in the room. The board constantly readjusts its sights for maximum impact.

Veteran ASCAP board member publisher John L. Eastman has served since 1997. He is cofounder (with Paul McCartney) and officer of MPL Communications, one of the largest independent publishers. Eastman, who is also a longtime music business attorney, views the

ASCAP board as "a disparate group of major publishers, independent publishers, classical—or otherwise specialized—publishers, and writers of current hits, great standards, country music, movie and television music, and classical composers, often with differing interests. Yet we all understand we have comity of interest and inevitably come together to support the rights of creators of music."

Jimmy Webb, author of "MacArthur Park," "By the Time I Get to Phoenix," and dozens of other standards, joined the board in 2000 and is now writer vice chair. He remembers his first few meetings as a baptism by fire.

> Over time I began to realize that my emergence onto the board fit quite neatly with the emergence of these peer-to-peer technologies, which is the biggest donnybrook on the face of the planet. What you saw at the outset was a certain amount of naïveté on the part of our community that people would probably behave in a vaguely civilized manner, and that was a gross misassumption by us. We didn't realize that we were about to eaten alive and left by the side of the road to die. I have been here for 11 years, and for 11 years we have been trying to figure out how to get into this game, not how to get rid of this game, but how to get into the game.

One of the game's first new major players was iTunes, which ASCAP eventually licensed. Said Webb,

> It wasn't a great deal, but we were in a position where we were thinking that if we get to license it then that's a victory. As an industry, we were scared of this thing. It's like a big monster in a dark room. Is it going to want to eat us or is it friendly and can we pet it? So I think at a certain point we regarded any kind of a licensing deal as a victory. We were also struggling with a circuit court on whether a download was a performance or not, and that took five or six years and we were told no, it's not. In my heart, I know that a download is a performance, but this is a problem when a new technology comes into the marketplace and the judiciary knows less about it than we do.

But the thing you learn about ASCAP and that many people have learned in the past is that we're not going away. We're not going to stop complaining about performances as long as our writers aren't being paid. We are going to be there. We were there when they invented the jukebox and we were there when they invented CDs and the fact of life is that we are going to be here until this thing is over, and if that means the rest of my life, then there is going to be another generation carrying on. We believe in our hearts that songwriters deserve to be reimbursed for what they do.

If distributions during this tumultuous time have remained high, Webb attributed that to "the tenacity of our board and some pretty drastic steps by management, with restructuring and the attempt to get our square footage down, to bring our operating ratio more in line."

Speaking at seminars across the country, Webb counsels the future songwriters of America to keep doing what they do best.

I tell them, we have to keep writing the best songs we can write, because the one thing that can't be replaced is the great American song. It's something we invented; it's something that belongs to us. It's something that's widely emulated and admired, counterfeited, copied, and stolen! Obviously, it's something of value, so the idea is we don't want to throw the baby out with the bathwater. Sometimes I repeat myself, but I have to go back to the idea that a good song is the fuel at the center of the reactor no matter what permutations occur technologically. God knows what this is all going to look like in 25 to 30 years. I think the kids are acutely aware of that fact. It's ironic to me that one of the things youngsters complain about is that music isn't as good as it used to be, and then on the other hand there is a recalcitrance for paying for music and it's like, don't you get it? You get what you pay for.

On the publisher side of the board, BMG Music North America president Laurent Hubert sees more common ground between music creators and technology people than is usually acknowledged.

In a world where music content has become widely available through an explosion of new media outlets, it is easy to forget that behind every song, there is a creator and an innovator. I choose this term, innovator, because too often the kind of innovation that dominates the headlines is technology-related innovations—however, I believe that the creative process is in itself a process of innovation, no different than a programmer writing a breakthrough code. The generally accepted view is that content owners and the technology sphere are different minded when in fact they share the same goal: to make our lives a little easier while creators try to make our world a little better, one song at a time. Against that backdrop and despite the natural tensions that can develop between music publishers and writers, ASCAP is a unique organization where we come together to defend the creator/innovator's rights.

"There's a whole group of people who feel like they're entitled to anything that's out there," said ASCAP board member Valerie Simpson. "It's kind of hard to change those minds now. We can fight the good fight, but I really believe we need to be doing a better teaching job on some younger people, who will consider that what they've created is valuable and they should be paid proportionately. Then there won't be so much of this 'I'm gonna give it away,' or 'I have the right to take it.'"

Simpson received an education herself when she joined the board, at the urging of Bergman and Quincy Jones, among others. "It was a little bit mind-boggling," she admitted of this early period of peeking behind the velvet rope at some of the things she'd never had to fully consider in her previous life as a songwriter. "The number of issues we're faced with is overwhelming, as well as the crises that come up where if you don't decide rightly money is lost."

You see the red flags, but then you go to sleep and you wake up and the check comes. Then suddenly you see what the problems are and why the checks may be getting smaller as opposed to getting bigger. Then you try to figure how to make the checks get bigger again. Then you try to figure out who are your friends and who are your enemies and how do you make friends out of your enemies, because you need to work together now. There were so many things that came into view that I just had no idea about.

Marilyn [Bergman] was very helpful in the beginning, because it's enough to make you say, "Do I really need to know all this?" The whole board was helpful. You realize you have these great songwriters who not only understand their craft but care about the preservation of the music. It means a lot that they can sit down when you say, "I don't really get this at all," and speak to you from the heart.

Wayland Holyfield ("Could I Have This Dance") was elected to the ASCAP board in 1990, the first country music writer to be accorded this honor. Although his mandate on the board is to represent the interests of all songwriters, it's understandable if the problems of country writers are uppermost in his mind. "We're all in the same boat whether it's R&B or hip-hop or pop," he said.

All genres are challenged, but country probably more than anything, because we have a whole lot of writers who are not artists. If you're an artist and you get hot, you can make a lot of money making personal appearances, but for the writers who are not artists, it's tough because there are fewer artists to take your songs and the airplay roster is smaller than it ever used to be. I don't think we have any oldies stations at all. Now you have the Clear Channels and the Citadels and all these people who own thousands of stations, and when they go into a market, they might own five stations and it's all a matter of content and market share and an oldies but goodies station doesn't fit their model. The only way you get airplay is on satellite radio. Your catalogue is still valuable, but it just doesn't pay as much. Ironically, there are more stations that play country music than any other format, but most of them are in rural areas where the income to that radio station compared to top two or three in Chicago might be four times less, so the payout is reflected according to that share.

ASCAP board member Barry Coburn, publisher of Nashville's Ten Ten Music, who numbers among his early signees Alan Jackson and Keith Urban, is a passionate defender of songwriters' rights. "We need performance income more than ever now," he said, "because we're not going to see the mechanical income, because we get paid for one in 20. The rest of them are stolen. I used to track Keith Urban and for every one of his songs we'd sell each day legit, we would have 19 or 20 stolen."

As much of a songwriter's haven as Nashville has traditionally been, it too has been devastated by the collapse of the record business and the new, lawless era of free music.

Coburn said,

I'm often really frustrated, particularly living in a community like Nashville, where every gas station attendant, every waitress, every waiter, every barkeep is a songwriter. Now there's not as many coming here as there used to be, because there's not as many writer deals as there used to be. But our president, Paul Williams, is such a great voice for ASCAP. I think he can rouse people to step up and do something—because I feel we've failed miserably to deal with this. It's such a big issue that the industry as a whole has got to get together and create one voice to challenge this. Paul has a different twist on things; he's self-deprecating, he's enthusiastic, he's a great salesman. He's got a history of understanding the music industry, the film and television industries, and he can stir up a lot more passion. That's what we need. At the ASCAP board meeting yesterday we were looking at how we can form alliances with other copyright stakeholders to put the brakes on this.

Succeeding Marilyn Bergman as ASCAP president and chairman of the board in 2009, Paul Williams, whose catalogue contains standards like "We've Only Just Begun" and "You and Me Against the World," can certainly look to these two song titles as part and parcel of his mission. The challenges are many and well known, but his job is to supply fresh energy and perspective to a century-old battle. "It's always a struggle," he said.

The Internet era is an interesting time for me to be president, because it's like being the head of a major publishing organization, with the invention of the printing press. Essentially, the impact of the Internet is as large socially as the invention of the printing press as far as making "content" available to the world. But it's interesting that if I send you a book from Amazon, I pay more for speedy delivery than I do for the book. On the Internet the value of content is diminished to the point of people wanting it for free. And that would remain a business model if we didn't seek to protect the music creator.

I get very Jiminy Cricket about this whole deal. The elegance of ASCAP to me is in this mystical mission, which is to maintain the quality of life for our writers. I don't think it's a losing battle. I'm really optimistic about it. I think there's a struggle. We're seeing radio come down and we're seeing satellite come up. We're watching cable remain flat. Flat is the new up. I think we'll be all right, but I know I'm really grateful for the time I was born. My songwriting career took off in the '70s. It was that magical time when songs still got covered, and if you had a hit all of a sudden you could have 600 licenses of a single song. It was also a unique time. I caught the end of Elvis's career and Ella Fitzgerald and Sinatra, and I even had a Bing Crosby cut, so it was absolutely the best time for a songwriter. So it's something of a challenge for me to try to put that piece of the puzzle back in for the writer who's working so hard today and in the future. That's the essence of my mission, to try to put at least part of that world back together again.

Paul Williams was asked to run for the board in the '80s, but wasn't elected. Hal David prodded him to run again over a decade later. Williams joined the board in 2001 and was elected vice president in 2007. In 2011, he was elected to his second term as president.

I saw it as a great opportunity to serve, but I had no idea how steep the learning curve would be. It's an amazingly long process. From Marilyn, from Hal, from everyone, the advice I got was to be yourself. I turned to Hal all the time. I turn to Marilyn. I turn to Jimmy Webb, who is vice chair. The board of ASCAP on both sides of the aisle is immensely passionate and informed. There are very highly paid CEO's of major firms that I don't think work any harder than the board of ASCAP.

One of the things that immediately surprised me was how supportive the board was. As the challenges of the Digital Age have increased, the level of commitment has increased. I don't see a lot of "What about me?" in the boardroom. I see a lot of "What about ASCAP?" When you think in terms of licensing in the digital world, and when you're working for the well-being of the music creator as your focus on the horizon, it's almost inevitable that ASCAP is included as a part of that equation.

I remember when I was hosting the Songwriters Hall of Fame dinner and they had to change the set, so they said, "Fill." I went out and I said, "I am newly elected as president and chairman of the board of ASCAP, but I want to remind you who I represent," because there were all these huge stars on stage. "Somewhere there is a lady writing on an electric keyboard with headphones on because she can't wake the baby in the next room. But she also doesn't want to be up all night because she has to get up and go to work tomorrow morning. That is who I'm representing. Someone who is perhaps almost making a living or trying to make a living with their music. So let's not forget that small business person with a head full of music and a heart full of dreams." The response was immense. People were coming up to me afterwards and saying, "I got chills when you were talking about her. I can see her. I can see her." That's my job, to make sure that when I'm talking to a congressman or senator, or when I sit down with the Register of Copyrights or somebody from the State Department talking about monies that we are not collecting from the Caribbean, that maybe you can see beyond me and see into the life of that woman. The young songwriter who is trying to build a life and feed a family.

As an itinerant actor and performer for much of his career, Williams is used to the rigors of the traveling lifestyle the ASCAP presidency requires. But it comes with a crucial difference.

> When my head hits the pillow now, I know that the next day what I will be doing can impact the lives of hundreds of thousands of people. This is a 24/7 job. I'm living on airplanes, but I also think in some ways that it is more joyous for me than when I was performing. I have never felt more useful in my life than I do right now. The fact is, I will go anywhere in the world if it will have a positive effect on the future of a music creator.

CHAPTER 10

FOLLOW THE DOLLAR

Although ASCAP's current payment system is painstakingly explained on the ASCAP website, it is still a source of confusion, even to the Society's most established writers. "It's fun to look at the ASCAP statements and see what's happening where," said multiple hit-maker Billy Steinberg (author of "Like a Virgin," "True Colors," and "So Emotional," among others). "It's all kind of mystical trying to interpret them. I try not to get too microscopic about it because you can't understand them. I just feel fortunate to earn royalties for my songs."

Even nearly 100 years ago, as soon as ASCAP had significant monies to distribute, the process of distributing the sum evenly and rationally was no less complex, no less a source of contention. The first shot across the bow was fired by the publishing contingent in 1920, squarely into the wallets of the songwriting community. With their number having dwindled to six, as against 150 writers, the rest of the publishers proposed a deal by which they would return en masse to ASCAP, if, and only if, the system of royalty payments were changed from its then one-third split between authors (lyricists), composers, and publishers, to a much more favorable (to the publishers) fifty-fifty. This compromise by the songwriters resulted in the solidification of an ASCAP that would dominate the performance rights landscape for the next twenty years. But even within the publishing ranks, to say nothing of the songwriter ranks, how this growing pile of revenue should be divided would become a source of semiannual, if not quarterly, review and discussion.

"Having thrown the original system of allotting the royalties to members out the window, some other method had to be devised," Raymond Hubbell wrote in his informal history of ASCAP. "Judges and juries were considered, auditing concerns were consulted, and many meetings were devoted to the matter, without any seemingly fair and honorable system appearing."

It was ASCAP founder and legal genius Nathan Burkan who sorted it out, creating two classification committees, one for publishers and one for writers. Both operated in similar fashion in their attempt to put a quantitative ranking on so ephemeral a beast as a song, establishing a number of classes into which they grouped songwriters or publishers of similar esteem. In the case of songwriters, along with several variables, including current popular status, they considered one's past catalogue and whether it contained any enduring standards. This led to a situation in which many a deceased composer's royalty checks, delivered to their respective estates, and many a long-retired lyricist's royalty checks, delivered to their respective vacation homes in Miami Beach, far outstripped the relative pittance paid a struggling young Turk basking in the glory of his or her first, and perhaps only, hit. Which led, in very short order, to a series of formalized protests by the growing ranks of young Turks agitating to overturn a system so obviously in favor of the old boys (and the occasional old gal).

As one of the founding old boys, Raymond Hubbell set forth the rationale for the original system, remarkably capturing both the immeasurable joys and inevitable sorrows of a songwriting career.

> Some of the biggest hit writers we had to catalogue hadn't written a rhyme or a bar of music since the Society started, and one of the toughest conditions that exist in rewarding musical merit is that while your composition this year may be pounded to death on radio and in all the movie houses, cafés, hotels, dance halls, clubs, etc. for five or six weeks, this time next year only six people will remember it, and only two (your mother and your wife) will know that *you* wrote it.

Now picture to yourself just how you would feel back in 1892 if you were Charles K. Harris and you'd written a blockbuster like "After the Ball," and along about 1914 you'd joined a Society for the good of everybody and stuck with it through fire and water until 1921, when it commenced to pass out a few dollars among all its members according to the number of their compositions, their nature and character, popularity, vogue; and the member's prestige, reputation, qualifications, standing, and service rendered; and you opened a letter containing a Class B or a Class C check!

After all, "After the Ball" is still "After the Ball." You were told so for 30 years by toastmasters, governors, senators, laundrymen, nursemaids, bartenders, flappers; the whole world sang it at you for ten years after you wrote it, and if you were still alive, well, you'd sort of look that Class C in the eye and say, "Who are you kidding"—wouldn't you? Now then, take about 250 members, each with an "After the Ball" or nearly one, and figure out how self-conscious you'd be if you had the responsibility of figuring out the relative value of each one of them to ASCAP. Many a song written long before ASCAP came into being is commercially valuable today. In fact, it is the countless thousands of past successes that make the vast reservoir of the ASCAP catalogue so extremely valuable to music users.

Another of ASCAP's founding fathers in his turn spoke out against the rating system, but for an entirely different reason. As noted by Hubbell, "Victor Herbert didn't like the system one bit." He was especially opposed to ranking musicians. "Hell," he said, "we're all writers. One's as good as another. Put the money all in one pot and divide it up equally, every three months. I don't want any more than any other member."

Although the ranking system, which at one point in the 1930s contained as many as 16 different letter classifications, eventually gave way to other, even more arcane and debatable configurations, Herbert's idealistic view of artistic equality has never been quite fulfilled. While he may have thought the output of a composer whose works were performed at Carnegie Hall easily on a par with that of a tin-eared Tin

Pan Alley hack, the credo of "follow the dollar" has survived a century of all such altruistic critiques. The argument was then, as it remains today, that royalties to writers are distributed in accordance with the fees paid by the particular establishment in which the music is predominantly heard. In the 1920s, Carnegie Hall and other "highbrow" venues paid nothing to ASCAP. By the 1930s radio was carrying the load, as it has to this day. Thus, in some form or fashion, if a song is not getting major media play with an earsplitting regularity, its writer (or writers), may feel underpaid by the prevailing ASCAP system.

Said ASCAP senior vice president and longtime chief economist Peter Boyle,

> The money from local TV is paid to local TV, cable to cable, radio to radio. There are areas where it's too costly to accurately obtain representative viable performance information relative to the license fees and it doesn't make sense to spend that much of the members' money to do so. Average license fees from bars and restaurants are well under $1000 a year, based on seating capacity. You could easily spend all that money trying to track certain performance information.

Because the rate structure is so different from radio and television, adding the digital world into the equation often adds nothing but paper. "Earnings-wise you can get 50 pages of statements that are worth five dollars," said Todd Brabec, former ASCAP membership director and 34-year veteran, who now runs a successful business with his brother Jeff, consulting on the vagaries of the copyright law and the Internet. "That means when you're going to get a royalty statement, you can have one statement for traditional radio that will pay you $400,000 and it'll just be one line on a statement. Then 50 pages with 50 lines each for Internet performances and it's 50 bucks."

When Brabec worked with Paul Adler in the membership department in the early '70s, he was involved when the board changed one of the more onerous distribution systems ASCAP has ever had, the Four Funds. "Up until 1960, the only way a writer could get paid at ASCAP was on the Four Funds, which averaged income over five or ten years," he said.

This system discriminated against newer writers, since only a small percentage of their earnings was based on current performances. Older writers liked the Four Funds, because payments were based in part on continuous quarters of membership, thus favoring their long years of service. It was also difficult to opt out of the Four Funds, since there were often a lot of back royalties tied up in the system that would then be lost. When Bob Dylan left ASCAP in 1995 to join SESAC, the Four Funds may have been one of the factors behind his defection. Far more likely a reason, however, was that Dylan was offered more than twice what he earned at ASCAP over a five-year period.

The smallest among American performing rights organizations, with a highly specialized repertoire of religious and classical music, SESAC had just changed ownership hands. The new regime, led by savvy entertainment veterans Freddie Gershon, Stephen Swid, and Ira Smith, was eager to make a splash in the pop world. "The business plan was to identify a songwriter who was also a recording artist who also controlled their own publishing," said ASCAP's executive vice president of licensing, Vincent Candilora, a 27-year SESAC veteran who played an active role in luring Dylan to the rival PRO.

> We also wanted someone who did not sit on the board of ASCAP, meaning they didn't have any real allegiance to ASCAP as an organization. The other aspect of it was in terms of them as a recording artist, that the peak of their careers was already past, so SESAC could evaluate the body of works that they created and put a guaranteed price on it. There was a short list. I don't know if there are many legendary songwriters and artists like Bob Dylan.

While members frequently switch alliances between BMI and ASCAP (and vice-versa), Dylan's defection in 1995 was particularly alarming, occurring as it did on the same day Neil Diamond followed suit. According to Candilora, this was not a coincidence. "Well, they were separate deals, and yet they were well aware that one wanted to make sure the other was also coming, so in a sense it was a tandem deal," he said.

Speaking to David Hinckley in New York's *Daily News*, on February 3, 1995, Freddie Gershon was understated when explaining the coup.

"Our goal is not to have the most copyrights, but to have a crème de la crème of indispensable music of the writers who define eras." The paper reported that the deals received by the two icons would "triple their previous songwriting earnings under five-year, no-cut contracts." Also bagged from ASCAP at the same time was *Seinfeld* composer Jonathan Wolff.

"The fellows who run SESAC are canny, tough businessmen," Fred Koenigsberg said. "It was always tiny; their performance and license fees were always a fraction of 1 percent of BMI or ASCAP. So these fellows said, 'We're so much smaller, if we want to get more licensees, all we have to get is a few white diamonds.' They don't have a consent decree; they can charge as much as they can get. No radio station in the world is gonna be able to play music without Dylan."

In the meantime, somewhat easing the pain of losing Dylan and Diamond, ASCAP has had great success in gaining signatures from former BMI affiliates James Taylor, Joni Mitchell, Billy Joel, and three of the four Beatles—lacking only John Lennon to complete the reunion.

With the industry stuck in the economic doldrums, a hit song-writer can still do very well at ASCAP, even with fewer songs reaching the charts, and those songs staying there longer (many of them for at least 20 weeks, which was almost unheard of in the '60s). "At the top end you are doing exceptionally well financially," said one ASCAP executive. "You could make a million dollars on a number one song, even with downloads, because traditional radio still pays a lot of money." In the current ASCAP model, a Bruce Springsteen makes no more per spin than a rank unknown. The only difference would be that a Springsteen song might be heard somewhere on a major station once every two hours, while the rank unknown is lucky to hear their song once, at four in the morning on a 5000-watt college station.

To monitor radio play, ASCAP makes use of new technologies that listen to 2500 stations, 24 hours a day, seven days a week—a marked improvement from the early days, when two women handled all the record keeping. "We would get sheets of paper from the radio stations or the nightclubs with the listing of the songs they'd played for the month, and another woman and I would record them," said one of them, the niece of J. C. Rosenthal (an early ASCAP office manager), Dorothy Gullish, who worked for ASCAP in their 45th floor offices at Rockefeller Center from 1937 to 1944. As late as the 1960s ASCAP employed people to sit in a room from nine to five each day, marking down on index cards each song they heard.

"We had people who went around the country and made tape recordings," said ASCAP's Peter Boyle. "And they'd ship the recordings back and we had people sitting under headphones listening to them. That was the only way we could get reliable information." As much as this might seem like the ultimate music fan's ultimate job description, Boyle disagreed. "It wasn't as much fun as it sounds, because those folks weren't just listening to the radio in real time. They would listen only until they could identify a song and then fast forward to the next song. It wasn't like singing to the Beach Boys and the Beatles all day long. If you did, you wouldn't meet the appropriate productivity results and you'd probably be let go."

Computerized services have since rendered that job obsolete. "We've changed the way we get radio and TV performance information," Boyle said.

Now you can make a digital fingerprint of a CD with high reliability. We used Mediaguide for a while and then switched to Media Monitors, which does similar things, but we were able to get performance information from them at a lower cost, which means it makes more money available for distribution. It's allowed us to increase our radio survey over the years by a factor of ten. We still maintain a staff to listen to samples for two purposes: to see if they're identifying the songs correctly, and to see they haven't missed things, because none of these technologies are perfect.

Television is a different story. The music isn't as easily discernible. Background music and underscore are designed to be beneath the action. You don't always hear the music clearly, because voice-overs might distort it and make it more difficult to recognize. So the television companies create cue sheets that identify all the musical compositions put into a TV show. Producers have to get sync rights, which is permission from members to put music into a film or a television show, so they create cue sheets to clear sync rights and provide a copy to us.

Since the '90s, we can get program schedules electronically and we can match program titles to cue sheets. For TV we used to have a 30,000-hour sample; now it's virtually everything that's on.

The Internet's a challenge because we're dealing with huge volumes. There are many more individual songs being performed than on radio or TV. On radio you've got a song going out to 50 or 100,000, 200,000 listeners, but they're all hearing the same song and there's only a certain amount of songs you can play per hour per day per week. On the Internet it's one song, one person, which makes it much more complicated. There we rely on the Internet companies to provide us with electronic databases of what they've performed over the course of the quarter—and on YouTube, Pandora, Spotify, and the like, you might have millions if not tens of millions of plays in a quarter.

ASCAP board member and SONGS Music Publishing CEO Matt Pincus, a publisher who came of age with the Internet era, well understands what copyright owners are now facing and appreciates the stability ASCAP provides in a time of uncertainty.

With the transition to a digital music market comes a metastasis of data, without commensurate revenue growth to date to fund the capacity to handle it. This creates a tremendous challenge for content creators and owners, and we are all working hard every day to find our footing in this new market paradigm. And then there is ASCAP. For 100 years, this great institution has been fighting to get fair pay for writers and publishers, matching performances to payments, and providing a home to the creative community. Through many disruptions in the music market—the advent of distributed recordings, the transition to radio, the introduction of the CD, and now the Internet economy—ASCAP has stood strong and gotten stronger. While no organization is immune to the challenges of the digital economy, ASCAP remains a steady hand—the vanguard for all of us.

Longtime television composer Alf Clausen (*The Simpsons, ALF*), who was elected to ASCAP's board of directors in 2013, noted key improvements and modernizations to ASCAP's system of processing performances and payments.

I've been an ASCAP writer member since 1970. My time in the Society has been filled with the most interesting turns, twists, and changes. One of the most beneficial to ASCAP members in general has been the change in royalty payment terms to four domestic payments and four international payments per year. The increased frequencies of payments have made life much easier for ASCAP songwriters, composers, and publishers, whose income can often be erratic and unpredictable.

Another important change has been the logging of performances by computer. The ASCAP logging system has been constantly improved through the years so that performances are now logged more accurately and more frequently than ever. All members benefit from the new, cutting-edge technology.

On broadcast radio, according to ASCAP's senior vice president for special projects, Seth Saltzman, more songs are being played than ever, in many more musical formats, even if fewer of them wind up with the traction necessary to become a major hit. This, despite the lethargy in the Top 40, where songs these days have been known to pitch a tent for upwards of a year or more. Said Saltzman, "There are still 13,000 radio stations. We survey millions of hours of radio, so we're paying many, many more writers. More songs are getting heard now. From where I sit, I like to have a lot of people who are getting a lot of play, because we need representation across all media types."

Vincent Candilora observed,

In the mid to late '60s, FM radio really started to take off. It found its way into automobiles, and our revenues and royalty distributions grew as FM radio grew. Then, as we got into the mid and late '70s, along came cable television. Then very specific program services like MTV, VH1, Country Music Television, and Music Choice were born. The difference with the cable services is the rate they pay us. So MTV, when it was music intensive, and the Music Choice channels pay a higher rate than the USA Network, which is more general entertainment.

The one constant is that more music is being used today than ever before, because there are so many new platforms to deliver it. When ASCAP and the music user can't agree on what a fair and reasonable rate is, they go to the Federal court in the Southern District of New York, and both sides argue their case before the judge, who listens to the arguments and then makes a determination as to what is a fair and reasonable rate.

In recent years, these cases have not gone in ASCAP's favor. Even the knowledgeable William C. Conner (1920–2009), who had formerly upheld the Society's claims in the district court, began to lean in the other direction in his later years.

Appointed to New York's Southern District Court by Richard Nixon in 1973, Conner immediately became involved in all matters ASCAP. As noted in his *New York Times* obituary: "Judge Conner's expertise in intellectual property issues was the principal reason he was given responsibility in the mid-1970s for overseeing a 1941 consent order governing the activities of ASCAP." In 2004, Conner approved ASCAP's pact with radio that provided for total fees of over $1.7 billion for the period 2001–2009. In 2007 Judge Conner did not side with ASCAP on the issue of whether a digital download was a performance. "The designation would have given songwriters an extra royalty," the article reported. In 2008, he trimmed ASCAP's request for 3 percent of revenues from songs streamed over AOL, Yahoo, and Real Networks down to 2.5 percent.

According to Vincent Candilora,

The fact that business models have changed also makes it a little difficult. When the Internet came along all of a sudden you could get access for free. Yeah, they had some advertising on the Web site, but it really wasn't any substantial revenue. But does that mean the use of somebody else's property should be for free? This goes back to what Oliver Wendell Holmes said years ago: if music weren't worth anything, people wouldn't use it. If it had no value, it would be given up.

In his newsletter, Todd Brabec observed some repercussions of recent court cases, and predicted more for the future.

ASCAP's income reached $995 million in 2009. That came down based primarily on the economy, and on these interim decisions, which have not been good. I think it was $924 million in 2010. The same thing is going to happen with BMI and SESAC, because if ASCAP loses a big case, it will be used as leverage against them. So everyone's income is going to start coming down, not significantly, but over time there is some concern, to say the least.

Although ASCAP's income rose again to record levels in 2011, it fell again in 2012, and the average ASCAP songwriter still feels woefully underpaid for his or her particular works.

"They want to get paid for every single performance," said Seth Saltzman.

I think the biggest misconception, unfortunately, for songwriters, is their idea of what every performance should be worth. "Hey, my song was on the radio, why didn't I get $100?" Well, your song was on the radio, but it was on the radio in Wisconsin at 3:00 in the morning on a college station that only pays us $500 a year in licensing fees. Or let's assume the station has some commercials. So they're maybe playing ten songs an hour if they're all music. Every hour, every day of the week, 365 days a year. They paid us $500 for the licensing fee. They paid us essentially a dollar a day. I now have 24 times 10, or 240 songs played during the day. Every song has one writer and one publisher, at least, probably two, maybe three. How thin a dime am I gonna spread?

Somebody comes to me and says, "I played a club last night, and it should be worth $100." Okay, time out. Let's say the club pays us $1000 a year, $3000, $4000! And they have live music five nights a week from 8:00 P.M. until 1:00 A.M. Every hour there's a new band playing nine, ten songs. What part of that do you think is worth $100? You're getting a proportion of the actual money we're receiving. ASCAP does bring in a lot of money, but it's representing 13,000 radio stations, 1300 television stations, hundreds of cable stations, thousands of nightclubs and restaurants. We help people understand—you got paid your proportional share. There's a lot of music happening!

In the 21st century, ASCAP has been able to continue revamping its payment system, due to revisions to its new consent decree. In 1960, the government had put in place certain requirements for ASCAP to meet in terms of how it surveyed performances and distributed royalties, via an amendment to the version of the ASCAP consent decree that was entered into in 1950. ASCAP's Richard Reimer referred to the 1960 amendment as "a mostly unwanted appendage to the 1950 consent decree." The 1960 amendment's dictates regarding royalty distribution—which were not prescribed in rival BMI's consent decree—significantly hampered ASCAP's ability to react fluidly to the changing marketplace until a revision in 2001.

"Until 2001, many of the changes involving the survey and distribution system had to be approved by the court," Reimer explained. "That is no longer the case. Our board of directors now establishes the manner in which royalties are being distributed to the membership and can make those changes at the board level when it deems it appropriate."

Reimer explained how the pool of income is dispersed among the membership. "In determining the value to be given individual performances, the highest rate is given to what is called a feature performance, a song played on the radio or sung by a performer on television." On TV a feature performance is valued at one credit. A theme or background music is valued at less than one credit, although in 2012, ASCAP's board approved more changes to the weighting formula for TV writers.

Seth Saltzman explained further how television music is valued.

Let's say on *Glee* somebody sings a full Lady Gaga song, the camera's on the kids; that's a feature performance, which earns 100 percent of a credit. Music in the background used to be 14 percent of a credit for every three minutes; now it's 60 percent. Theme music used to be 20 percent; now it's 60 percent. We're constantly adding new surveys. When I first started here we used to do a very small sample from television for performances to pay royalties. We now do a complete census: every local station, every cable service, the networks.

Where the computations get more complex is with ASCAP's reliance on radio play as a proxy for performances in hotels, bars, and restaurants. Also, touring performers who play smaller venues and have limited airplay suffer in this system. "The individual bars and restaurants don't pay ASCAP very much money in licensing fees, so you can't ask them to pay two or three or ten times what they're paying in license fees to pay for your survey cost," Richard Reimer said. "But there are elements of performances in the live setting where we *do* get survey data and *do* pay on a census basis. For example, live concerts. The 300 top-grossing tours of the year report their playlists to us, and we use that for a basis for distribution."

By far the vast majority of the membership, however, play their songs, or have them played by someone else, in much less auspicious venues, Reimer noted.

If you're talking about somebody who's just starting out and appears at a neighborhood coffeehouse, playing their own music, the coffeehouse may pay us $750 a year in license fees. What percent would you pay to a performer who's playing five or six songs in one night? What amount could you afford to distribute to them? Not much. But if the songwriter becomes popular and they get radio airplay, then they'll generate royalties. It's a matter of how you can best allocate your resources.

Recently, however, the number crunchers at ASCAP have come up with a way to further reward those performers who work in niche genres, like folk, blues, cabaret, or jazz, and whose songs add prestige to the literature of music, but are not generally entered in the Top 40 steeplechase. In addition to the ASCAP Plus program (founded in the mid-1960s to provide cash and recognition to writers who create music that is performed in venues beyond the scope of the ASCAP performance surveys), which makes its awards once a year, now there's On Stage, which pays quarterly. "Traditionally, we've paid the top 300 grossing concert venues and the opening acts, but that excludes a lot of people who play at smaller clubs," said Membership's Brendan Okrent. "In Europe and Canada they make these payments. Now ASCAP has figured out a way for people to report these small-venue gigs through the Member Access digital system and we're paying out money quarterly."

No matter how much or how little is shown on their royalty statements, one continuing source of pride among the membership is how much of ASCAP's resources go toward fighting the various legal battles they've been embroiled in throughout their 100-year existence—battles that have historically increased the monies available to be dispersed to songwriters. With technology running laps around the law, as it often does, the last few years have seen multiple Internet concerns being hauled before the courts to face the music.

"The last major legal victory was the AOL case [in 2008]," said Reimer, referring to a rate case that also includes Yahoo and RealNetworks.

Usually it's ASCAP's burden, initially, to determine what we believe the fee should be and how it should be calculated. In the mid-'90s, when the Internet came on the scene, we offered an agreement that was essentially modeled on our radio agreement—you'd go to a Web site and they had the ability to transmit music via the Internet. So on your computer you were hearing music. We also offered an alternative form of license, a form of rate calculation that allowed people to pay a percentage based on their total costs of operation. That wasn't terribly successful; people resisted, so ultimately we evolved a percentage of revenue rate, which had been the norm, and in addition a way of calculating the license fee based on the number of what we called "sessions." If the session lasted more than an hour, they calculated the fee on that basis. When we offered that to Yahoo and AOL and RealNetworks, they said, "No, that's not going to work for us; we want something else." So we went on to the litigation phase. This case first went to court in 2006; we had a preliminary ruling in 2007 on one aspect of the proceeding, and we had a decision in 2008. An appeal was filed and we're waiting for the decision from the Court of Appeals. If we win this, it's not necessarily a windfall; there are no windfalls. What we're doing in this instance is building the marketplace for use of music, valuing it for this new marketplace. You start at ground zero and you build up. You can't predict what the outcome is going to be until you know what the decision is. If it is reversed it could go up on appeal again.

Which is exactly what happened in September 2010, when the appellate court overturned the case, sending the issue into further litigation that ultimately was settled. "The performance area remains in a state of flux," the Brabec brothers wrote in their newsletter. "Settlement agreements with the various major players may result in negotiated rather than court-set license fee formulas and fees."

One major concern of the membership is the age-old question of who pays more for a given performance, ASCAP or BMI—especially on the occasion when an ASCAP writer collaborates with a BMI writer and finds differing royalties paid out on the same song. Said ASCAP's Saltzman,

> I don't know for certain how BMI does it, as I do not know how they apply their rules in every situation. I can guess and I can estimate. Sometimes BMI will direct money very specifically, saying, "We're going to give more value to a particular type of music this quarter." If all of a sudden country music is getting outpaid wildly by BMI it may be because BMI decided to juice up the value on it. At the end of the day it's mostly a wash. It's not that in any one area ASCAP is outpaying or BMI is outpaying forever. It just doesn't make sense. We'd lose too many members. With the income being almost equal these days between ASCAP and BMI, if BMI is paying country music heavily, somebody's getting hurt. So the TV guys may be crying, "How come my ASCAP cowriter earned so much more than I did?" Well, BMI decided to give the money to country music.

For members of either performance rights organization, a tidal shift in the way music is used and paid for may now be in the process of changing the essential paradigm of how songwriters make a living, vastly complicated by the new business model facing streaming (listening) and download (purchasing) sites like Pandora and Spotify. Nevertheless, for the lucky ones who can create an enduring hit, the rewards are still plentiful. Consider Jason Mraz, author of the radio staple "I'm Yours," which not only won the ASCAP pop award in 2010 for airplay, but broke the record for weeks on the chart, remaining on the Hot 100 for an amazing 76 weeks. "I was just with my financial advisor about a week ago," he said—checking up on his ASCAP statements. "Every so often I call and ask her for permission to do something. We were doing a little remodeling of our studio and I got nervous about some of the things that I was doing because it could get costly. I said, 'I haven't worked very much in the last year. Is it okay that I do this?' She didn't tell me my exact ASCAP numbers, but she said, 'Yeah, I think you're going to be okay.'"

Airplay and royalties at ASCAP are generally interdependent and the system, if imperfect, makes sense for most ASCAP members. The members of ASCAP who write concert (or what used to be called "classical") music deal with a set of unique circumstances. Certainly, concert music is fairly hard to find on ASCAP's top two sources of performance royalties (radio and television). "We are underrepresented on radio, for sure," said ASCAP board member and composer Stephen Paulus. "Concert music is normally played on one little station on the far left of the radio dial—the type of station that's not heavily sampled. A large percentage of the music played on those stations is centuries old—in other words, in the public domain—and contemporary composers really have to compete for airtime. So, I can have a piece played five days in a row that's an hour long and there's a good possibility that it won't show up."

The Oscar- and Pulitzer Prize–winning composer John Corigliano, one of Paulus' colleagues on ASCAP's Symphony and Concert Committee, knows all about the paucity of airplay for classical or concert compositions. Back in the '60s, among Corigliano's other esteemed accomplishments, he was at the leading edge of radio as the music director of the independent WBAI in New York City. "Nothing exists like that now," he said, "although satellite radio and the Internet are good places for a contemporary composer to get airplay, because a lot of people have told me they heard my music that way."

All public performances are weighted according to duration and number of players involved. "If I've written a piece for chorus and orchestra that's one hour long, that receives a larger royalty than a 15-minute piece for a string quartet," said Paulus.

"For symphonic performances and recital performances we've always done a complete census," said Peter Boyle, ASCAP senior vice president and chief economist.

> If you have a live professional performance that was licensed and paid in the concert field, you're going to get paid. For similar performances at colleges and universities we have a sample survey. We take a certain amount of dates out of the year, and any performances on those dates are paid. Several years ago the people who write music for concert bands and wind ensembles pointed out that colleges and universities are really the only places this genre of concert music has a chance of being performed. Because in every sample survey you're going to have some variability from year to year, we said, "We think we can expand this in a cost-effective way." It didn't change the way we weighted them, but instead of having one out of every ten performances, we processed all ten. So these composers had some guarantee that if they had a performance they'd get paid and their earnings would have less variability from year to year.

Fran Richard, former vice president of concert music at ASCAP, noted:

> The minute I got here I understood that if the license fee is not paid, we can't credit the composers. So I made a very fast alliance with the people who license our field and the concert crediting department that credits our members when there is a performance. You need to have a license fee from the venue in hand before anybody can get paid. The members send thousands and thousands of printed concert programs every year and we check whether it's a licensed venue, so it can go right

away to crediting, or whether it has to go to the licensing representatives to go and find the venue. Concerts are taking place all over and we have to look for them everywhere to license them.

ASCAP works hard to entice new members into the fold, said Richard, now a consultant. With the Society approaching its 100th year, out of nearly 500,000 members, there are about 20,000 in the concert field. "We take an inventory every year," Richard said.

We have to have the next generation of creative new composers; otherwise we can't issue a license. It's our job to find and recruit very gifted young people. We welcome them with open arms, and when we hear something or see something, we contact them and invite them to join the Society.

One wonderful resource we have is The ASCAP Foundation's Morton Gould Young Composer Competition. For anyone who thinks that concert music in America is dead, you need to be here at deadline time when all the submissions must be in. In 2011 we had 730 applications. It was an amazing number of wonderful scores and compositions with great variety. Every year we have a Concert Music Awards event and we honor the composers who won and those who received honorable mention. It is not easy to win, and some of those who have received honorable mention are just a shade away from winning. At the Concert Music Awards, we put the winners on the stage and introduce their bio, with their photo and even an audio snapshot of their piece. There are publishers sitting in the audience and many other people looking to discover new talent.

While the concert music world has particular challenges, some are universal for all music creators. "I think the bottom line for most ASCAP members is the same: is my check getting larger—or am I even getting a check?" said Stephen Paulus.

I've been hearing from more people that they are getting recognized. More people are taking advantage of the ASCAP Plus Awards. I think we're doing a better job of educating young composers with workshops. We're getting people to become more serious. We teach people to think of themselves as a professional from the get-go.

Jim Kendrick pointed to the ASCAP awards ceremonies as a good place to network. "At the Young Composer awards, a lot of people in the field will come to celebrate the honorees, greet their colleagues, and make new friends," he said.

Despite the challenges, Kendrick was optimistic about the future of concert music.

This is actually a very exciting time for younger groups—in years of existence, not necessarily in age. Having said that, the obvious funding challenges are quite real. We should be doing a lot more with exposing young people to classical music, as used to be the case. But the field is not shrinking. At each meeting of the Symphony and Concert Committee, Stephen Paulus and myself, plus a number of other publishers not on the board, get a list of the new concert composers and publishers signing up, and it's enormous. The ASCAP Adventurous Programming Awards are presented at the annual conferences of the League of American Orchestras, Chamber Music America, and Chorus America as a thank-you and also as an encouragement for various orchestras, ensembles, chamber groups, choruses, and presenters to show there's recognition for innovative programming.

Kendrick and Paulus, along with Alex Shapiro, a composer who has her own publishing company, have presented composer seminars to educate and inform the next generation entering the field. "The Philadelphia Music Project hosted a brunch for composers who came from all over the area for the seminar," said Paulus. "It was standing room only, about 100 people. That kind of event makes us see that composers are hungry for knowledge about copyright. I didn't know thing one about copyright when I went to school. What is a copyright and how do you protect your work? We want all composers to understand their basic rights, how best to protect them, and how to grow a successful catalog."

That question has been the leitmotif over the decades since the inception of ASCAP, and it continues to loom as large as ever in the face of the newest and most wide-reaching vehicle for conveying music to date: the Internet.

CHAPTER 11

PLAYBACK AND FAST FORWARD

With the coming of the new millennium and the advent of the Internet, where information (and music) supposedly demands to be free, ASCAP's business model has been seriously challenged. With the economy driving down advertising revenue for radio and network TV, with cable struggling to survive and the Internet overturning traditional music payment models, some have suggested that the ultimate survival of the venerable giant may be in jeopardy.

Clearly, those who indulge in this manner of thinking have no recollection of ASCAP's historic endurance.

Even though the copyright revision act of 1909 gave songwriters the right to collect a fee for the public performance of their work, and compensation should their copyrights be infringed upon; and even though the best of them banded together in a Society to collect those fees, and to enforce their rights through the courts if necessary, joining hands with many of the most powerful publishers in the business, in the early going, this was all but a moot point. Hotel, restaurant, and club owners were simply not going to shell out good money for something they were accustomed to getting for free, even if it was Irving Berlin at the door with a copy of the legal documents in his hand. With all the original excitement the founders drummed up at the Hotel Claridge in 1914 having dissipated by 1917, the publishers started defecting. As the Broadway wags had long predicted, there was just too much money in the sale of sheet music to antagonize the very places that exposed the work to a wider audience.

Before it even began, ASCAP appeared to be finished.

After Supreme Court Justice Oliver Wendell Holmes weighed in on the subject in ASCAP's favor in 1917, the tide began to turn, ever so slowly, and the publishers came back. But it would take four more years before there was enough in the till to start paying any ASCAP members a portion of their due; and by then movie theater owners were claiming they were exempt from such payments. A few years later, radio broadcasters decided the law shouldn't apply to them, either. This brought about another round of lawsuits.

If any of them had gone the wrong way, it could surely have spelled the end of ASCAP.

In the 1920s and early '30s, with Prohibition driving the nightlife of the populace underground and into the arms of the criminal element, ASCAP field representatives were often regarded as far more dangerous to the proprietors when they came calling with their licenses. For the remainder of the decade, from Maine to Oregon, states attempted to pass laws forbidding ASCAP to collect fees within their borders. On one occasion the president of ASCAP was jailed for extortion while vacationing in Arizona. Meanwhile, the broadcasting industry had the ear of the Justice Department, attempting to nail ASCAP for antitrust violations. A trial balloon of a case never got off the ground. But the broadcasters weren't finished. With negotiations for a new contract stalled and ASCAP threatening to take all their music off the air, they began developing their own rival society behind the scenes. It was possible that 1941 would dawn without the music of Cole Porter and Oscar Hammerstein piped into the kitchens and bedrooms and living rooms of America.

If that ever happened, how would ASCAP survive?

With a war going on overseas, and the upstart Broadcast Music Incorporated supplying radio programs with songs from Argentina and Brazil, and songs by writers deemed not qualified for membership in ASCAP, few people in the listening audience seemed to care or even notice. ASCAP caved in, signing a new contract with the broadcasters after a nine-month holdout, taking a huge hit to distributions. But within a few years they were flush again—until the government picked up on the antitrust suit, and a bunch of movie house owners won a landmark decision against them in 1947, knocking out one of the biggest sources of performance income and leading to a consent decree in 1950.

With BMI cornering the market on country music and rhythm and blues, while ASCAP was slow to acknowledge the changing marketplace, it seemed but a matter of time before ASCAP and its old-fashioned parlor tunes would be put out to pasture, along with the Ziegfeld Follies and the jitterbug.

Instead of welcoming the inevitable arrival of rock 'n' roll, ASCAP spent the '50s and much of the '60s taking BMI to court, losing case after case. It similarly failed to gain any traction with the jukebox industry. It ceded the Nashville territory. It tried to bar its members from writing with anyone from BMI. From their lofty offices, the board of directors issued statements decrying the state of the art of popular music.

Only a few of them understood that if ASCAP couldn't attract a new generation of songs and songwriters, it would cease to exist.

Once these saner heads prevailed and ASCAP turned the corner in the early '70s, modernizing their attitudes, a level of equanimity reigned. For about a minute. Suddenly, network television decided it shouldn't have to pay ASCAP. Then local television stations thought they should be exempt. Several crucial cases raged through the courts for twenty years.

The fate of ASCAP hung in the balance.

In the '90s, religious broadcasters decided they were certainly outside the purview of the copyright law. Restaurant and club owners rejoined the fray. Meanwhile, inside the Society office politics exploded into a vast reorganization that threatened ASCAP at the core. There were tears and layoffs, and Napster just up the road.

Which is to say that ASCAP has lived on this razor's edge for the past hundred years and is still guided by the same defining quest to protect the right granted by Theodore Roosevelt in 1909 and affirmed by Justice Holmes in 1917. The current counsel for the board, Fred Koenigsberg, summed it up in this famous quote: "The price of liberty is eternal vigilance."

In the same 2009 issue of the in-house magazine, *Playback*, in which Paul Williams assumed the mantle of the presidency from Marilyn Bergman, the headline read: "Record Collections for Members in 2008." The article stated:

Consistent with its history of leadership on behalf of music creators, ASCAP earlier this year reported a record level of money collected for its members in 2008. Representing nearly 350,000 lyricists, songwriters, composers, and publishers of music from every genre, the member-owned organization generated over $933 million while making royalty payments of more than $817 million. It also reported an all-time low operating expense ratio of 11.3 percent.

A year later the figure had risen again. Membership was up to 380,000. Collections topped out at $995 million, with payments to members a resounding $883 million (over $300 million of that from foreign affiliates). "Music is performed in more ways by more businesses than ever before," John LoFrumento told *Playback*. "That expanded music use, combined with dramatic ASCAP membership growth, market share increases, and effective strategic management, have led to stunning revenue and distribution growth for 2009. Looking to 2010 and beyond, our challenge is to obtain fair rates for the increasingly valuable public performance right over Internet and wireless devices."

LoFrumento delivered those figures in April 2010, at a membership meeting prior to ASCAP's fifth annual "I Create Music" Expo. On the morning of the last day, as part of a heavyweight industry panel, LoFrumento was less enthusiastic about 2010. "In the US, the rates that we apply on licensing are lower than they would be in foreign territories," he said. "Given our business environment, it's very difficult for us to raise those rates, but there comes a time when we in ASCAP need to fight to get those rates raised. This year it's a perfect storm, because all of our major traditional media contracts are up for negotiation."

LoFrumento noted that revenues were down at all of these traditional licensing sources. "I remember when I came to ASCAP in 1981," he said.

The fledgling cable services yielded us about $4,000,000. Last year, we received $164 million from the cable industry. And many of those cable services are up again for negotiation. Besides their traditional business, which is dependent upon advertising revenues and subscription revenues, cable is moving into the Internet, it's moving into wireless, it's moving into cellular phones. So when we sit down to negotiate, it's no longer a simple matter. The scope of their license is so much greater. The rates they paid us in the past must now reflect these additional uses of music.

In the beginning, ASCAP offered new media services experimental licenses whose purpose was to give them the space to grow. Now these services are making significant money. But some don't believe they should pay anything at all. We have a licensee who for the past three, four years prior to 2009 offered us $70,000 for all music use over a four-year period of time. We took them to rate court, and the judge on an interim-fee basis gave us a $70,000-a-month rate, $840,000 for one year.

There are, however, other challenges. ASCAP believes that a download should be considered a performance—as is the case in nearly every other country in the world. However, to date, the courts have ruled against us. In addition, the court ruled against ASCAP's premise that a ringtone should also be considered a performance.

Later in 2010, some of those negotiations concluded and some of those court decisions were rendered. In addition to reversing the decision on AOL, Yahoo, and RealNetworks, the U.S. Court of Appeals for the Second Circuit also weighed in on whether music downloads and ringtones could be considered performances.

Beyond making its case in court, ASCAP determined that the pre-eminence of the Internet clearly demanded a full-scale escalation of its legislative efforts—beginning with the expansion of its lobbying activities. Ben Palumbo had served as ASCAP's lobbyist since the '80s, covering both the Democrats and the Republicans. In 2002, following the election of President George W. Bush, ASCAP decided it needed to bring on someone who could concentrate on the Republicans. Palumbo said, "I continued to do the Democrats and also a number of key Republicans with whom I'd had very close relationships over the years, like Hatch, and Henry Hyde, who took over as chairman."

"I was on the board when we changed our attitude toward lobbying in Washington," the publisher Nicholas Firth said.

The board had been very effective lobbying the Democratic majority, including the Clinton White House. When I came on the board I said I thought it would be a good idea to get a Republican lobbyist. In fact, I was the guy who got the introduction to a firm called Quinn-Gillespie, and Gillespie ended up as George Bush's right-hand man in the White House, so I think that was quite helpful. I also think it showed ASCAP behaving in a businesslike fashion.

Harriet Melvin became the point person for handling the Republican legislators. "We have a very recognizable name now on both sides of the aisle," she said. Rather than a strictly Republican-Democrat or liberal-conservative debate, Melvin finds her opponents lined up more state by state.

Where we run into people who oppose us it's not because of party affiliation, or where they are in the political spectrum; it's really where they're from. If you're from Silicon Valley, you have a different take than the people in Nashville. People in Montana, for instance, are usually property rights people. But digital technology companies have plants and call centers all over the country. So it all depends on your constituency and your core beliefs.

Former ASCAP president/chairman Marilyn Bergman, who presided over the Society during the early Internet years, made a different point. "We're fortunate to have some chairmen of some committees that hold our fate in their hands who are understanding," she said of the state of Congress in regard to copyright in the new Wild West of the Digital Age. "But it's taken them a while, too. They're learning along with us. It's a very complicated business and I think we have to be patient."

Alec French, ASCAP's current Democratic lobbyist, is tasked with educating the lawmakers in Congress on the nuances of the copyright law. Especially germane is the advantage many potential new licensees have taken of the fine points in ASCAP's court-mandated licensing process. "Because ASCAP operates under a consent decree, we don't have the ability to claim that someone has stolen our copyrighted works and is performing them illegally," he said.

If they have simply said, "I want a license," they don't have to pay us anything. They don't have to have a deal with us up front as long as they have applied for a license. Even if it takes them four or five years to get it through rate court, they can be in a place where they are not infringing the performance right. At the end of the road, if their business model is a failure and they don't have any revenue, they were able to get that music for free.

Another issue that makes it difficult for ASCAP is, in the old world, a new business model would come along and the rate court would figure out what the rate would be, and once the rate was set it worked across the business line. Nowadays, YouTube is saying, "We're not like anyone else." Yahoo goes, "We're not like anyone else." Pandora—"We're not like anyone else." And so it's gone from a couple of cases that go on for a while but set a rate to an incredible litigation burden on ASCAP with all these new businesses coming along, claiming to be totally different. If all these new media services were simply going to be add-ons to existing revenue streams, the fact that the courts may not value it the way we want them to value it, its net would still be a positive. The concern is that the big sustaining performance royalty sources of today may be eviscerated by these new media sources, which don't look like they're going to pay as much money. So it's kind of exchanging, to paraphrase something an old boss of mine said, analog dollars for digital dimes. If overall revenue goes down, does it get replaced by the performance royalties paid by the Internet Web sites? Not based on the rates currently being set.

Without a doubt the best champions for the rights of music creators before members of Congress are the songwriters themselves. "The one thing songwriters have going for them is who they are," said David Israelite, the president and CEO of the National Music Publishers Association (NMPA).

When you walk into a member of Congress' office and you can say you represent someone who writes songs in America, then it doesn't matter that we don't have as many lobbyists as the opponents do. We can touch a place in the heart of that member

of Congress. So lobbying efforts before Congress are more important than ever, and they need the backing of all songwriters.
To me, one letter from a songwriter is more important than
a high-paid lobbyist wandering around the halls of Congress.

And a visit from a songwriter can be even more effective.

Josh Kear, coauthor of several Grammy Award–winning hits, including "Need You Now" for Lady Antebellum and "Before He Cheats"
for Carrie Underwood, and Dan Wilson, producer and coauthor of
Adele's massive "Someone Like You," both participated in a 2013 in-
terview/performance event on Capitol Hill before an audience of legislators and their aides. For Kear, 38, who had a publishing deal for
ten years before gaining his first hit, it was a great opportunity to give
something back to ASCAP. "I care deeply about ASCAP," he said. "I've
been a member from even before I got my first publishing deal." Not
surprisingly, he found a lot of music fans among the politicians he met.

> Everybody likes music. But what you find out is how little they
> actually know about how it works. There's a misconception,
> even with the general public, that a songwriter who has a song
> on a big album is making the same kind of money as the star
> is making. It's not even close. Let's say two songwriters write
> a song on a platinum-selling album; they'd each make roughly
> $20,000 from mechanicals. Especially for beginning writers
> it's hard to make any kind of a living off mechanicals. It all
> comes from radio and the other usages of your songs, which
> is where ASCAP comes in. They've become extremely vital
> to writers because those other performances end up being
> your lifeblood.
>
> The group we talked to the most were the Congressional
> staff people, who are the ones doing all the research. That
> group is more the age 20s and 30s crowd. So they might care
> a little more deeply about what's been on the radio lately, but
> they're also the generation that was raised in the environment
> of "Why am I paying very much for music?" They're the ones
> we need to educate the most. Afterwards, we talked directly
> to some members of the Judiciary Committee, which does the

earliest voting on what's going to come up before the Congress and the Senate. Quite a few were new members who are starting from scratch, not just on this issue, but on a lot of issues. That's a lot of information to take in all at once. You not only need to know what's happening now, you need the history of what's been leading up to this.

When the writer of a hit song is the one making the presentation, the impact can be immense. "It's important when you can talk to a congressmen and mention a song they care about," said Kear.

When Dan Wilson comes into a meeting and he's talking about "Someone Like You," that's a song that's meant a lot to a lot of people over the last couple of years. So they instantly feel a connection to him. And that song might not have been written. At the end of our meeting we asked for questions. We had a moment of silence where nobody was saying anything and I said, "I'd like to close this by saying that silence you're hearing right now, that's the soundtrack of your life if songwriters don't get to make a living and get to keep doing what they're doing."

One of the most important ways that ASCAP engages the attention of members of Congress is via The ASCAP Foundation's annual "We Write the Songs" musical shows at the Library of Congress in Washington, DC. Officially conceived as a celebration of the partnership between the Library and The ASCAP Foundation in establishing an extensive archive of materials relating to the historic and cultural impact of ASCAP and its members, "We Write the Songs" has brought a wide variety of songwriters across musical genres to the Library's Coolidge Auditorium stage each May since 2009. The shows have featured performances by the leading writers and performers of every popular music style as well as by ASCAP board members, including Marilyn (and Alan) Bergman, Bruce Broughton, Hal David, Dan Foliart, Wayland Holyfield, Dean Kay, Johnny Mandel, Valerie Simpson (and Nick Ashford), Jimmy Webb, and Paul Williams.

"We Write the Songs" also brings senators and representatives into the process by having them introduce the performers from their respective districts/states. This tradition has served to strengthen the bonds between those who write the songs and those who write the laws. Illustrative of the impact of this unique collaboration is the comment of Representative Mel Watt of North Carolina, following the May 2013 installment of this event, before a House Judiciary Subcommittee hearing:

> Earlier this week I attended the "We Write the Songs" event at the Library of Congress. The auditorium was packed with an audience transfixed on the skillfully crafted lyrics and the astonishing performances—including an electrifying performance that earned a standing ovation from the audience for a young group out of my home state of North Carolina—the Carolina Chocolate Drops. Bearing in mind the Chairman's call for a comprehensive review of copyright law in the digital era, I left the event with an even more passionate view that our copyright system must preserve and protect the rights of the creators of the music, books, games, movies, and other forms of intellectual ingenuity that enrich each of us individually and all of us collectively as a nation.

ASCAP board member Bruce Broughton, who has participated in this event, emphasized its value:

> Contact with lawmakers is an important part of service on the board. Each year, the ASCAP board "walks the halls of Congress," visiting legislators to talk about ASCAP, trying to secure support on issues that are important to ASCAP's members. For the past few years, The ASCAP Foundation has put on a Congressional event called "We Write the Songs" at the Library of Congress. Three years ago, my wife, Belinda, and I performed *Silverado* for an enthusiastic crowd of senators and congressmen, a very exciting evening for us, as we shared the stage with other songwriters who were performing their own classic works for the members of Congress. The program has become a positive annual highlight on Capitol Hill that

George Maxwell, a prominent New York music publisher, was elected as ASCAP's first president at the Society's first official meeting on February 13, 1914. He served until 1924.

Gene Buck, a lyricist and illustrator of sheet music, became ASCAP's second president in 1924. His 18-year term coincided with the explosive growth of radio and talking pictures as new media for music. Buck served until 1942.

Deems Taylor—a leading concert music composer, music critic, and radio personality—took the reins as ASCAP president from 1942 to 1948. He is fondly remembered as the narrator of the classic 1940 Walt Disney animated film *Fantasia*.

Fred E. Ahlert, a hit songwriter, was ASCAP president from 1948 to 1950. Ahlert was the composer of "I'll Get By (As Long as I Have You)," "Mean to Me," and "Walkin' My Baby Back Home."

Otto Harbach, lyric writer for operettas and musical theater, served as ASCAP president from 1950 to 1953. Among his best-known songs are "Smoke Gets in Your Eyes" (music by Jerome Kern) and "Indian Love Call" (written with Oscar Hammerstein II, Rudolf Friml, and Herbert Stothart).

Paul Cunningham, a lyricist and former vaudeville entertainer, was ASCAP president from 1956 to 1959, between Stanley Adams' two terms.

Stanley Adams, a lyricist, was ASCAP's longest-serving president, holding the office twice—from 1953 to 1956 and from 1959 to 1980. Adams wrote the English-language lyrics to "What a Diff'rence a Day Made," a hit in the 1930s, 1950s, and 1970s. (Photo by Arnold Newman)

Hal David, an Oscar- and Grammy-winning lyricist best known for his long string of hits with composer Burt Bacharach, was ASCAP president from 1980 to 1986. David's songs include "Raindrops Keep Fallin' on My Head," "Alfie," and "Walk On By."

Morton Gould, a Pulitzer Prize–winning composer, conductor, and Grammy Award–winning recording artist, was ASCAP president from 1986 to 1994. (Photo by RJ Capak)

Marilyn Bergman, an Oscar- and Grammy-winning lyricist, led the Society as ASCAP president and chairman from 1994 to 2009. She and her husband, Alan Bergman, are the lyric-writing team behind such hits as "The Windmills of Your Mind," "The Way We Were," and "You Don't Bring Me Flowers." (Photo by Spike Nannarello)

Left: Paul Williams, an Oscar- and Grammy-winning songwriter, recording artist, and actor, became ASCAP president and chairman in 2009. His hit songs include "We've Only Just Begun," "Evergreen," "The Rainbow Connection," and "You and Me Against the World." (Photo by Alan Mercer)

Bottom: At the first ASCAP Foundation Musical Theatre Workshop in New York in 1979, artistic director Charles Strouse (*right, front*) is joined by Broadway great Stephen Sondheim (*left, front*). (Photo by Sam Teicher)

Right: Don Schlitz, one of country music's most successful songwriters, joined ASCAP in 1978. Schlitz's hits include "The Gambler" and "When You Say Nothing at All." (Photo by Jim McGuire)

Bottom: ASCAP president Hal David (*left*) presents the ASCAP Founders Award to Motown superstar and ASCAP songwriter Stevie Wonder in Detroit in 1984.

ASCAP president Hal David (*left*) presents the ASCAP Founders Award to former Beatle Paul McCartney at a ceremony in New York in 1985. (Photo by Sam Teicher)

ASCAP's annual Pop Awards Dinner honors the writers and publishers of the most performed pop songs of the previous year. Pictured at the 1987 Pop Awards are (*left to right*) Stevie Wonder, Barbra Streisand, ASCAP president Morton Gould, and Lionel Richie. (Photo by Lester Cohen)

ASCAP publisher and vice chairman Irwin Z. Robinson (*left*) greets Senate Judiciary Committee member Senator Ted Kennedy at an ASCAP dinner in Washington in 1998. (Photo courtesy of Irwin Z. Robinson)

Country superstar Garth Brooks was presented with the ASCAP Golden Note Award by ASCAP president and chairman Marilyn Bergman at an all-star tribute on Capitol Hill in 2002. (Photo by Focused Images Photography)

Hip-hop great Jay-Z receives the ASCAP Golden Note Award from ASCAP president and chairman Marilyn Bergman at the ASCAP Rhythm & Soul Awards in Los Angeles in 2005. (Photo by Lester Cohen)

Billy Joel was recognized with the ASCAP Foundation Champion Award in 2006 for his support of music education. The ASCAP Foundation's president, Marilyn Bergman, presented the award in New York. (Photo by Kevin Mazur)

Superstar and ASCAP member Beyoncé (*second from left*) was honored as Woman of the Year at the 2009 annual Billboard Women in Music Awards Luncheon in New York. On hand to show support were (*left to right*) ASCAP VP of membership Nicole George, ASCAP senior VP of industry affairs Karen Sherry, ASCAP board member Valerie Simpson, and ASCAP senior VP of marketing Lauren Iossa. (Photo courtesy of Billboard)

ASCAP members Bill Withers (*left*) and Justin Timberlake appearing on a panel at the 2010 ASCAP "I Create Music" Expo in Los Angeles. The '70s singer-songwriter icon and the contemporary superstar compared and contrasted their experiences as recording artists and music creators. (Photo by Rick Miller)

ASCAP president and chairman Paul Williams with Speaker of the House Nancy Pelosi at The ASCAP Foundation's "We Write the Songs" show at the Library of Congress in 2010. (Photo by John Harrington)

Stephen Schwartz (*right*), the composer-lyricist of *Godspell*, *Pippin*, and *Wicked*, is honored in 2011 with the ASCAP Foundation Richard Rodgers Award for his lifetime contributions to American musical theater. Presenting the award is musical theater composer Adam Guettel, the grandson of Richard Rodgers. (Photo by Scott Wintrow)

Lyle Lovett performing at the 2011 edition of "We Write the Songs," the annual concert at the Library of Congress. The shows celebrate the ASCAP Collection at the Library—a gift by The ASCAP Foundation of documents, photos, sheet music, and other artifacts. (Photo by John Harrington)

Participants along with ASCAP staff and industry professionals taking part in the ASCAP Television & Film Scoring Workshop with Richard Bellis (*front row, third from right*) in 2012. (Photo by April Rocha)

Top: ASCAP songwriter and board member Jimmy Webb (*left*) with ASCAP Foundation Harold Adamson Lyric Award recipient and fellow Oklahoman John Fullbright in 2012. (Photo by Scott Wintrow)

Right: Jason Mraz accepts the ASCAP Foundation Champion Award in New York in December 2012. Mraz was recognized for leadership in such social causes as human equality, environmental protection, and arts education. (Photo by Scott Wintrow)

The ASCAP Foundation Morton Gould Young Composer Award recipients, with presenters, judges, other honorees, and ASCAP board members and staff, on stage at Manhattan's Merkin Hall in 2013. (Photo by RJ Capak)

Latin music superstar Marc Anthony (*left*) with his friend soccer star David Beckham, who presented the Founders Award to Anthony at the ASCAP Latin Music Awards in Los Angeles in 2012. (Photo by Frank Micelotta/PictureGroup)

Congressman John J. Conyers (*center*) ranking member of the House Judicia Committee, met at his Capitol Hill of with (*left*) ASCAP songwriter Siedah Garrett and (*right*) ASCAP CEO John LoFrumento in May 2013. (Photo by George Tolbert IV)

Rising Nashville-based singer-songwriter Brandy Clark is pictured on stage at the 2013 ASCAP Expo "Writers Jam." Clark, cowriter of the country hits "Mama's Broken Heart" and "Better Dig Two," drew a spontaneous standing ovation from the audience after her powerful performance. (Photo by Brian Dowling/Invision)

provides Congress the best picture of who we are and what we do.

These days Washington is a serious part of ASCAP's agenda and budget. "We have a tremendous grassroots network of ASCAP members," Karen Sherry explained.

> So at a moment's notice, if we're told, "You've got to see this senator from Illinois and convince him to vote for the legislation," we galvanize our people in Illinois and we say, "You call the senator and you go and see him." We've found that grassroots is essential; legislators respond to their constituents, because they are the people who voted them in and can vote them out. ASCAP is bipartisan. We support anybody who supports music rights. We have this huge network that's at the ready when we need it. We've used it many times in the past; we continue to use it today, and we're continually expanding it.
>
> We also help to set up individual appointments with legislators for one-on-one sessions to tell them about our issues. The good news is that ASCAP members place a very high value on the Society's advocacy activities and are very responsive when we reach out to them—as we have done so many times over the years. One example is Lyle Lovett, the eclectic singer-songwriter from Texas. Back in 2001, he very effectively testified on ASCAP's behalf before the House Subcommittee on Courts, the Internet and Intellectual Property about royalty payments for digital music performances. Further, more and more, music creators are also taking it upon themselves to speak out on issues affecting their rights.

However, the copyright debate has been somewhat skewed in recent years by consumer and industry groups who have been very vocal in seeking to diminish creators' rights. An example of the new reality was the 2012 defeat of the Stop Online Piracy Act (SOPA) and the Protect Intellectual Property Act (PIPA), which sought to curtail the proliferation of foreign Web sites engaged in piracy. Said the NMPA (National Music Publishers Association) president and CEO, David

Israelite, "Both bills were limited to dealing with Web sites that are foreign-based whose primary purpose is to steal."

If you were to ask the average person who heard about this, they would have no ability to tell you what it was about, because all they heard was that it was going to shut down the Internet or censor the Internet. And if you're a songwriter or a music publisher, it is a tremendous problem that foreign-based Web sites are in the business of stealing your property and making money off it, and it's very hard to do anything about it.

So for the songwriters who were part of a larger music co-alition, which was part of a larger content community coalition, who all were in favor of these bills, it's a real step backward to see what happened. Through a great deal of misinformation and scare tactics, the people who control the pipes were able to generate an enormous amount of outcry from people who I don't think were properly informed about the legislation, and Congress reacted to that. So we find ourselves having to start over with the challenge of what do you do about these Web sites that are based overseas that are stealing our content? We clearly have lost a great deal of time, and we've invested a lot of money and effort, and we're gonna have to take another crack at it. They control the pipes, so when you're able to shut down Web sites as a way to get your message out, it's unfortunate. Songwriters don't have the option of shutting down their music to get your attention. That's the whole point: they can't control what happens once it gets up on the Internet. So we're at a big disadvantage in trying to raise the profile of this issue to the masses, compared to the huge corporations that are on the other side of this fight.

In the long run, the question of how consumers will want to experience music in the future—whether streaming will replace owning, with sites like Rhapsody, Spotify, Pandora, YouTube, and countless others dominating the marketplace—becomes even more important to songwriters. "Internet companies have a viewpoint that somehow there should be different rules that apply to the Internet than apply to everywhere else in the world," said Israelite.

The argument I love is when people say, "When you steal music, you're just making a copy of the original; you're not taking the original. It isn't like stealing a car, because if you steal a car, you deprive the original car owner of having that car. But if you copy someone's music, that person still has their copy; you just have another copy. Therefore, it's not stealing." They completely ignore the economic chain, where the person who created that music only gets paid when people purchase it, and if everybody made a copy they couldn't do what they do.

The issue of music on the Internet continued to dominate the media in 2012. In February, Bill Keller of the *New York Times* weighed in: "This is a complicated subject that has been turned into simplistic sloganeering by rival vested interests dressed up as the saviors of freedom. . . . Content makers would be crazy to let the Internet be stunted as a force for invention, mobilization, and shared wisdom. . . . At the same time, online companies would be crazy to let piracy kill off the commerce that supplies quality material upon which even free sites like Wikipedia depend."

Former ASCAP board member Jimmy Jam, who has cowritten and coproduced hits with his partner Terry Lewis for Janet Jackson, Mariah Carey, Mary J. Blige, and others, would agree with Keller's assessment.

Creatively we're in a great place. There's a lot of kids who have a love of music and are interested in learning to play instruments. That side of it is being cultivated, a great next wave of singers and songwriters and producers, and we get a chance to work with them every day. The actual industry is probably a little more murky, because legal digital downloads haven't offset the decline in physical sales. I'm encouraged by all the young talent, but we have to make sure there's an industry where they can make a living doing it. I'd hate for it just to become something you do as a hobby on the side. It shouldn't be that. You should be able to make a living doing it if you're good at it. On the industry side, we still have a long way to go. But I think it will weed itself out because at the end of the day music is really important.

It's particularly important to the people who are manufacturing the hardware, because, as dazzling as the hardware is, it's meaningless without the content that goes with it. I think we're getting a little better with the tech side. I don't think there's as much of a disconnect between the tech side and the creative side as there used to be. The tech side recognizes that rather than exploit music to sell their product, they should partner with us. We're doing partnerships with tech companies that realize when they launch their new technology they're going to need music to go with it. That's one of the things myself and Terry [Lewis] have been exploring. Let's get in deals with these people where there's a value attached to what we do and the people we bring in and let's make sure these people get paid while you show off your great new technology.

Jam sees the disconnect as generational, and also as one between artists and their fans, typified by the feeling among the young that bands can always make up their lost sales and airplay royalties on the road. Putting aside the economics of whether this is true, pure songwriters don't have the option of touring and selling T-shirts; they only make money when someone buys their song or plays it on the air.

"The songwriter used to be the best compensated," Jimmy Jam reflected. "Now it's totally reversed. If an artist wants to put their music out for free and if they're the songwriter, they can make their income from other sources. If you're just a songwriter you need to get compensated for when it gets played."

When music was physical, it was more valued because you actually held something in your hand. Of course it costs money, I'm holding it in my hand. When downloading happened, you were just getting a digital file. It was nothing you could hold in your hand. A whole generation has no idea about intellectual property. Hopefully, we can catch the next generation. One of the reasons I got involved in board service is that I have kids who are musically inclined and I would love [it] if they decide to go into music. How would it look for me to discourage them from becoming songwriters?

Clearly, discouraging the next generation is not an option for either Jimmy Jam or ASCAP—which means that ASCAP, once again, must leave no stone unturned.

LoFrumento commented,

I still believe that the licensing of music will be required in the future. But I also believe ASCAP must continue to be more than a licensing organization in order to be relevant. We are responsible for a rapidly growing membership. We help our members develop their craft and their careers. We take some of our promising new talent and we put them in showcases. We advocate for their rights in Washington. We make the point that songwriters and publishers count. We undertake infringement litigation on their behalf. We identify what music is being performed and where it's performed and make sure that the royalties go into the pockets of our members.

With the introduction of the increased use of technology in our survey systems, the Society has been able to achieve our lowest operating ratio to date, and that is 11.3 percent—which places ASCAP in the forefront of PROs around the world.

The 2011–2012 period found John LoFrumento tackling a restructuring very similar to the one that greeted him upon his arrival to the position in 1994. "Back in 2009 we did $995 million; in 2010 we dropped to $930 million. In 2011 we came up a bit, to around $975 million," LoFrumento said. "The last three years have been hard on morale. Our people see what's happening in the music business and they worry. Another thing is we've slowed our salary growth, and slowed down bonus payments, because we see change happening and we believe it's not to the advantage of the people we serve to continue to raise salaries if the distributions are dropping."

As a result of this restructuring process, ASCAP's total staff went down from 664 at the end of 2008 to 485 at the end of 2012. LoFrumento said, "My ultimate need is service to the members. It's not service to my employees, or service to myself; it's service to the songwriters, composers, and publishers. By taking more money out of the operational cost of ASCAP, we're making our distributions more valuable to members."

According to LoFrumento, ASCAP revenue in 2012 came to almost two-thirds from TV, radio, and cable, and a third from foreign affiliates. New media represents approximately $25 million in domestic licensing fees.

ASCAP's fiscal year has always been strongly bolstered by royalties received from abroad, and the Society's dealings with PROs around the world matter more than ever. ASCAP's long relationship with Britain's PRS runs deep and is based on their similar philosophies of ownership by songwriters and publishers. Said Roger Greenaway, executive vice president, international:

> Like ASCAP, PRS has writer members and publishing members who are members of their Board, so, like ASCAP, they're actually run by their members. ASCAP has always had a sister relationship with PRS. PRS has a registration form, and when you register a title with PRS, there is a SESAC box, a BMI box, and an ASCAP box. Now, if you check any of these boxes, your copyright will go through one of those three societies in America, but if you don't tick it, it automatically goes to ASCAP. Historically, we have the default.

Some performers, however, bypass PRS completely, wanting to get their money from the United States more quickly. "It was a big deal when we were able to get Paul McCartney with the Wings catalogue," said Paul Adler.

> PRS was not delighted by the fact that ASCAP and BMI had offices in the UK. But we were not trying to get them to become members of ASCAP; we were just trying to get them to license in America through ASCAP. Eventually the bigger acts wanted to get money faster than they would have by going through PRS. If they made a lot of money in the United States, they didn't want to wait for ASCAP to pay PRS and then for PRS to pay it to them. So they became members of ASCAP directly for the United States.

Back in the '70s and '80s ASCAP saw a need to more closely monitor how its members were being protected abroad, leading to the practice of making "technical visits," which were really audits to determine whether American songs were being properly identified overseas. These days, technical visits are the province of the London office. "We have Society visits to make sure things are being distributed properly and that the money's not left behind," said Bob Candela, a 23-year ASCAP veteran, who is now senior vice president and CFO.

> It's less of an audit now. It's more amicable and professional on both sides than it was years ago. Then, it was more like, "If you don't find it, I'm not giving it to you." Now we're more in tune as to what were expecting. We know more about their deals and their structure. Since the late '90s we've used WID—Worldwide International Database. Years ago they'd get cue sheets in, now a lot of them are sent from producers electronically. We get paid for movies internationally, while we don't pay for cinema in the United States. But we can't get paid if we don't get all the information as to what songs are in what shows. Before, they had to do it manually; now a lot of things are auto-matched. We have a joint venture with BMI called RapidCue, which is an electronic cue sheet format that has standardized the industry.

Candela elaborated on the complexities of international distribution.

> We receive about $2 million a year from Russia, $80,000 from India, and $56,000 from China. If we were receiving full value for performing rights from those places, we could easily be getting 10 to 15 percent more income annually. Ninety percent of the music in China is Chinese, but even of the 10 percent that's not, most of it is lost to piracy. We do well with Japan, but Japan's had some problems because of the earthquakes and the tsunami; a lot of bars and restaurants got wiped out, so as they're rebuilding, the Japanese society decided they weren't going to collect for a year or so to give everybody a chance to regrow their business. We did something similar to that with the victims of Katrina down in New Orleans. We gave them a free pass for a year on their licensing.

According to Candela's latest figures, the European countries (among them Britain, France, Germany, Spain, Greece, Ireland, and the Netherlands) were the source of $139 million, or 41 percent of the total; the United Kingdom alone brought in $49 million. The top five countries for American performances overseas were the United Kingdom, France, Canada, Germany, and Japan. "The concern overseas is economic," said Candela.

> But we haven't seen ASCAP performances and repertory dropping over there. If you take the fluctuations of the currency out of the equation, we've had a 1–2 percent growth. We think that may flatten out a little bit. The world economy is volatile, for sure. You just hope there's more and more sources to draw from to make up any shortfalls anywhere else. Brazil has really taken off; its income has doubled in the last six years. Australia has picked up. Now if we could just pick up Cuba and China, and get a little more from Russia . . .

As the CEO, John LoFrumento is confident about the future. "The question really is 'How should ASCAP be positioned as we go forward?'" he said. "We will soon be 100 years old. If at that time all we can say about ourselves is 'We are 100 years old,' then we're in deep trouble. What we should be able to say about ourselves is 'We are in the first year of another 100-year run.' That's what we have to prepare ourselves for."

ASCAP publisher board member Zach Horowitz, Chairman and CEO of the Universal Music Publishing Group, finds ASCAP's 100-year story inspiring and envisions a continuing role and relevance for the Society as it moves into its second century.

> ASCAP's centennial anniversary is a remarkable testament to the enduring and indispensable service the organization provides for those who create music. For 100 years, regardless of how, where, or when music is performed, there's been one constant—that ASCAP will continually evolve to monitor those performances and ensure that songwriters, composers, and music publishers are fairly compensated. In an era of massive and complicated technological changes that have dramatically altered the way music is consumed and enjoyed, the need for ASCAP has never been more apparent, the opportunities never so great. At a time when music is performed billions of

times each year, in ways not imaginable when songwriters like Jerome Kern and Irving Berlin started ASCAP in 1914, the passion, commitment, and dedication of the organization to its members is a continual source of inspiration for all of us who sit on the board. We know ASCAP's invaluable contribution to the music community will continue in the decades to come.

Veteran music publisher Martin Bandier agrees. Currently the CEO and chairman of the board of the new EMI/Sony/ATV and a longtime ASCAP board member, Bandier stated:

> The world has changed and the good news is that ASCAP has changed with it. Their priorities are always the same: to license their repertoire and to maximize revenue in a fair and reasonable manner for their membership. They've done a great job of moving ahead with respect to that, but always there are bumps in the road when you're dealing with the kind of savvy digital licensing people who sometimes look to take advantage of the works created by authors and composers and owned by publishers. But ASCAP is fighting the good fight on behalf of all those people.
>
> Performance rights organizations are very important in today's world. They were in the past as well, but even more so today. Because the uses of music are so diverse. In the music publishing business you only have a handful of revenue streams: money from selling records, downloads, money from licensing of songs for commercials and film and TV, and then you've got performance income, which is growing to become the largest segment of the income. So for writers and publishers there's nothing more important than a PRO. That's why we really have to cherish an American institution like ASCAP for the work they do.

In many ways, ASCAP's value is even more incalculable today than when it was founded. Back then ASCAP's only responsibility was making sure an Irving Berlin or a Jerome Kern got paid. As complicated and exhausting a task as that might have been, today, all you have to do is attend an event like the Expo or one of the inspirational awards cer-emonies under the auspices of The ASCAP Foundation to see how that mission has expanded, putting ASCAP at the forefront of nurturing the arts. You can read it in the eyes of the young winners and runners-up, or the young strivers who want to follow in the footsteps of their idols.

No one has a better handle on the songwriters' ultimate quest than ASCAP's current leader, Paul Williams.

> The way I see it there are three levels of payment for a song-writer. The first is that sense of self-knowledge and that kind of do-it-yourself therapy that takes something out of the center of your chest that is bothering you or delighting you, and gives you the chance to understand it a little better. The second thing is where all of a sudden I connect with another human being, not by what is different with me but what I have in common with that person. When all of a sudden they respond to what I've written with a "Me, too." There's an amazing sense of inclu-sion there for you when you suddenly become part of the family of man. I refer to it as the heart payment for a songwriter. It's someone coming up and saying, "My mom was a single mom and 'You and Me Against the World' was a really important song to her and she used to hold me on her lap and sing it," or "We got married to 'We've Only Just Begun' or 'Evergreen.'" A by-product of having a hit is the third level, when you can put food on the table for your family, which is innately important to getting somebody to continue to make music as more than a hobby. Those are amazing moments for a songwriter, but the first two really can't exist without that third level of keeping the payment system alive, which is what we're doing here.

And in the end, as it was at the beginning, ASCAP will be there to do the protecting. Perhaps master lyricist Johnny Mercer, in an ob-servation of more than 40 years ago, expressed most succinctly the essence of ASCAP: "I would say that ASCAP is the Magna Carta of the author and composer . . . the Declaration of Independence of the creative mind . . . and the Social Security of the free spirit."

ASCAP LEADERSHIP THROUGH THE YEARS

ASCAP Presidents

George Maxwell (1914–1924)
Gene Buck (1924–1942)
Deems Taylor (1942–1948)
Fred E. Ahlert (1948–1950)
Otto A. Harbach (1950–1953)
Stanley Adams (1953–1956)
Paul Cunningham (1956–1959)
Stanley Adams (1959–1980)
Hal David (1980–1986)
Morton Gould (1986–1994)
Marilyn Bergman (1994–2009)
Paul Williams (2009–present)

ASCAP Board Members

W= Writer; P = Publisher

Stanley Adams (W)	1944–1994
Richard Adler (W)	1963–1966
Fred E. Ahlert (W)	1933–1953
Harold Arlen (W)	1969–1975
Martin Bandier* (P)	1993–1998, 2007–Present
Samuel Barber (W)	1968–1973
Jack Beeson (W)	1991–1994
Frederick Belcher (P)	1914–1917

Richard Bellis* (W)	2007–Present
Marilyn Bergman* (W)	1985–Present
Irving Berlin (W)	1914–1920
Charles Bernstein (W)	2007
Elmer Bernstein (W)	2003–2004
Louis Bernstein (P)	1914–1962
John Bettis (W)	1995–2003
Irving Bibo (W)	1924–1927
Caroline Bienstock* (P)	2008–Present
Freddy Bienstock (P)	1995–2008
E. F. Bither (P)	1917–1933
Victor Blau (P)	1965–1968
Henry Blossom (W)	1917–1920
Susan Borgeson (P)	1995–1997
Joanne Boris (P)	1998–2005
Ben Bornstein (P)	1920–1922
Saul H. Bornstein (P)	1921
Saul H. Bourne (P)	1921–1957
Mrs. Saul Bourne (P)	1957–1958
J. J. Bregman (P)	1935–1947
J. K. Brennan (W)	1928
Leon Brettler (P)	1962–2001
Arnold Broido (P)	1972–1979, 1981–2007
Bruce Broughton* (W)	2003–Present
Gene Buck (W)	1920–1956
Arnold D. Burk (P)	1969
R. H. Burnside (W)	1917–1918
John Cacavas (W)	1993–2001
Irving Caesar (W/P)	(W) 1929–1945, (P) 1947–1967
Sammy Cahn (W)	1977–1993
Harry Carroll (W)	1914–1917
Jacques R. Chabrier (P)	1968–1974
Salvatore T. Chiantia (P)	1968–1985
Desmond Child* (W)	2013–Present
Alf Clausen* (W)	2013–Present
Barry Coburn* (P)	2007–Present
Cy Coleman (W)	1966–2004

Willie Colón (W)	1994
Frank H. Connor (P)	1946–1971
Aaron Copland (W)	1973–1976
Robert Crawford (P)	1930–1937
Paul Creston (W)	1960–1968
Paul Cunningham (W)	1946–1960
Hal David (W)	1974–2012
Reginald De Koven (W)	1917
Bud G. De Sylva (W)	1922–1930
Howard Dietz (W)	1959–1966
Walter Donaldson (W)	1930–1932
Walter Douglas (P)	1922–1924, 1931–1938
Louis Dreyfus (P)	1964–1967
Max Dreyfus (P)	1914–1964
Jacob Druckman (W)	1976, 1981–1989
George Duke (W)	2011–2013
George W. Duning (W)	1972–1984
John L. Eastman* (P)	1997–Present
Sammy Fain (W)	1979–1989
Ernest R. Farmer (P)	1971–1980, 1983–1988
Roger Faxon (P)	2005–2012
W. Rodman Fay (P)	1927–1930
Leo Feist (P)	1914–1917
Nicholas Firth (P)	1994–2007
Walter Fischer (P)	1924–1946
George Fisher (P)	1931–1941
Dan Foliart* (W)	2009–Present
Ron Freed (P)	1984–1986, 1989–1995
William Gallagher (P)	1970–1971
L. Wolfe Gilbert (W)	1941–1944, 1953–1970
E. Ray Goetz (W)	1914–1920
John Golden (W)	1914–1915
Leonard Golove (P)	1979–1982
Bernard Goodwin (P)	1951–1957, 1959–1963
Morton Gould (W)	1959–1996
Donald Gray (P)	1942–1956
John Green (W)	1981–1988

Name	Years
Arthur Hamilton (W)	1969–2001
Oscar Hammerstein II (W)	1939–1960
Otto A. Harbach (W)	1920–1927, 1929–1963
Charles K. Harris (P)	1921–1930
Silvio Hein (W)	1914–1928
Ray Henderson (W)	1942–1951
Victor Herbert (W)	1914–1924
Sidney Herman (P)	1975–1992
Donna Hilley (P)	1994–2005
Louis A. Hirsch (W)	1917–1924
George V. Hobart (W)	1914–1920
David Hockman (P)	2005–2007
Wayland Holyfield* (W)	1990–1999, 2002–Present
Zach Horowitz* (P)	2012–Present
James Newton Howard (W)	2004–2006
John Tasker Howard (W)	1945–1958
Raymond Hubbell (W)	1914–1941
Laurent Hubert* (P)	2011–Present
Mark Isham (W)	2001–2002
Arthur Israel (P)	1965–1966
Jimmy Jam (W)	1996–1999, 1999–2007
William Jerome (W)	1914–1925
David Johnson (P)	2007–2011
Gus Kahn (W)	1927–1930
Ronald S. Kass (P)	1969
Dean Kay* (P)	1989–Present
Chuck Kaye (P)	1982–1986
Jerome Keit (P)	1919–1932
James Kendrick* (P)	2007–Present
Gustave Kerker (W)	1914–1923
Jerome Kern (W)	1924–1929, 1932–1942
Buddy Killen (P)	1983–1991, 1991
A. Walter Kramer (P/W)	(P) 1941–1942, (W) 1943–1956
Alex C. Kramer (W)	1954–1959
Burton Lane (W)	1985–1996
George Lee (P)	1970–1971
Edgar Leslie (W)	1931–1941, 1947–1953

Leeds Levy* (P)	1985–1991, 1992–Present
Lou Levy (P)	1963–1968
Julie Lipsius (P)	1995–1997
Ballard MacDonald (W)	1920
Glen MacDonough (W)	1914–1923
John K. Maitland (P)	1968–1969
Henry Mancini (W)	1967–1971
Johnny Mandel (W)	1989–2011
Keith Mardak (P)	1987–1994
Edward B. Marks (P)	1921–1923
Gerald Marks (W)	1970–1980
John D. Marks (P)	1957–1960
Frederick Martens (W)	1924–1932
Arnold Maxin (P)	1965–1969
George Maxwell (P)	1914–1931
Joseph McCarthy (W)	1921–1929
Jimmy McHugh (W)	1960–1969
John McKellen (P)	1992–1994
Evan Medow (P)	2007
Peter Mennin (W)	1966–1971
Johnny Mercer (W)	1940–1941
George W. Meyer (W)	1920–1923, 1932–1958
Jack Mills (P)	1924–1964
Douglas Moore (W)	1957–1960
Jay Morgenstern (P)	1987–2007
Edwin H. Morris (P)	1932–1935, 1936–1939, 1961–1974
Edward Murphy (P)	1979–1983
R. F. Murray (P)	1941–1945
John J. O'Connor (P)	1938–1949
Geoffrey O'Hara (W)	1941–1945
Abe Olman (P)	1946–1956
Stephen Paulus* (W)	1990–1995, 1996–Present
Ralph Peer II (P)	1985–1994
Vincent Persichetti (W)	1971–1974
Matt Pincus* (P)	2012–Present
Stuart Pope (P)	1971–1984
David Raksin (W)	1995–2003

David Renzer (P)	1999–2011
Howard S. Richmond (P)	1966–1970
J. J. Robbins (P)	1933–1935, 1938–1946, 1950–1956
Irwin Z. Robinson* (P)	1972–2009, 2010–Present
Mary Rodgers (W)	1995–1999
Richard Rodgers (W)	1929–1930, 1941–1947, 1960–1974
Sigmund Romberg (W)	1930–1939
Wesley H. Rose (P)	1967–1984
Michael Sammis (P)	2011–2012
Lester Santly (P)	1945, 1947–1951
Gustave Schirmer (P)	1914–1915, 1930–1958
Rudolph Schirmer (P)	1914
Arthur Schwartz (W)	1959–1984
Stephen Schwartz (W)	2004–2009, 2012–2013
Maurice Scopp (P)	1956–1965
Larry Shayne (P)	1970–1982
Alan L. Shulman (P)	1971–1975
Elie Siegmeister (W)	1977–1990
Lester Sill (P)	1978–1993
Edward Silvers (P)	1971–1979
Valerie Simpson* (W)	2007–Present
Harry B. Smith (W)	1914–1917
Stephen Sondheim (W)	1994
John Philip Sousa (W)	1924–1932
Kathy Spanberger (P)	1997–1999, 2001–2010
Oley Speaks (W)	1924–1943
Herman Starr (P)	1935–1936, 1939–1964
Michael Stewart (P)	1975–1988
Cameron Strang* (P)	2011–Present
Rudolph Tauhert (P)	1959–1971
Billy Taylor (W)	1975–1978
Deems Taylor (W)	1933–1965
Virgil Thomson (W)	1975–1982
M. E. Tompkins (P)	1924–1927
Adolph Vogel (P)	1957–1972
Will Von Tilzer (P)	1914–1919, 1921–1941
Harry Warren (W)	1929–1933

Ned Washington (W)	1957–1976
Henry Waterson (P)	1914–1919, 1921–1922
Jimmy Webb* (W)	1999–Present
Norman Weiser (P)	1974–1977
Paul Williams* (W)	2001–Present
Jay Witmark (P)	1914–1930
Reynold Wolf (W)	1920–1922
Doug Wood* (W)	1999–Present
Jack Yellen (W)	1951–1968
Joseph Young (W)	1926–1939

*Current board member (as of November 2013)

ASCAP MEMBERSHIP ACTIVITIES

ASCAP "I Create Music" Expo

Launched in 2006 and held annually in Los Angeles, the ASCAP "I Create Music" Expo is the first and only national conference dedicated to songwriting and composing. Selling out in its inaugural year, the Expo immediately provided a unique opportunity for songwriters, composers, publishers, producers, and those in the industry that support them to come together in an unprecedented way to share their knowledge and expertise. In the Expo's short history, the innovative programming offered to attendees has grown to include celebrity Q&As, master classes, songwriting and composing workshops, publisher and business panels, one-on-one sessions, DIY career-building workshops, showcases and performances, song feedback panels, state-of-the-art technology demos, and leading music industry exhibitors.

Some of the biggest names in music, from both the creative and the business sides, have participated in the ASCAP Expo. Headliner interviews have included Katy Perry, Ne-Yo, Stargate, Carly Simon, the Smeezingtons (Bruno Mars, Philip Lawrence, Ari Levine), Lindsey Buckingham interviewed by Sara Bareilles, Quincy Jones interviewed by Ludacris, Justin Timberlake and Bill Withers, John Mayer, Ann and Nancy Wilson (Heart), Jeff Lynne, Jon Bon Jovi and Richie Sambora, Jackson Browne, Steve Miller, Randy Newman, and Tom Petty.

New York Sessions

ASCAP brings its top songwriters, composers, and producers together for a full day devoted to the craft, creativity, and business of being a music creator. Sessions combine insightful panels featuring top writers and musicians with master classes and product demonstrations, all to help strengthen participants' skills, knowledge, and connections.

The inaugural New York Sessions event in 2009 featured a special keynote interview with Grammy Award–winning singer-songwriter Rob Thomas (Matchbox Twenty). New York Sessions has also brought such notable names as Kerry "Krucial" Brothers, Carvin & Ivan (Karma Productions), Sam Hollander, Nico Muhly, Adam Schlesinger, Maria Schneider, Stargate, and Gregg Wattenberg.

Showcases

Through its extensive roster of showcases throughout the year, ASCAP offers promising songwriters opportunities to get their music heard by fans and industry professionals.

- **Sundance/ASCAP Music Café**—The annual Sundance/ASCAP Music Café celebrates the role of music in film with an eclectic mix of songwriters and artists, from legendary icons to rising stars, all handpicked by ASCAP. Past participants include the All-American Rejects, Sara Bareilles, Andrew Bird, the Civil Wars, Shawn Colvin, Donovan, Melanie Fiona, the Fray, Gin Blossoms, Guster, Glen Hansard and Markéta Irglová, Emmylou Harris, Wyclef Jean, Flying Lotus, Richard Marx, Ingrid Michaelson, Jason Mraz, Graham Nash, Matt Nathanson, Mike Posner, Grace Potter and the Nocturnals, Johnny Rzeznik (Goo Goo Dolls), Damien Rice, LeAnn Rimes, Josh Ritter, Rodriguez, Silversun Pickups, Stephen Stills, Rufus Wainwright, Dan Wilson, and Neil Young.
- **ASCAP Presents . . . at South by Southwest**—The Society handpicks the acts on its own stages and sponsors various other events at the annual South by Southwest Music Festival. Acts that have played on ASCAP's SXSW stages include the Cadillac Black, the Carolina Chocolate Drops, Kendrick Lamar, John Mayer, Katy Perry, the Rescues, the Temper Trap, T.I., Vampire Weekend, and Dan Wilson.
- **ASCAP Presents . . . Quiet on the Set**—Designed to focus attention on the cornerstone of the music business—the song itself—these showcases feature emerging talent and established artists and writers in an intimate setting, while also providing an opportunity

for members and industry executives to network. Past Quiet on the Set participants include Joseph Arthur, Jonatha Brooke, Reeve Carney, Deana Carter, Desmond Child, Ben Harper, John Mayer, Martin Sexton, Sixpence None the Richer, Allen Shamblin, Jill Sobule, Rufus Wainwright, and the Weepies.

- **ASCAP Music Lounge at the Nashville Film Festival**—Since 2010 ASCAP's Nashville office has booked the ASCAP Music Lounge at this premier film festival. Past participants include Escondido, the Wild Feathers, Katie Herzig, Mikky Ekko, Alyssa Bonagura, and Keegan DeWitt.
- **Women Behind the Music Events**—The Rhythm and Soul team selects up-and-coming ASCAP members to perform at these regular events honoring female pioneers in the music industry.
- **Sponsored Stages**—ASCAP presents selected artists in showcases at major music festivals and conferences like CMA Music Festival, CMJ Music Marathon, Folk Alliance, Noise Pop, and the Mill Valley Film Festival.

Panel Appearances

ASCAP books informative panels with prominent ASCAP members at a variety of conferences and festivals nationwide, including

- *Billboard/The Hollywood Reporter* Film and TV Music Conference
- San Diego Comic Con
- WonderCon
- Los Angeles, AFI, and Napa Valley Film Festivals

Song Camps

ASCAP's exclusive song camps bring together top ASCAP writers, producers, and recording artists with the goal of crafting demos that are ready to pitch to labels and publishers.

- **Château Marouatte**—Since 2011 ASCAP has hosted an intensive songwriter retreat at the idyllic Château Marouatte in France, owned by industry legend Miles Copeland. Participating song-writers have included Johntá Austin, Dave Bassett, Michelle Bell, Billboard, Claudia Brant, Chris DeStefano, Theron "Neff-U" Feemster, Ellie Goulding, Tom Higgenson (Plain White T's), Brett James, Hillary Lindsey, Mika, Justin Parker, Mike Posner, Lindsey Ray, Priscilla Renea, Shea Taylor, and Greg Wells.

· **Latin Song Camps**—The ASCAP Latin department regularly holds song camps across the US and in Mexico, and in collaboration with prominent writers in other genres. Past invitees include Aureo Baqueiro, Claudia Brant, Ferra, Gabriel Flores, Amaury Gutiérrez, Yoel Henríquez, Juan José Hernández, Koko, Natalia Lafourcade, Carlos Marmo, Fernando Osorio, Jorge Luis Piloto, Bobby Pulido, Dany Tomas, Mónica Vélez, and Wise.

· **Music City Trifecta**—ASCAP's Nashville office hosts a three-day song camp bringing together ASCAP's finest country, pop, and Christian writers. Past participants include Greg Becker, Billboard, Chris DeStefano, Ben Glover, Ashley Gorley, Catt Gravitt, JT Harding, Brett James, Mike Krompass, Hillary Lindsey, Shane McAnally, Autumn Rowe, Shane Stevens, Troy Verges, and Justin Weaver.

Networking Events

· **Love Fest**—Every year, ASCAP's songwriting elite gathers at a private home in Los Angeles for this invitation-only soiree. It brings together creative types (no suits allowed) in a casual atmosphere to hang out, network, and plant the seeds for future generations of hit songs.

· **Hollywood Hit Makers and Gotham City Hit Makers**—A series of intimate networking events in Los Angeles and New York for young, on-the-verge writers and producers in the pop and rhythm and soul genres.

· **Sundance Composer-Filmmaker Cocktail Party**—ASCAP's film and TV music team puts together an annual mixer at Sundance for ASCAP composers and filmmakers, with the goal of fostering creative partnerships.

Educational Events

- **Music Business 101**—A series of informational and educational sessions where guest speakers address topics such as performing rights, publishing, A&R, and breaking into the business. Geared toward new and up-and-coming writers, these sessions provide ample time for audience questions. All Music Business 101 events are free and open to the public, and are held at various times throughout the year in New York, Los Angeles, Atlanta, Nashville, and Miami.
- **Building Your Team**—ASCAP's Rhythm and Soul team curates this ongoing series of panels, focused on helping music creators assemble the perfect team to boost their careers. Workshops are held year-round in various cities.
- **"Check It Out" Series**—Held regularly in Atlanta, this series gives budding writers and producers the opportunity to have their music critiqued by successful professionals and industry experts, all in front of a live audience.
- **ASCAP Twitter Q&A's**—ASCAP hosts an ongoing series of interactive Twitter Q&A's with experts from all over the music industry map. Past Q&A sessions have put the public in direct contact with prominent managers, A&R execs, music supervisors, and producers for casual and informative Twitter chats.

Workshops

- **GPS Project**—ASCAP's GPS Project stands for "Guidance from Publishers for Songwriters" and puts the emphasis on getting the best of Nashville's unsigned writers in front of the city's vibrant publishing community. Participating writers are paired with a series of six publishers for meetings designed to help them develop their writing and solidify their professional relationships.
- **ASCAP Television & Film Scoring Workshop with Richard Bellis**—ASCAP offers a one-of-a-kind experience for aspiring film and television composers. Twelve selected participants have an opportunity to record an original composition with an "A list" of Hollywood professionals, including a 60-piece orchestra of LA's finest on a major studio film scoring stage, with a legendary scoring

mixer, professional music editors, copyists, and composers acting as coaches and mentors. In addition, there are "From the Horse's Mouth" sessions with studio executives, agents, attorneys, and music supervisors. Graduates of the workshop are some of today's most active film and TV composers, including Jim Dooley, Rob Duncan, Trevor Morris, Atli Örvarsson, Scott Starrett, Joseph Trapanese, and Austin Wintory.

ASCAP OnStage

The ASCAP OnStage program offers ASCAP members the opportunity to receive royalties when their music is performed live at venues of any size throughout the country. Members provide the basic details of the performance; then OnStage payments come through their normal quarterly ASCAP distribution.

ASCAP Plus Awards

The ASCAP Plus Awards program provides cash and recognition to writers who create music with a value beyond the scope of performance surveys. It rewards writer members of all genres whose works were performed in unsurveyed media as well as writer members whose catalogues have prestige value. ASCAP Plus Awards are available to writers who received less than $25,000 in domestic performance royalties in the previous calendar year.

THE ASCAP FOUNDATION AND ITS PROGRAMS

The following represent ASCAP Foundation programs established prior to 2013—a legacy of ongoing programs for music education, talent development, awards, and recognition supported by ASCAP Foundation donors for almost four decades.

1975

The ASCAP Foundation is incorporated in June after the estate of Jack Norworth, writer of "Take Me Out to the Ballgame," leaves a bequest with instructions to create a program to honor and support young composers.

1979

The ASCAP Foundation Young Composer Awards for composers under 30 (which in 1998 became the ASCAP Foundation Morton Gould Young Composer Awards) are underwritten by the Jack and Amy Norworth Memorial Fund.

The ASCAP Foundation Raymond Hubbell Award is established in memory of Mr. Hubbell, one of ASCAP's founding members and the writer of "Poor Butterfly," by a trust from Estelle Hubbell, his widow. This award is given to a college music composition student.

The ASCAP Foundation Pop Songwriters Workshop is established on the East and West Coasts; a third is started later in Nashville. Each workshop features prominent guests from various facets of the music business and is designed to enrich participants' knowledge of the industry, help them establish contacts and confidence, and expand their collaborative partnerships. The West Coast workshop was renamed in 1995 to honor industry pioneer Lester Sill; the East Coast version was renamed in 2013 after the great songwriter Jerry Ragovoy.

The ASCAP Foundation Musical Theatre Workshop series is initiated under the leadership of Charles Strouse (*Bye Bye Birdie, Annie*). From 1992, the workshop continues under the leadership of Stephen Schwartz (*Pippin, Wicked*).

1982

The ASCAP Foundation Richard Rodgers Award is established by Dorothy Rodgers to recognize musical theater veterans. Mr. Rodgers, together with his main collaborators, Lorenz Hart and Oscar Hammerstein II, wrote Broadway classics that include *Oklahoma!* and *The Sound of Music*. The award is supported by an endowment from the Rodgers Family Trust.

1983

The ASCAP Foundation Louis Dreyfus Warner/Chappell City College Scholarship is established to honor Mr. Dreyfus, cofounder of the U.S. Division of Chappell Music (now part of Warner/Chappell Music). The scholarship, jointly funded by The ASCAP Foundation, the City College of New York, and the Jean and Louis Dreyfus Foundation, recognizes a composition student.

1984

The ASCAP Foundation Commission Program is created to spotlight and develop the talent of emerging composers.

The ASCAP Foundation Ira Gershwin Award at LaGuardia High School in New York City is established with funds from the Gershwin family in memory of Mr. Gershwin, the lyricist of "I Got Rhythm," "Someone to Watch Over Me," and "The Man That Got Away."

1985

The ASCAP Foundation Rudolf Nissim Prize is established by a bequest under the will of Dr. Rudolf Nissim, former director of ASCAP's foreign department. This prize goes to an ASCAP member composer for a concert work that requires a conductor and has not been previously performed.

1986

The ASCAP Foundation Max Dreyfus Scholarship is established to encourage musical theater composers. It is funded by the Max and Victoria Dreyfus Foundation in memory of Mr. Dreyfus, a former publisher board member and mentor to many musical theater legends.

The ASCAP Foundation Boosey & Hawkes Young Composer Award Honoring Aaron Copland at LaGuardia High School in New York City is established. It is funded by Boosey & Hawkes, publisher for Mr. Copland, who composed *Appalachian Spring* and *Billy the Kid*.

1987

The ASCAP Foundation Michael Masser Scholarship is initiated to assist young songwriters/musicians with funding from Michael Masser, composer/producer of such songs as "The Greatest Love of All" and "Saving All My Love for You."

The ASCAP Foundation receives a bequest from Florence Bennett Cunningham, the wife of ASCAP president Paul F. M. Cunningham, with the instruction that the royalties from her husband's works are to aid worthy American composers of musical compositions.

1990

The ASCAP Foundation Louis Armstrong Scholarship at the Aaron Copland School of Music at Queens College is established to support a jazz composition student. It is funded by a grant from the Louis Armstrong Educational Foundation in memory of Mr. Armstrong, one of the leading American musicians of the 20th century.

1991

The ASCAP Foundation Berklee College of Music Songwriter-in-Residence master classes are initiated.

The ASCAP Foundation Frederick Loewe Scholarship at New York University's Tisch School of the Arts is created in memory of the composer of *My Fair Lady* with a grant from the Frederick Loewe Foundation. This scholarship encourages young musical theater writers.

1992

The ASCAP Foundation Leiber & Stoller Music Scholarships are established on both coasts with gifts from Jerry Leiber and Mike Stoller, the writers of "Jailhouse Rock" and "Hound Dog."

1995

The ASCAP Foundation Sammy Cahn Award is established by ASCAP in Mr. Cahn's memory to encourage new lyricists. It is now funded by a gift from Tita Cahn in memory of Mr. Cahn, who wrote "High Hopes" and "Call Me Irresponsible."

The ASCAP Foundation receives a major bequest from the estate of Rosalie Meyer, widow of Joseph Meyer ("California, Here I Come"), to encourage young composers and support the efforts of senior composers.

The ASCAP Foundation Leo Kaplan Award is initiated for the top-ranking Morton Gould Young Composer Award recipient. It is funded through the Leo Kaplan family in memory of Mr. Kaplan, former ASCAP special distribution advisor, juror, and music lover.

1997

The ASCAP Foundation Lifetime Achievement Awards are created and supported by the Rosalie Meyer Fund to recognize senior composers and lyricists.

The **ASCAP Foundation Leonard Bernstein Composers Fund**, to assist young composers, is established with a grant from ASCAP in celebration of the 70th birthday of Mr. Bernstein, composer of *West Side Story.*

The **ASCAP Foundation/Disney Musical Theatre Workshop** is established in Los Angeles to provide musical theater writers the opportunity to present their original works-in-progress for professional critique. The workshop is funded in part by Walt Disney Feature Animation. After a change of sponsorship in 2011, it was renamed the ASCAP Foundation/DreamWorks Musical Theatre Workshop.

1998

The **ASCAP Foundation John Denver Music Scholarships supported by BMG/Cherry Lane** at Perry-Mansfield Performing Arts School and Camp in Colorado are initiated in memory of Mr. Denver, who wrote "Take Me Home, Country Roads." The scholarships are now supported by BMG/Chrysalis, John Denver's publisher, and the ASCAP Foundation Irving Caesar Fund.

The **ASCAP Foundation Music Teacher Recognition Award** is initiated to recognize outstanding music teachers. It is supported by the Rosalie Meyer Fund.

The **ASCAP Foundation Musical Theater Development Program** is established with a grant from the Johnny Mercer Foundation in memory of Mr. Mercer, who wrote "Ac-Cent-Tchu-Ate the Positive" and "Come Rain or Come Shine."

1999

The **ASCAP Foundation Fresh Air Fund Camps Program** is initiated, providing instruments and composer instructors to inner-city children at New York camps throughout the summer.

The **ASCAP Foundation Louis Armstrong Jazz Scholarships Honoring Duke Ellington at UCLA** are inaugurated in the year of Mr. Ellington's centennial. The scholarships are funded through a grant by the Louis Armstrong Educational Foundation in memory of Mr. Ellington, who wrote "It Don't Mean a Thing If It Ain't Got That Swing."

The ASCAP Foundation New York University Film Studies Fellowship in Florence, Italy, is initiated to broaden film composition students' understanding of their role in film.

The ASCAP Foundation Louis Armstrong Award Honoring W. C. Handy at Mount Vernon H.S. in Mount Vernon, New York, is created for W. C. Handy's 125th birthday. The award is funded by a grant from the Louis Armstrong Educational Foundation in memory of Mr. Handy, who wrote "St. Louis Blues" and lived in the Mount Vernon area in his later years.

The ASCAP Foundation receives a major bequest from the estate of Charles Kingsford, who wrote "The Ballad of John Henry," to promote the composition of art songs in the Romantic tradition through a commissions program.

The ASCAP Foundation Benny Davis Musical Theater Prize at the University of Miami is endowed through a bequest from Gilda Davis in memory of Mr. Davis, writer of "Baby Face."

2000

The ASCAP Foundation "In the Works" musical theater initiative is established in partnership with the Kennedy Center and subsequently with CLO/Carnegie Mellon to ensure that promising new musicals undergo further development with an eye toward eventual production.

The ASCAP Foundation Livingston & Evans Music Scholarship, supporting aspiring songwriters and musicians, is established with funding from Jay Livingston and Ray Evans, writers of "Mona Lisa" and "Que Será, Será."

The ASCAP Foundation "Music in the Schools" Program is launched in partnership with the Diane Warren Foundation and the VH1 Save the Music Foundation. This initiative ensures that students have quality music to play as they learn their instruments. Alfred Music Publishing, Inc. provides the printed music materials.

The **ASCAP Foundation** receives a major bequest from the estate of Audrey Nelson, daughter-in-law of Ed G. Nelson, writer of "I Apologize," for the support of music education and talent development for young composers.

2001

The **ASCAP Foundation Jerry Herman Legacy Series**, funded by composer and lyricist Jerry Herman, who wrote *Hello, Dolly!* and *Mame*, is established to bring the American musical theater heritage to students across the country.

The **ASCAP Foundation Henry Mancini Music Fellowships** are established with funding from Ginny Mancini in memory of Mr. Mancini, who wrote "Days of Wine and Roses" and "Moon River." These scholarships provide support for film and television composition students at universities nationwide.

The **ASCAP Foundation** receives a major bequest from the estate of John DeVries, writer of "Oh! Look at Me Now," for the education and support of young musicians via composer-in-residence programs at schools and special grants.

2002

The **ASCAP Foundation Young Jazz Composer Awards** are established to encourage the creation of new jazz works.

The **ASCAP Foundation Living Archive Project** is initiated to videotape prominent ASCAP songwriter and composer members to document their place in music history and the music industry. This project is funded through a gift from the Cain Foundation, directed by Wofford Denius.

The **ASCAP Foundation Fran Morgenstern Davis Scholarships** are established for students at Manhattan School of Music. These scholarships are funded by a gift from Joan and Jay Morgenstern, a recording and music publishing veteran, to honor the memory of their daughter.

The **Heineken Music Initiative/The ASCAP Foundation Grant Program for R&B Songwriters** assists up-and-coming songwriters in selected local markets with career advancement to develop new musical talent. The awards are supported with a grant from the Heineken Music Initiative.

2003

The Richard Adler–ASCAP Foundation Musical Theater Development Program is initiated at the Perry-Mansfield Performing Arts School and Camp in Colorado to nurture new composers, lyricists, and librettists. This is funded through a gift from Richard Adler, Broadway musical writer of *The Pajama Game* and *Damn Yankees*.

The ASCAP Foundation receives a bequest from Lola Brockman, daughter of James Brockman, who wrote "I'm Forever Blowing Bubbles," for the support of music education and talent development for young composers.

The ASCAP Foundation Rudy Pérez Songwriting Scholarship is established with a gift from songwriter Rudy Pérez, one of the top producers of Latin music. This scholarship is presented to an aspiring Latino songwriter who demonstrates potential to produce creative and original work and also demonstrates financial need.

The ASCAP Foundation Eunice and Hal David Instructor-in-Residence Award is established. This award provides funding to support the work of an outstanding music instructor at the Los Angeles County High School for the Arts. Hal David, ASCAP and ASCAP Foundation board member and lyricist for such great standards as "Raindrops Keep Fallin' on My Head," "Do You Know the Way to San Jose," and "Alfie," together with his wife, Eunice, funds this program.

2004

The ASCAP Foundation Steve Kaplan TV & Film Studies Scholarship is created by the Kaplan family in memory of Steve Kaplan, an award-winning film and television composer whose talents and credits span 25 years and encompass multiple genres. The scholarship encourages the career development of aspiring film and television composers by providing financial support for participants in ASCAP's annual film scoring workshop in Los Angeles.

The ASCAP Foundation/Disney Musical Theatre Workshop is established in Chicago to provide musical theater writers the opportunity to present their original works in progress for professional critique. The workshop is funded by Peter Schneider and the Chicago Department of Cultural Affairs.

The ASCAP Foundation Harold Arlen Musical Theater Award and the ASCAP Foundation Harold Arlen Film & TV Award, to assist songwriters and lyricists, are established by Sam and Joan Arlen in celebration of the centennial year of Harold Arlen, composer of "Over the Rainbow" and "Stormy Weather."

The ASCAP Foundation David Rose Award is established with a gift from the Rose Family Trust to honor television- and film-scoring great David Rose. Rose's best-known works include the instrumental standards "Holiday for Strings" and "The Stripper," music for *Bonanza* and *Little House on the Prairie*, and decades of work with radio and television star Red Skelton. The award is presented to a composer working toward a career in scoring for film and/or television who is participating in ASCAP's Television & Film Scoring Workshop.

The Heineken USA/ASCAP Foundation Latin and Pop/Rock Grant Program is launched. This grant program benefits emerging Latin and pop/rock music songwriters in selected markets. The awards are supported with a grant from Heineken USA.

The ASCAP Foundation is selected by the National Endowment for the Arts as one of only 10 organizations nationwide to receive a grant in a new initiative, the pilot phase of Summer School in the Arts.

The ASCAP Foundation is named the final beneficiary of all of Irving Caesar's assets (copyrights), including those held under his lifetime trust and those retained in his wholly owned publishing company, as well as his memorabilia. Irving Caesar was a prolific and beloved lyricist who wrote hundreds of songs, including "Tea for Two," "Just a Gigolo," "Swanee," and "Animal Crackers in My Soup."

2005

The ASCAP Foundation Charlotte V. Bergen Scholarship is established and is awarded annually to the top ASCAP Foundation Morton Gould Young Composer age 18 or under. This scholarship is made possible by the Frank and Lydia Bergen Foundation and is named in memory of their daughter, Charlotte, a lover of classical music. The scholarship is to be used for music study at an accredited college or music conservatory.

The ASCAP Foundation Children Will Listen program in honor of ASCAP member and musical theater great Stephen Sondheim (*West Side Story, Gypsy, Pacific Overtures, A Little Night Music*) is established to provide the musical theater experience to a generation of students who might not otherwise have this opportunity.

The ASCAP Foundation Creativity in the Classroom curriculum for grades 3, 4, and 5 is designed to help students recognize their own creative work and understand their rights as owners of intellectual property as well as the ethics of protecting and respecting the creative property of others. The premise of the program, as conceived by former ASCAP president Marilyn Bergman, is to encourage students to label their own creative work with the copyright symbol, the year, and their name, just as they would see on any published, professional creative work.

2006

The ASCAP Foundation Robert Allen Award is established and is presented annually to an aspiring ASCAP songwriter participating in ASCAP's New York Paul Cunningham Songwriters Workshop. It is named in honor of Robert Allen, composer of many classic pop songs, including "It's Not for Me to Say" and "Chances Are," and is funded by a gift from Patty Allen in memory of her husband.

The ASCAP Foundation Irving Berlin Summer Camp Scholarship is created to honor American songwriter Irving Berlin, who wrote such classics as "God Bless America" and "White Christmas." This scholarship makes the summer music camp experience possible for a young music creator who may otherwise not have this opportunity, and is funded by a gift to The ASCAP Foundation from the Irving Berlin Charitable Fund, Inc.

The ASCAP Foundation Leon Brettler Award is presented to a singer-songwriter participating in an ASCAP Foundation Nashville Songwriters Workshop. It is funded through a gift from Michael and Doug Brettler, and by the music publishing firm Shapiro, Bernstein & Co., in memory of Leon Brettler (1926–2001), who helmed Shapiro, Bernstein & Co. and served on the ASCAP board of directors for nearly 40 years.

The ASCAP Foundation Life in Music Award is established. This award recognizes the efforts of veteran music creators who have made significant contributions to our nation's music culture. This program is funded by a bequest under the will of Rosalie Meyer, the widow of Joseph Meyer, a longtime ASCAP member whose standards include "If You Knew Susie."

The ASCAP Foundation Irving Burgie Scholarship to support an aspiring African-American songwriter from the New York City area is established. It is funded by Irving Burgie in celebration of the 50th anniversary of his song "Day-O."

The ASCAP Foundation Champion Award is established and presented to an ASCAP member who is "making a difference" through social action on behalf of worthwhile causes, including music education, or who has demonstrated exceptional efforts in humanitarianism. Recipients include Billy Joel, John Mellencamp, Judy Collins, Susan and Tony Bennett, Arlo Guthrie, Jason Mraz, and Ne-Yo.

2007

The ASCAP Foundation Harold Adamson Lyric Award is established and presented annually to aspiring lyricists who participate in an ASCAP or ASCAP Foundation workshop in musical theater, pop, and/or country. Recipients must demonstrate talent and an intelligent and sensitive use of language, an ability that the heirs of the late lyricist Harold Adamson, writer of "Time on My Hands" and "An Affair to Remember," seek to recognize and foster in future generations. It is funded by Harold Adamson's royalties.

The ASCAP Foundation Jamie deRoy & Friends Award is established. This award is presented to an ASCAP songwriter (either a composer, a lyricist, or a team of writers) whose work has been of a high and consistent level of professionalism. This award for outstanding work, dedication, and craftsmanship, is funded by the Jamie deRoy Charitable Trust.

The ASCAP Foundation BMG/Cherry Lane Scholarship in Honor of Quincy Jones is established. This scholarship supports the work of a college or university student majoring in music who demonstrates talent and proficiency in the areas where Quincy Jones has made his mark: composing, arranging, producing, conducting, and performing. The scholarship is funded by BMG/Cherry Lane.

The ASCAP Foundation Joan and Irwin Robinson Scholarship is established by Irwin Z. Robinson and his wife, Joan. The scholarship supports a music business undergraduate or graduate student at New York University who demonstrates leadership, knowledge, dedication, skill, and career potential. Irwin Z. Robinson is vice president of industry affairs for the Richmond Organization.

2008

The ASCAP Foundation Cy Coleman Award is established by Shelby Coleman in memory of her husband. Cy Coleman wrote many pop standards, including "Witchcraft" and "The Best Is Yet to Come," as well as hit Broadway scores such as *Wildcat* ("Hey, Look Me Over"), *Little Me* ("Real Live Girl"), *Sweet Charity* ("Big Spender"), *Seesaw* ("It's Not Where You Start"), *I Love My Wife*, *The Will Rogers Follies*, and *The Life*. The award provides funds for readings of new musicals.

2009

The ASCAP Foundation Cole Porter Award is established with a gift to The ASCAP Foundation from the Cole Porter Musical and Literary Trusts, to be presented annually to an ASCAP or unaffiliated member who writes music and lyrics, whose work shows promise, and who has participated in the ASCAP Foundation Musical Theatre Workshop. The award honors the memory of Porter, who wrote such classics as "I Get a Kick out of You" and "Night and Day."

The ManUp4Kids educational program and Anthem Award are established at The ASCAP Foundation by Grammy Award–winning ASCAP songwriter/producer Desmond Child. The program provides low-income families the opportunity to attend music, theater, and cultural events within their community that would otherwise be unattainable. The Anthem Award supports a promising songwriter. Child, who was inducted into the Songwriters Hall of Fame in 2008, has over 70 Top 40 singles to his credit, including "Angel," "I Was Made for Loving You," "Livin' on a Prayer," "Livin' la Vida Loca," and "Dude Looks Like a Lady."

The ASCAP Foundation Jay Gorney Award is established Jay Gorney's wife, Sondra, and Jay's son, Dr. Roderic Gorney, to commemorate Jay's career and legacy. Gorney, a longtime ASCAP member and composer, along with lyricist E. Y. "Yip" Harburg wrote the 1930s classic "Brother, Can You Spare a Dime?," which became the anthem of the Great Depression. The Jay Gorney Award is presented for an original song judged on its social conscience or social significance as well as overall craft, artistry, and compositional elements.

The ASCAP Foundation Scholarship in Honor of Louis Armstrong is established and is presented to an outstanding student of jazz composition at either Manhattan School of Music or the New School for Jazz and Contemporary Music. The scholarship is underwritten by a grant from the Louis Armstrong Educational Foundation.

2010

The ASCAP Foundation Michelle and Dean Kay Award is established to support careers in music, particularly for those who concentrate their efforts in the Los Angeles area. Dean Kay is currently president and CEO of his own Demi Music Corp. and its affiliates, Lichelle Music Company and Yak Yak Music. Michelle Kay is vice president and CFO of the company. Dean is also a successful songwriter, having had hundreds of his compositions recorded, including "That's Life" by Frank Sinatra.

The ASCAP Foundation Barbara and John LoFrumento Award is established by ASCAP's CEO and his wife, Barbara, to support music and music therapy programs for autistic learners in New York's Eastchester School District. These weekly programs involve hundreds of students with autistic spectrum disorders and other developmental delays in the creative art of making music, with a specific focus on accomplishing goals for personal growth and improved social abilities.

The ASCAP Foundation Joe Raposo Children's Music Award is established by the family of Joe Raposo to honor his legacy. The award supports emerging talent in the area of children's music. Raposo, one of the creators of *Sesame Street* and its first and longtime musical director, wrote music for such diverse talents as Kermit the Frog, Frank Sinatra, Ray Charles, Dr. Seuss, Barbra Streisand, and Cookie Monster. "Sing," "It's Not Easy Bein' Green," and the "Sesame Street Theme" are among the songs that earned Raposo five Grammys and multiple gold and platinum albums.

Songwriters: The Next Generation, a partnership between The ASCAP Foundation and the John F. Kennedy Center for the Performing Arts, is established, in memory of Dr. Billy Taylor, to showcase the work of four emerging songwriters and composers in a free concert on the Kennedy Center's Millennium Stage. This program is made possible by the ASCAP Foundation Bart Howard Fund.

2011

The ASCAP Foundation Louis Prima Award is established by Gia Prima, wife of Louis, and her friends and longtime counsel at Riker, Danzig, Scherer, Hyland & Perretti LLP, and is presented to a talented vocalist or musician attending the New Orleans Center for the Creative Arts. Louis Prima was honored with the first Grammy Award for best performance by a vocal group for his rendition of "That Old Black Magic" in 1958. He recorded many popular favorites, including compositions of his own such as "Jump, Jive, an' Wail" and "Sing, Sing, Sing." Louis Prima passed away on August 24, 1978.

The ASCAP Foundation Freddy Bienstock Scholarship and Internship is established by ASCAP board member and Carlin America CEO Caroline Bienstock, along with her mother, Miriam Bienstock, and brother, Robert, COO of Carlin America, to honor the memory of publishing great and ASCAP board member Freddy Bienstock. Bienstock dedicated his life to the music industry as a music publishing and record company executive and founded Carlin America Music Publishing, whose catalogue includes more than 100,000 titles spanning a wide variety of musical genres. The scholarship in his name provides a tuition-based cash award to an NYU student interested in music publishing who completes a full-time summer internship at Carlin America.

The ASCAP Foundation Mary Rodgers/Lorenz Hart Award is established by Mary Rodgers to honor the legacy of lyricist Lorenz "Larry" Hart, who together with composer Richard Rodgers produced a roster of hit shows including *Jumbo, On Your Toes, Babes in Arms, I Married an Angel, The Boys from Syracuse,* and *Pal Joey.* The award is presented annually to an ASCAP member who is a promising musical theater lyricist. A composer/lyricist team is also eligible.

The ASCAP Foundation "Reach Out and Touch" Award in Honor of Nick Ashford is established by Ashford's partner in life and musical collaborator, Valerie Simpson. Ashford & Simpson, who collaborated on such iconic R&B songs as "Ain't Nothin' Like the Real Thing," "You're All I Need to Get By," "Ain't No Mountain High Enough," and "Reach Out and Touch (Somebody's Hand)," began writing songs together in 1964. The award was established to advance the careers of promising songwriters by providing financial assistance for professional recordings of their work.

The ASCAP Foundation Bart Howard Songwriting Scholarship at Berklee College of Music is established to honor the memory of longtime ASCAP member Bart Howard. This tuition-based scholarship recognizes the talent, professionalism, musical ability, and career potential of a Berklee student majoring in songwriting. Bart Howard (1915–2004) was a prolific composer who wrote over 200 songs, most notably "Fly Me to the Moon," which has been performed by hundreds of singers, including Frank Sinatra, Ella Fitzgerald, Peggy Lee, and Diana Krall.

The **ASCAP Foundation** is named as a major beneficiary of all royalties and copyrights from the musical works of ASCAP composer and lyricist Bart Howard.

2012

The **ASCAP Foundation Young Jazz Composer Awards**, an annual program for jazz composers, receives a major, multiyear financial commitment from the Herb Alpert Foundation. To honor that commitment, the program, established in 2002, has been renamed the Herb Alpert Young Jazz Composer Awards.

The **ASCAP Foundation Jimmy Van Heusen Award** is established by his family to honor his legacy. Van Heusen was one of the most accomplished songwriters from the mid-20th century, with countless hits sung and recorded by such American vocal icons as Frank Sinatra, Bing Crosby, Lena Horne, and Rosemary Clooney. Some of his most popular songs were written for movies: "Swinging on a Star," "All the Way," "High Hopes," and "Call Me Irresponsible." The ASCAP Foundation Jimmy Van Heusen Award is presented to an outstanding, promising composer who has participated in the ASCAP/NYU Television and Film Scoring Workshop.

The **ASCAP Foundation "Sunlight of the Spirit" Award** is established by Paul Williams and his wife, Mariana. The award is presented to an individual who is exemplary in substance abuse recovery and in music creativity. Paul Williams is an Oscar-, Grammy-, and Golden Globe–winning Hall of Fame songwriter and president and chairman of the board of ASCAP and The ASCAP Foundation. Recognized as one of America's most gifted lyricists and composers, Williams has written songs, including "We've Only Just Begun," "You and Me Against the World," and "The Rainbow Connection," recorded by artists as varied as Elvis Presley, Frank Sinatra, Barbra Streisand, REM, Tony Bennett, the Dixie Chicks, Jason Mraz, and Kermit the Frog.

The **ASCAP Foundation Vic Mizzy Scholarship** is established by the Mizzy Jonas Family Foundation to honor the veteran film and TV composer-lyricist Vic Mizzy, who created the beloved TV theme songs for *The Addams Family* and *Green Acres*, among many other musical achievements. Vic Mizzy was a proud and lifelong member of ASCAP, joining the organization in 1938. The scholarship assists a deserving graduate student of film and television scoring at New York University's Steinhardt School.

"We Write the Songs" Concerts

Each year since 2009, The ASCAP Foundation and the Library of Congress have jointly celebrated the ASCAP Collection at the Library of Congress with a concert called "We Write the Songs." Presented at the Library's historic Coolidge Auditorium, the event features ASCAP songwriters and composers performing their own music before an audience of members of Congress, Congressional staffers, and other Washington dignitaries.

Those who have appeared onstage at these concerts are Jessi Alexander, Nick Ashford & Valerie Simpson, Alan Bergman, Elvin Bishop with Mickey Thomas, Stephen Bishop, Bruce Broughton with Belinda Broughton, Irving Burgie, the Carolina Chocolate Drops, Mary Chapin Carpenter, Felix Cavaliere, Tracy Chapman, Roger Cook & Roger Greenaway, Hal David, Jackie DeShannon, Dion DiMucci, Barry Eastmond with Freddie Jackson, Dino Fekaris, Dan Foliart, Siedah Garrett, Arthur Hamilton, Albert Hammond, Wayland Holyfield, Brett James & Hillary Lindsey & Gordie Sampson, Dean Kay, Tom Kelly & Billy Steinberg, Lyle Lovett, Monica Mancini, Johnny Mandel with Karrin Allyson, Melanie, Ray Parker Jr., Don Schlitz, Stephen Schwartz, J. D. Souther, Chris Stapleton, Jim Weatherly, Jimmy Webb, Tom Whitlock with Terri Nunn, Paul Williams, and Bill Withers with Elisabeth Withers & Kori Withers.

Success Stories

Pop

- **John Mayer** received the 2001 ASCAP Foundation Sammy Cahn Award and has won seven Grammy Awards on 18 nominations, along with many Radio Music Awards, MTV Video Music Awards, and number one singles.

- **Daniel Mackenzie** received the ASCAP Foundation Sammy Cahn Award in 2004 and was nominated for an Emmy for scoring Disney's *Monster House*. He has written and produced songs for Joss Stone, including "All I Want for Christmas." His album *Dan Dan Doodlebug* won the 2009 Just Plain Folks Music Organization award for best children's album and earned him another ASCAP Foundation award as the 2010 recipient of the Joe Raposo Children's Music Award.
- **Rosi Golan**, an Israeli-born singer-songwriter, received the ASCAP Foundation Robert Allen Award in 2006. Her song "Follow the Arrow" was featured in a J. C. Penney commercial that took over the Christmas season in 2009. In 2012, her music was heard on television shows such as *The Vampire Diaries* and *Grey's Anatomy*.
- **Reeve Carney**, ASCAP singer-songwriter and a participant in the 2007 ASCAP Foundation Lester Sill Songwriters Workshop, started a band with his brother called Carney, which opened for U2 and Arcade Fire. He has also released a series of albums and recently starred as Peter Parker in the Broadway musical *Spider-Man: Turn Off the Dark*.
- **Oren Lavie**, co-recipient of the 2009 ASCAP Foundation Sammy Cahn Award, was nominated for a Grammy in 2010 for his song "Her Morning Elegance" in the best short form music video category.
- **Nick Howard**, winner of the 2009 Robert Allen Award, capped off a 150-show world tour by winning Season 2 of *The Voice of Germany*. His third studio album, *Stay Who You Are*, contains his latest single, "Unbreakable," which peaked at number one on the German, Austrian, and Swiss iTunes charts.
- **John Fullbright**, winner of the 2012 ASCAP Foundation Harold Adamson Lyric Award, received a 2012 Grammy nomination for his debut release album, *From the Ground Up*. He was signed by BMG Chrysalis that same year.

Film and TV

- **Jim Dooley** attended the ASCAP Television & Film Scoring Workshop in 1999 and in 2008 received an Emmy Award for his work on the TV show *Pushing Daisies*. He now writes for Hans Zimmer at his Remote Control Productions.

- **Trevor Morris**, a participant in the 1999 ASCAP Television & Film Scoring Workshop, has won two Emmy Awards and two Gemini Awards for his compositions on the television productions *The Tudors*, *The Borgias*, and *The Pillars of the Earth*. He is currently a composer at Hans Zimmer's Remote Control Productions.

- **Michael Bearden**, an ASCAP Television & Film Scoring Workshop alum from 2000, was named band leader of TBS's show *Lopez Tonight*, starring George Lopez, in 2009. Bearden also worked as the music supervisor, composer, and associate producer of the documentary *Michael Jackson's This Is It*. Bearden has worked with a multitude of artists, including Mary J. Blige, Christina Aguilera, Ricky Martin, Destiny's Child, Jennifer Hudson, Usher, India.Arie, Shakira, Brian McKnight, and Jennifer Lopez.

- **Didier Lean Rachou**, an alumnus of the ASCAP Television & Film Scoring Workshop in 2000, completed a score for *Powder Blue*, a movie starring Forest Whitaker and Jessica Biel. He has also contributed scores to *Aquaman*, *Mercy Reef*, *How to Rob a Bank*, and several episodes of *Sex and the City*. Rachou also scored the TV series *Storm Chasers* for the Discovery Channel.

- **Robert Duncan**, who took part in the 2001 ASCAP Television & Film Scoring Workshop, was among ASCAP's Primetime Emmy Award nominees in 2013 for *Last Resort*, his third Emmy nomination. He has been the composer for a number of successful television series, including *Castle*, *Missing*, *The Unit*, *Lie to Me*, and *Buffy the Vampire Slayer*'s final season. His other work includes the films *Shattered* and *Into the Blue 2: The Reef*. His previous two Emmy Award nominations were for Outstanding Music Composition for a Miniseries, Movie or a Special (Original Dramatic Score) for *Missing* (2012) and Outstanding Music Composition for a Series (Original Dramatic Score) for *Castle* (2009).

- **Mateo Messina**, an ASCAP Television & Film Scoring Workshop alum from 2005, has put together an impressive string of feature film successes, including *Young Adult*, *Up in the Air*, the Oscar-nominated *Butter*, *Thank You for Smoking*, and *Juno*, which earned him a Grammy Award. His television accolades are equally robust, including *The Office*, *Fairly Legal*, *Perfect Couples*, and *The Ex List*.

He was also commissioned to score the 2008 holiday campaign for Victoria's Secret. His most recent project is the feature film *The Angriest Man in Brooklyn.*

- **Brian Byrne**, 2006 ASCAP Television & Film Scoring Workshop alum and recipient of the ASCAP Foundation Steve Kaplan TV & Film Studies Scholarship in 2007, received the award for Best Original Score at the seventh annual Irish Film & Television Awards in 2010 for his work on the film *Zonad.* He also scored *The Good Doctor* and *Albert Nobbs*, and serves as the conductor/arranger for Bono when he tours internationally. He has contributed piano and arrangement work to the films *Sex and the City 2*, *The Spirit*, and *In America*, as well as lending those same talents to Katy Perry, Chaka Khan, Michael Bolton, and Van Morrison.

- **Austin Wintory**, an ASCAP Television & Film Scoring Workshop alumnus from 2008, has scored many films, including the award-winning Jordanian film *Captain Abu Raed.* It is his video game scoring, however, that defines his career. He scored *flOw* and *Monaco*, which led him to his most notable score, for the game *Journey.* The game was so successful that the soundtrack of Wintory's work was released, peaking at 116 on the *Billboard* charts, the second highest of any video game music album to date. He received a Grammy nomination for it, the first time a video game music album has ever received a nod from the Grammys.

- **Joseph Trapanese**, who attended the 2009 ASCAP Television & Film Scoring Workshop, received a 2006 Henry Mancini Music Fellowship and the 2009 Harold Arlen Film & TV Award. He specializes in collaboration with pop writers, as shown by his partnerships with Daft Punk to compose the score for *Tron: Legacy*, with Mike Shinoda of Linkin Park for the soundtrack of *The Raid*, and with Daniel Licht composing for the series *Dexter.* He recently cowrote the score for the film *Oblivion.*

Jazz

- **James McBride** received the inaugural (1996) ASCAP Foundation Richard Rodgers New Horizons Award. McBride is a saxophonist who tours with his six-piece jazz/R&B band and works as a sideman with jazz legend Jimmy Scott and others. He has written songs (music and lyrics) for Anita Baker, Grover Washington Jr., Pura Fé, Gary Burton, and even for the PBS television character Barney. He received the Stephen Sondheim Award for his musical *Bo-Bos*, cowritten with playwright Ed Shockley. His Riffin' and Pontificatin' tour was captured in a 2003 Comcast television documentary, and he has been featured on national radio and television programs in America, Europe, Australia, and New Zealand. In addition to his musical talents, McBride is also an accomplished author and screenwriter. His landmark memoir, *The Color of Water*, spent two years on the *New York Times* bestseller list and has been published in 16 languages; his third novel, *The Good Lord Bird*, was published in 2013 and won the National Book Award. He is an ASCAP Foundation board member.

- **Remy and Pascal Le Boeuf**, multiyear recipients of ASCAP Foundation Young Jazz Composer Awards, have also received awards from the National Foundation for Advancement in the Arts, *Downbeat Magazine*, and the International Songwriting Competition. The *New York Times* said in 2009, "This group has an impressively self-assured new album. *House Without a Door* reaches for the gleaming cosmopolitanism of our present era." Their latest album is *Remixed*.

- **Grace Kelly** has received five ASCAP Foundation Herb Alpert Young Jazz Composer Awards (2007, '08, '10, '11, '13) and has performed with Lee Konitz, Phil Woods, Dave Brubeck, Hank Jones, Wynton Marsalis, Kenny Barron, Harry Connick Jr., and countless others. After releasing eight full-length albums, she released her first single, "Sweet Sweet Baby," which has made it to number 10 on the *Billboard* Smooth Jazz Songs chart. The *Downbeat* Critics Poll named her one of the "Alto Saxophone Rising Stars" at age 16, the youngest artist ever to be named to the music poll.

- **Garth Neustadter**, a 2011 ASCAP Foundation Young Jazz Composer Award recipient and winner of the 2012 David Rose Award, became one of the youngest composers to receive a Primetime Emmy Award, for his score for the PBS *American Masters* documentary *John Muir in the New World*.

Musical Theater

- **Jeanine Tesori** attended the ASCAP Foundation Musical Theatre Workshop and received the 1997 ASCAP Foundation Richard Rodgers New Horizons Award. Tesori has written four Tony Award–nominated scores, including *Twelfth Night, Thoroughly Modern Millie, Shrek the Musical,* and *Caroline, or Change,* as well as scoring Disney films such as *Shrek the Third, Mulan II,* and *The Emperor's New Groove II: Kronk's New Groove.*

- **Andrew Lippa** received the 1999 ASCAP Foundation Richard Rodgers New Horizons Award and has written music and lyrics for many Broadway and off-Broadway plays. He was nominated for a Grammy in 2000 for *You're a Good Man, Charlie Brown,* and he received a Tony nomination in 2010 for best original score for *The Addams Family.*

- **Glenn Slater** received the 2000 ASCAP Foundation Richard Rodgers New Horizons Award and in 2008 was nominated for a Tony Award along with his collaborator Alan Menken for best original score for *The Little Mermaid.* He followed that with another Tony nomination for *Sister Act* in 2011 for best score, and won a Grammy in 2012 for best original song written for visual media for his song "I See the Light" from the animated Disney film *Tangled,* which he cowrote with Alan Menken.

- **Peter Mills,** the recipient of the 2003 ASCAP Foundation Richard Rodgers New Horizons Award, won the 2010 Kleban Foundation's annual prize for most promising musical theater lyricist. Mills' credits include *Golden Boy of the Blue Ridge, The Pursuit of Persephone, Illyria, The Alchemists,* and *The Taxi Cabaret.*

- **Michael Korie (lyricist) and Scott Frankel (composer)** received the 2006 ASCAP Foundation Richard Rodgers New Horizons Award. Korie and Frankel wrote the music and lyrics for the Tony-nominated *Grey Gardens,* which appeared on Broadway in 2006/07.

- **Lin-Manuel Miranda,** the recipient of the 2007 Richard Rodgers New Horizons Award, won four Tony Awards in 2008 and a Grammy for best musical show album in 2009 for his musical *In the Heights,* which he cowrote and starred in. He also cowrote the music and lyrics for the Tony-nominated *Bring It On: The Musical.*

- **Matthew Sklar,** a 2010 recipient of the ASCAP Foundation Richard Rodgers New Horizons Award and an alumnus of the ASCAP Foundation/Disney Musical Theatre Workshop, was nominated for a Tony Award for best original score for *The Wedding Singer.* His musical *Elf* opened on Broadway for the holiday season in 2010 and returned in 2012/13.
- **Matt Gould and Griffin Matthews,** recipients of the 2010 ASCAP Foundation Michelle and Dean Kay Award and the Harold Adamson Lyric Award, will have the world premiere of their musical *Witness Uganda* at the American Repertory Theater at Harvard University in February of 2014. The musical, for which Gould and Matthews won the 2012 Richard Rodgers Award, will be directed by renowned Broadway director Diane Paulus (*Pippin, The Gershwins' Porgy and Bess*).
- **Benj Pasek and Justin Paul,** recipients of the 2011 ASCAP Foundation Richard Rodgers New Horizons Award, had a production of their original musical *Dogfight* produced at Second Stage Theatre in New York in 2012. *Dogfight* won the 2013 Lucille Lortel Awards for outstanding musical and choreography, and it received a Drama League Award nomination for outstanding production of a musical and Outer Critics Circle Award nominations for best off-Broadway musical, best score, and best book. Another one of their original musicals, *A Christmas Story: The Musical,* also received best musical and original score Tony nominations in 2013. Their original "Caught in the Storm" was performed on NBC's *Smash.*
- **Marcy Heisler,** the recipient of the 2012 Mary Rodgers/Lorenz Hart Award and, along with her writing partner, Zina Goldrich, a 2002 recipient of the ASCAP Foundation Richard Rodgers New Horizons Award, received the $100,000 Kleban Prize for lyric writing in 2012. She and Goldrich are preparing for the opening of their new Broadway musical, *The Great American Mousical.*
- **Alan Zachary and Michael Weiner,** recipients of the 2012 Richard Rodgers New Horizons Award, had their new musical, *Secondhand Lions,* debut at Seattle's 5th Avenue Theater in September 2013. Their play *First Date* opened on Broadway in July 2013.

Concert Music

- **David Lang** received an ASCAP Foundation Morton Gould Young Composer Award in 1979 and received a Pulitzer Prize in 2008 for his work *The Little Match Girl Passion*.
- **Melinda Wagner** received an ASCAP Foundation Morton Gould Young Composer Award in 1982 and won a Pulitzer Prize in 1999 for her work *Concerto for Flute, Strings, and Percussion*.
- **Elliot Goldenthal** received an ASCAP Foundation Commission in 1988 and won an Academy Award for best original score in 2002 for the movie *Frida*.
- **Jennifer Higdon** won the 2010 Pulitzer Prize in music for her Violin Concerto, which premiered on February 6, 2009, in Indianapolis, Indiana. She received two Morton Gould Young Composer Awards (in 1991 and 1992), and The ASCAP Foundation commissioned her first orchestra piece, a work honoring Morton Gould for the Portland Symphony. Higdon also won a Grammy for best contemporary classical composition in 2010 for her Percussion Concerto. She currently holds the Milton L. Rock Chair in Composition Studies at the Curtis Institute of Music in Philadelphia.
- **Nico Muhly** received an ASCAP Foundation Morton Gould Young Composer Award in 2000. In 2008 he wrote the original film score for *The Reader*, and his opera *Two Boys* was staged by the English National Opera in 2011 and the Metropolitan Opera in 2013.

ASCAP AND OSCAR

Since the Academy of Motion Picture Arts and Sciences introduced the Academy Award for Best Original Song in 1934, these members of ASCAP and foreign affiliates have won the Oscar in that category.

1934
"The Continental" (*The Gay Divorcee*)
Con Conrad, Herb Magidson

1935
"Lullaby of Broadway" (*Gold Diggers of 1935*)
Al Dubin, Harry Warren

1936
"The Way You Look Tonight" (*Swing Time*)
Dorothy Fields, Jerome Kern

1937
"Sweet Leilani" (*Waikiki Wedding*)
Harry Owens

1938
"Thanks for the Memory" (*The Big Broadcast of 1938*)
Leo Robin, Ralph Rainger

1939
"Over the Rainbow" (*The Wizard of Oz*)
Harold Arlen, E. Y. Harburg

1940
"When You Wish Upon a Star" (*Pinocchio*)
Leigh Harline, Ned Washington

1941
"The Last Time I Saw Paris" (*Lady Be Good*)
Oscar Hammerstein II, Jerome Kern

1942
"White Christmas" (*Holiday Inn*)
Irving Berlin

1943
"You'll Never Know" (*Hello, Frisco, Hello*)
Mack Gordon, Harry Warren

1944
"Swinging on a Star" (*Going My Way*)
Johnny Burke, Jimmy Van Heusen

1945
"It Might as Well Be Spring" (*State Fair*)
Oscar Hammerstein II, Richard Rodgers

1946
"On the Atchison, Topeka and the Santa Fe" (*The Harvey Girls*)
Johnny Mercer, Harry Warren

1947
"Zip-a-Dee-Doo-Dah" (*Song of the South*)
Ray Gilbert, Allie Wrubel

1948
"Buttons and Bows" (*The Paleface*)
Ray Evans, Jay Livingston

1949
"Baby, It's Cold Outside" (*Neptune's Daughter*)
Frank Loesser

1950
"Mona Lisa" (*Captain Carey, U.S.A.*)
Ray Evans, Jay Livingston

1951
"In the Cool, Cool, Cool of the Evening" (*Here Comes the Groom*)
Hoagy Carmichael, Johnny Mercer

1952
"High Noon (Do Not Forsake Me, Oh My Darlin')" (*High Noon*)
Dimitri Tiomkin (SACEM), Ned Washington

1953
"Secret Love" (*Calamity Jane*)
Sammy Fain, Paul Francis Webster

1954
"Three Coins in the Fountain" (*Three Coins in the Fountain*)
Sammy Cahn, Jule Styne

1955
"Love Is a Many-Splendored Thing" (*Love Is a Many-Splendored Thing*)
Sammy Fain, Paul Francis Webster

1956
"Whatever Will Be, Will Be (Que Será, Será)" (*The Man Who Knew Too Much*)
Ray Evans, Jay Livingston

1957
"All the Way" (*The Joker Is Wild*)
Sammy Cahn, Jimmy Van Heusen

1958
"Gigi" (*Gigi*)
Alan Jay Lerner, Frederick Loewe

1959
"High Hopes" (*A Hole in the Head*)
Sammy Cahn, Jimmy Van Heusen

1961
"Moon River" (*Breakfast at Tiffany's*)
Johnny Mercer, Henry Mancini

1962
"Days of Wine and Roses" (*Days of Wine and Roses*)
Henry Mancini, Johnny Mercer

1963
"Call Me Irresponsible" (*Papa's Delicate Condition*)
Sammy Cahn, Jimmy Van Heusen

1965
"The Shadow of Your Smile" (*The Sandpiper*)
Johnny Mandel, Paul Francis Webster

1968
"The Windmills of Your Mind" (*The Thomas Crown Affair*)
Alan and Marilyn Bergman/Michel Legrand (SACEM)

1969
"Raindrops Keep Fallin' on My Head" (*Butch Cassidy and the Sundance Kid*)
Burt Bacharach, Hal David

1972
"The Morning After" (*The Poseidon Adventure*)
Al Kasha*

1973
"The Way We Were" (*The Way We Were*)
Alan and Marilyn Bergman/Marvin Hamlisch

1974
"We May Never Love Like This Again" (*The Towering Inferno*)
Al Kasha*

1975
"I'm Easy" (*Nashville*)
Keith Carradine

1976
"Love Theme from *A Star Is Born* (Evergreen)" (*A Star Is Born*)
Barbra Streisand, Paul Williams

1977
"You Light Up My Life" (*You Light Up My Life*)
Joe Brooks

1981
"Arthur's Theme (Best That You Can Do)" (*Arthur*)
Burt Bacharach, Christopher Cross*

1982
"Up Where We Belong" (*An Officer and a Gentleman*)
Buffy Sainte-Marie*

1983
"Flashdance . . . What a Feeling" (*Flashdance*)
Irene Cara, Keith Forsey, Giorgio Moroder

1984
"I Just Called to Say I Love You" (*The Woman in Red*)
Stevie Wonder

1985
"Say You, Say Me" (*White Nights*)
Lionel Richie

1986
"Take My Breath Away" (*Top Gun*)
Giorgio Moroder, Tom Whitlock

1987
"(I've Had) The Time of My Life" (*Dirty Dancing*)
John DeNicola, Donald Markowitz, Franke Previte

1988
"Let the River Run" (*Working Girl*)
Carly Simon

1989
"Under the Sea" (*The Little Mermaid*)
Howard Ashman*

1990
"Sooner or Later (I Always Get My Man)" (*Dick Tracy*)
Stephen Sondheim

1991
"Beauty and the Beast" (*Beauty and the Beast*)
Howard Ashman*

1992
"A Whole New World" (*Aladdin*)
Tim Rice (PRS)*

1993
"Streets of Philadelphia" (*Philadelphia*)
Bruce Springsteen

1995
"Colors of the Wind" (*Pocahontas*)
Stephen Schwartz*

1996
"You Must Love Me" (*Evita*)
Tim Rice (PRS), Andrew Lloyd Webber (PRS)

1997
"My Heart Will Go On" (*Titanic*)
James Horner*

1998
"When You Believe" (*The Prince of Egypt*)
Stephen Schwartz

1999
"You'll Be in My Heart" (*Tarzan*)
Phil Collins (PRS)

2001
"If I Didn't Have You" (*Monsters, Inc.*)
Randy Newman

2002
"Lose Yourself" (*8 Mile*)
Luis Resto*

2003
"Into the West" (*The Lord of the Rings: The Return of the King*)
Annie Lennox (PRS), Howard Shore, Fran Walsh (APRA)

2004
"Al Otro Lado Del Río" (*The Motorcycle Diaries*)
Jorge Drexler (SGAE)

2006
"I Need to Wake Up" (*An Inconvenient Truth*)
Melissa Etheridge

2007
"Falling Slowly" (*Once*)
Glen Hansard (IMRO), Markéta Irglová (IMRO)

2010
"We Belong Together" (*Toy Story 3*)
Randy Newman

2011
"Man or Muppet" (*The Muppets*)
Bret McKenzie (APRA)

2012
"Skyfall" (*Skyfall*)
Paul Epworth*

*Shared credit not licensed by ASCAP

APRA—Australasian Performing Right Association
IMRO—Irish Music Rights Organisation
PRS—Performing Right Society
SACEM—Société des Auteurs, Compositeurs et Éditeurs de Musique
SGAE—Sociedad General de Autores y Editores

ASCAP RECIPIENTS OF THE PULITZER PRIZE

In Music

- 1944: Howard Hanson, Symphony No. 4 ("Requiem")
- 1945: Aaron Copland, *Appalachian Spring*, ballet
- 1946: Leo Sowerby, *The Canticle of the Sun,* for chorus and orchestra
- 1949: Virgil Thomson, *Louisiana Story*, film score
- 1950: Gian Carlo Menotti, *The Consul*, opera
- 1951: Douglas Stuart Moore, *Giants in the Earth*, opera
- 1952: Gail Kubik, *Symphony Concertante*, for trumpet, viola, piano, and orchestra
- 1955: Gian Carlo Menotti, *The Saint of Bleecker Street*, opera
- 1956: Ernst Toch, Symphony No. 3
- 1958: Samuel Barber, *Vanessa*, opera
- 1959: John La Montaine, Piano Concerto No. 1 ("In Time of War")
- 1963: Samuel Barber, Piano Concerto
- 1972: Jacob Druckman, *Windows*, for orchestra
- 1975: Dominick Argento, *From the Diary of Virginia Woolf,* for medium voice and piano
- 1976: Ned Rorem, *Air Music*, for orchestra
- 1977: Richard Wernick, *Visions of Terror and Wonder*, for mezzo-soprano and orchestra
- 1978: Michael Colgrass, *Déjà Vu*, for percussion and orchestra
- 1980: David Del Tredici, *In Memory of a Summer Day*, for soprano and orchestra
- 1985: Stephen Albert, Symphony No. 1 ("RiverRun")
- 1986: George Perle, Wind Quintet No. 4, for flute, oboe, clarinet, horn, and bassoon

- 1990: Mel D. Powell, *Duplicates: A Concerto for Two Pianos and Orchestra*
- 1991: Shulamit Ran, Symphony
- 1992: Wayne Peterson, *The Face of the Night, the Heart of the Dark*, for orchestra
- 1995: Morton Gould, *Stringmusic*, for string orchestra
- 1996: George Walker, *Lilacs*, for voice and orchestra
- 1997: Wynton Marsalis, *Blood on the Fields*, oratorio
- 1999: Melinda Wagner, *Concerto for Flute, Strings, and Percussion*
- 2001: John Corigliano, Symphony No. 2, for string orchestra
- 2002: Henry Brant, *Ice Field*, for large and small orchestral groups
- 2004: Paul Moravec, *Tempest Fantasy*, for clarinet, violin, cello, and piano
- 2007: Ornette Coleman, *Sound Grammar*, jazz album
- 2008: David Lang, *The Little Match Girl Passion*, for chorus
- 2010: Jennifer Higdon, Violin Concerto
- 2011: Zhou Long, *Madame White Snake*, opera
- 2013: Caroline Shaw, *Partita for 8 Voices*

In Drama (Musical Theater)

- 1932: *Of Thee I Sing*—Ira Gershwin
- 1950: *South Pacific*—Richard Rodgers, Oscar Hammerstein II
- 1962: *How to Succeed in Business Without Really Trying*—Frank Loesser
- 1976: *A Chorus Line*—Marvin Hamlisch
- 1985: *Sunday in the Park with George*—Stephen Sondheim
- 1996: *Rent*—Jonathan Larson

In Journalism (Music Criticism)

- 2002: Justin Davidson, *Newsday*—"For his crisp coverage of classical music that captures its essence."

Special Posthumous Citations in Music

- 1998: George Gershwin—"commemorating the centennial year of his birth, for his distinguished and enduring contributions to American music."
- 1999: Edward Kennedy "Duke" Ellington—"commemorating the centennial year of his birth, in recognition of his musical genius, which evoked aesthetically the principles of democracy through the medium of jazz and thus made an indelible contribution to art and culture."

ASCAP AND TONY

These members of ASCAP and foreign affiliates have won Tony Awards from the American Theatre Wing and the Broadway League for *Best Original Score, #Best Musical, and †Best Revival of a Musical.

1949
Kiss Me, Kate *#
Cole Porter

1950
South Pacific *#
Oscar Hammerstein II, Richard Rodgers

1951
Guys and Dolls #
Frank Loesser

1952
The King and I #
Oscar Hammerstein II, Richard Rodgers

1953
Wonderful Town #
Betty Comden, Adolph Green/Leonard Bernstein

1954
Kismet #
George Forrest, Robert Wright

1955
The Pajama Game #
Richard Adler, Jerry Ross

1956
Damn Yankees #
Richard Adler, Jerry Ross

1957
My Fair Lady #
Alan Jay Lerner, Frederick Loewe

1958
The Music Man #
Meredith Willson

1959
Redhead #
Dorothy Fields, Albert Hague

1960
The Sound of Music #
Oscar Hammerstein II, Richard Rodgers

1961
Bye Bye Birdie #
Lee Adams, Charles Strouse

1962
How to Succeed in Business Without Really Trying #
Frank Loesser

No Strings *
Richard Rodgers

1963
A Funny Thing Happened on the Way to the Forum #
Stephen Sondheim

1964
Hello Dolly! *#
Jerry Herman

1966
Man of La Mancha *#
Joe Darion, Mitch Leigh

1968
Hallelujah, Baby! *#
Betty Comden, Adolph Green/Jule Styne

1969
1776 #
Sherman Edwards

1970
Applause #
Lee Adams, Charles Strouse

1971
Company *#
Stephen Sondheim

1972
Two Gentlemen of Verona #
John Guare, Galt MacDermot (CAPAC)

Follies *
Stephen Sondheim

1973
A Little Night Music *#
Stephen Sondheim

1974
Gigi *
Alan Jay Lerner, Frederick Loewe

1976
A Chorus Line *#
Marvin Hamlisch (cowriter)

1977
Annie *#
Martin Charnin, Charles Strouse

1978
Ain't Misbehavin' #
Thomas "'Fats" Waller

On the Twentieth Century *
Betty Comden, Adolph Green/Cy Coleman

1979
Sweeney Todd: The Demon Barber of Fleet Street *#
Stephen Sondheim

1980
Evita *#
Tim Rice, Andrew Lloyd Webber (PRS)

1981
42nd Street #
Al Dubin, Harry Warren

1984
La Cage aux Folles *#
Jerry Herman

1986
The Mystery of Edwin Drood *#
Rupert Holmes

1987
Les Misérables *#
Alain Boublil, Herbert Kretzmer (PRS), Claude-Michel Schönberg

1988
The Phantom of the Opera #
Andrew Lloyd Webber (PRS)

1989
Jerome Robbins' Broadway #
Leonard Bernstein, Irving Berlin, Sammy Cahn, Moose Charlap, Betty Comden, Adolph Green, Morton Gould, Oscar Hammerstein II, Carolyn Leigh, Richard Rodgers, Stephen Sondheim, Jule Styne

1990
City of Angels *#
Cy Coleman, David Zippel

1991
The Will Rogers Follies *#
Cy Coleman, Betty Comden, Adolph Green

1992
Crazy for You #
George Gershwin, Ira Gershwin

1994
Passion *#
Stephen Sondheim

Carousel †
Richard Rodgers, Oscar Hammerstein II

1995
Sunset Boulevard *#
Andrew Lloyd Webber (PRS)

Show Boat †
Jerome Kern, Oscar Hammerstein II

1996
Rent *#
Jonathan Larson

The King and I †
Richard Rodgers, Oscar Hammerstein II

1998
Ragtime *
Stephen Flaherty, Lynn Ahrens

The Lion King #
Lebo M, Jay Rifkin, Julie Taymor, Hans Zimmer

1999
Parade *
Jason Robert Brown

Fosse #
Richard Adler, Leon Barry, Irving Berlin, Lew Brown, Bob Crosby, Cy
Coleman, Howard Dietz, Dave Dreyer, Mort Dixon, Dorothy Fields, G.
Harrell, Bob Haggart, Ray Henderson, Al Jolson, Bert Kalmar, Stanley
Lebowsky, Frederick Loewe, Johnny Mercer, Cole Porter, Louis Prima,
Andy Razaf, Gil Rodin, Billy Rose, Jerry Ross, Arthur Schwartz, Stephen
Schwartz, Ted Snyder, Frederick Tobias, Harry Warren, Richard Whiting

Annie Get Your Gun †
Irving Berlin

2000
Contact #
Clifford Burwell, James Cavanaugh, Dion DiMucci, Eddie Durham,
Lorenz Hart, Jack Lawrence, Tom Maxwell, Russ Morgan, Mitchell
Parish, Louis Prima, Richard Rodgers, Larry Stock, Charles Trénet
(SACEM)

Kiss Me, Kate †
Cole Porter

2001
42nd Street †
Harry Warren, Al Dubin

2002
Urinetown *
Mark Hollmann, Greg Kotis

Thoroughly Modern Millie #
Dick Scanlan, Jeanine Tesori

Into the Woods †
Stephen Sondheim

2003
Hairspray *#
Marc Shaiman, Scott Wittman

2004
Assassins †
Stephen Sondheim

2005
The Light in the Piazza *
Adam Guettel

La Cage aux Folles †
Jerry Herman

2006
The Drowsy Chaperone *
Lisa Lambert (SOCAN), Greg Morrison (SOCAN)

The Pajama Game †
Richard Adler, Jerry Ross

2007
Company †
Stephen Sondheim

2008
In the Heights *#
Lin-Manuel Miranda

South Pacific †
Richard Rodgers, Oscar Hammerstein II

2009
Hair †
James Rado, Gerome Ragni, Galt MacDermot (SOCAN)

2010
Memphis *#
David Bryan, Joe DiPietro

La Cage aux Folles †
Jerry Herman

2011
The Book of Mormon *#
Trey Parker, Matt Stone

Anything Goes †
Cole Porter

2012
Once #
Glen Hansard (IMRO), Markéta Irglová (IMRO)

The Gershwins' Porgy and Bess †
George and Ira Gershwin, DuBose Heyward

2013
Pippin †
Stephen Schwartz

CAPAC—Composers, Authors and Publishers Association of Canada
IMRO—Irish Music Rights Organisation
PRS—Performing Right Society
SACEM—Société des Auteurs, Compositeurs et Éditeurs de Musique
SOCAN—Society of Composers, Authors and Music Publishers of
Canada

ASCAP AND GRAMMY

Starting with the first presentation of a Gramophone Award by the National Academy of Recording Arts and Sciences in 1959 to recognize outstanding achievement in the music industry, these members of ASCAP and foreign affiliates have won the Grammy Award for Song of the Year.

1958
"Nel Blu Dipinto Di Blu (Volare)"
Domenico Modugno (SIAE)

1960
"Theme from *Exodus*"
Ernest Gold

1961
"Moon River"
Johnny Mercer, Henry Mancini

1963
"Days of Wine and Roses"
Johnny Mercer, Henry Mancini

1964
"Hello, Dolly!"
Jerry Herman

1965
"The Shadow of Your Smile"
Paul Francis Webster, Johnny Mandel

1968
"Little Green Apples"
Bobby Russell

1974
"The Way We Were"
Alan and Marilyn Bergman, Marvin Hamlisch

1975
"Send in the Clowns"
Stephen Sondheim

1976
"I Write the Songs"
Bruce Johnston

1977 (tie)
"Love Theme from *A Star Is Born* (Evergreen)"
Paul Williams, Barbra Streisand

"You Light Up My Life"
Joe Brooks

1978
"Just the Way You Are"
Billy Joel

1979
"What a Fool Believes"
Kenny Loggins, Michael McDonald

1980
"Sailing"
Christopher Cross

1981
"Bette Davis Eyes"
Jackie DeShannon*

1984
"What's Love Got to Do with It?"
Terry Britten (PRS)*

1985
"We Are the World"
Lionel Richie*

1986
"That's What Friends Are For"
Burt Bacharach*

1987
"Somewhere Out There"
James Horner*

1989
"Wind Beneath My Wings"
Jeff Silbar*

1991
"Unforgettable"
Irving Gordon

1993
"A Whole New World (Aladdin's Theme)"
Tim Rice (PRS)*

1994
"Streets of Philadelphia"
Bruce Springsteen

1996
"Change the World"
Gordon Scott Kennedy, Tommy L. Sims*

1997
"Sunny Came Home"
Shawn Colvin, John R. Leventhal

1998
"My Heart Will Go On"
James Horner*

1999
"Smooth"
Rob Thomas*

2000
"Beautiful Day"
Adam Clayton, David Evans, Larry Mullen Jr., Paul Hewson (all IMRO)

2001
"Fallin'"
Alicia Keys

2003
"Dance with My Father"
Luther Vandross, Richard Marx

2004
"Daughters"
John Mayer

2005
"Sometimes You Can't Make It on Your Own"
Adam Clayton, David Evans, Larry Mullen, Jr., Paul Hewson (all IMRO)

2006
"Not Ready to Make Nice"
Natalie Maines, Dan Wilson*

2008
"Viva la Vida"
Guy Berryman, Jonathan Buckland, Will Champion, Chris Martin (all PRS)

2009
"Single Ladies (Put a Ring on It)"
Thaddis Harrell, Beyoncé Knowles, Terius Nash, Christopher Stewart

2010
"Need You Now"
Dave Haywood, Josh Kear, Charles Kelley*

2011
"Rolling in the Deep"
Paul Epworth*

2012
"We Are Young"
Nate Ruess, Jeff Bhasker, Andrew Dost*

*Shared credit not licensed by ASCAP

IMRO—Irish Music Rights Organisation
PRS—Performing Right Society
SIAE—Società Italiana degli Autori ed Editori

NOTES

Chapter 1: Herbert's Victory

1 *February 13, 1914*: While this date is agreed upon by all the major sources, several of them differ on the exact chronology of events leading up to the date, and on who did the leading.

In his self-published, informal history of ASCAP, *From Nothing to Five Million a Year* (Washington, DC: Library of Congress, 1937), the last surviving founder (at the time of the book's writing; Hubbell died in 1954), Raymond Hubbell, credits himself with bringing Victor Herbert to the table at Lüchow's one rainy October night in 1913, along with publisher George Maxwell, lawyer Nathan Burkan, and others, for what turned out to be a preliminary session to discuss the formation of a society of songwriters and publishers. As corroborated in Herbert's biography, *A Life in Music*, by Edward N. Waters (New York: Macmillan, 1955), p. 434, Victor was at first reluctant to attend, but finally embraced the notion vociferously. And so ASCAP was born, with the first lawsuit to test its powers brought by John Philip Sousa in 1915; Herbert followed suit later that year, against Shanley's restaurant for their unauthorized playing of "Sweethearts," in October of 1913, from his then current operetta.

In Isaac Goldberg's collaboration with Isidore Witmark, *From Ragtime to Swingtime: The Story of the House of Witmark* (New York: Lee Furman, 1939), pp. 371–376, Burkan, Maxwell, and Witmark himself, brother of original founder Jay, all have stronger leading roles, but the date of ASCAP's inception is changed by three months, with the initial discussions being held on a similarly blustery afternoon in January of 1914 at the Lambs Club, where Herbert suggests they adjourn for dinner at Lüchow's. In this book, Herbert hears "Kiss Me Again" at Shanley's early in 1914, sparking his idea for a lawsuit.

In a later article in *Billboard* from 1939, "Jay Witmark Recalls Early ASCAP Days," Witmark repeats the "Kiss Me Again" story, in which he also includes his brother's account of the earlier meeting at the Lambs Club in 1914, leading to the February 13 meeting in which ASCAP was chartered.

In an article in the January 1933 issue of *Fortune Magazine*, Herbert hears "Sweethearts" at Shanley's in the autumn of 1913. But the article has the first meeting taking place in March of 1914 at Lüchow's. In part two of the Alva Johnston profile of Gene Buck that appeared in the December 24, 1932, issue of the *New Yorker*, Victor walks into Shanley's and institutes his lawsuit before founding ASCAP. Leonard Allen's article in the October 1940 issue of *Harper's Magazine*, entitled "The Battle of Tin Pan Alley," follows the same chronology as the *New Yorker*.

Hazel Meyer in her book *The Gold in Tin Pan Alley* (Philadelphia: J. B. Lippincott, 1958), pp. 76–84, uses the Witmark account, dating the meeting at Lüchow's to January 1914. She also has Herbert forming ASCAP expressly for the purpose of rushing into a lawsuit, forgetting that it was Sousa who first filed suit.

Several sources refer to the Puccini influence as "nostalgic" or "legend," but it sounds perfectly plausible to me. Even Waters acknowledges Puccini's role in educating Herbert about performance rights, though he only mentions a 1910 meeting of the two titans (p. 433), while Meyer refers to the 1913 meeting that supposedly led Herbert to the immediate founding of ASCAP (p. 77). Puccini also appears in the biography of future ASCAP president Deems Taylor, *Deems Taylor: A Biography*, by James A. Pegolotti (Lebanon, NH: Northeastern University Press, 2003), p. 264, although here his meeting with George Maxwell takes place as early as 1907. It is sourced from an article by Mark Murphy, "Play for Pay," from *Hearst's International Combined with Cosmopolitan*, June 1951, p. 138.

1   "A tax on music": From Hubbell, *From Nothing to Five Million a Year* (p. 27). When Joe Weber, head of the American Federation of Musicians, responded to the Hotel and Restaurant Association ads that claimed that paying songwriter royalties to ASCAP amounted to "a tax on music" by advising bands to forgo playing ASCAP music and publishers to refrain from supplying bands with said music, most of these publishers then decided to drop out of ASCAP.

2 *ASCAP distributed its first royalty payments*: Royalty figures are from Leonard Allen, "The Battle of Tin Pan Alley" (p. 521); 2012 figures are from ASCAP's 2012 Annual Report (ASCAP.com).

3 *"Meet Me Tonight in Dreamland"*: Referenced in *Tin Pan Alley: The Composers, the Songs, the Performers, and Their Times*, by David A. Jasen (New York: Donald I. Fine, 1988), pp. 65–66.

3 *One young banjo player from Milwaukee*: *Yesterdays*, by Charles Hamm (New York: W. W. Norton, 1983), pp. 284–300. Also in *After the Ball: Forty Years of Melody*, by Charles K. Harris (New York: Frank-Maurice, 1926), p. 206.

5 *The black composer Scott Joplin*: Jasen, *Tin Pan Alley*, p. 29. Also in *America's Musical Life*, by Richard Crawford (New York: W. W. Norton, 2001), p. 726.

5 *As Jerome Charyn wrote*: *Gangsters and Gold Diggers: Old New York, the Jazz Age, and the Birth of Broadway*, by Jerome Charyn (New York: Thunder's Mouth Press, 2005), pp. 33–35.

5 *Ziegfeld's main squeeze, the sexy Anna Held*: Although the description of Anna Held as sexy is indisputable, some were taken aback by her legendary eyes. In fact, the old-time sheet music Web site Parlorsongs.com goes as far as to call her facial features reminiscent of the bug-eyed comedian Marty Feldman, in an essay called "Florenz Ziegfeld and His Fabulous Follies" (2004), bringing to mind the Silly Willy song "Marty Feldman Eyes," a parody of the Jackie DeShannon–penned hit for Kim Carnes, "Bette Davis Eyes."

6 *But even major music publishers*: Vivid descriptions of early Tin Pan Alley, including the life and times of a song plugger, are provided by publisher E. B. Marks in his memoir *They All Sang: From Tony Pastor to Rudy Vallee* (New York: Viking, 1934), pp. 9–21.

7 *Al Jolson himself went straight from the synagogue*: Al Jolson's humble beginnings at McGurk's are found in *World of Our Fathers*, by Irving Howe (New York: Harcourt Brace Jovanovich, 1976), p. 559, and are mentioned by Ben Yagoda in "Lullaby of Tin Pan Alley," *American Heritage Magazine*, October/November 1983.

7 *a niggling affair*: Vaudeville managers' machinations to stamp out payola are mentioned in *American Popular Music Business in the 20th Century*, by Russell Sanjek and David Sanjek (New York: Oxford University Press, 1991), p. 8.

7 *But in 1909, when the new Copyright Act was passed*: The early history of performing rights societies is captured in Nicholas Firth's

extensive printout, "Informal History of Music Publishing," in which it's noted that the first case that tested the rights of a songwriter to receive a royalty for the public performance of his music was brought by a Frenchman, Ernest Bourget, who wandered into a Parisian café one night in 1850, accompanied by his collaborators, Victor Parizot and Paul Henrion, to find a song of theirs being played by the house orchestra. Refusing to pay for his drinks as compensation for this blatant piracy, Bourget was brought to court by the owner. Citing the French copyright act of 1791, the court decided in Bourget's favor, and thus, a year later, the first performing rights organization, the Société des Auteurs, Compositeurs et Éditeurs de Musique (SACEM), was born. Italy followed suit in 1882, with the creation of the Società Italiana degli Autori ed Editori (SIAE); among the members of its first board of directors was the composer Giuseppe Verdi, whose works were published by the venerable Italian firm of G. Ricordi— also the publisher of Giacomo Puccini, the composer of *La Bohème* and *Madama Butterfly.*

7   *but not before producing a number two single of the title song*: All song chart positions from *Pop Memories 1890–1954: The History of American Popular Music*, by Joel Whitburn (Menomonee Falls, WI: Record Research, 1986).

8   *One published account*: Hazel Meyer, *The Gold in Tin Pan Alley*, p. 77.

8   *the extravagant sum of $15,000*: The figure cited in Victor Herbert's victory against the *Musical Courier* is from *Tin Pan Alley: A Chronicle of American Popular Music*, by Isaac Goldberg (New York: Frederick Ungar, 1930), pp. 222–224.

8   *Burkan . . . would go on to make a career for himself*: According to the blog Jefferson Market Courthouse in New York, Mae West hired Burkan to represent her in court when her play *The Pleasure Man* was closed down for being obscene. "Celebrities who counted on Burkan's legal muscle included Charlie Chaplin, Al Jolson . . . New York Mayor Jimmy Walker, as well as the embattled gangster Arnold Rothstein." Although he won acquittal for West, Burkan's subsequent legal fees bankrupted her ("Enter the Dragon-Slayer," jeffersonmarketcourthouseny.blogspot.com, November 7, 2006).

11 *the nascent and short-lived Authors' and Composers' Copyright League*: This group was formed in 1908 primarily to help lobby Congress during the debates preceding passage of the revised Copyright Act. In

From Ragtime to Swingtime, by Isidore Witmark and Isaac Goldberg, Witmark presents himself as a leading force in the early discussions, along with Victor Herbert and their lawyer, Nathan Burkan (pp. 294–311). There is also a nice description of the Aeolian case (pp. 296–297).

11 *Herbert was concerned*: Another good summary of all the classic cases is given in "Portrait of the Artist as a Young Pirate," by Tom Barger, Dmusic.com, October 2, 2004.

11 *this defining statement from the public record*: For a full summary of all the comments on the various cases captured in the *Congressional Record*, see Edward Waters, *Victor Herbert: A Life in Music* (pp. 334–345).

13 *It was this essential task*: See Hubbell, *From Nothing to Five Million a Year*, for a guest list and description of the event (pp. 1–3).

16 *Even the typist he'd hired*: On December 12, 1979, Bruce Smith of the *Daily News* reported on the mystery of ASCAP's first typewriter. It was a Remington Standard No. 7 taken from the nearby offices of publisher Jerome H. Remick & Co. one Saturday morning in 1914 by ASCAP songwriters Malvin Franklin ("Little Brown Jug") and E. Ray Goetz ("Me and My Gal"). "At a brief noontime ceremony at the ASCAP Building across from Lincoln Center, the typewriter was finally returned."

Chapter 2: Buck Stops Here

19 *In Chicago, Manny Hartman*: "Manny Hartman can properly be termed an ASCAP pioneer. From his law offices he began the Titanic struggle of licensing Chicago and as his job was the whole Middlewest, he appointed and tutored and its different State representatives" (Hubbell, *From Nothing to Five Million a Year*, pp. 44–45).

19 *Writing in the* ASCAP Journal: Herman Greenberg joined ASCAP in 1920 as a field representative for "the New York Metropolitan district." The article, "Selling ASCAP," is from the *ASCAP Journal*, 1937 (pp. 17–20). "It was at this time necessary for us to establish branch offices throughout the United States and to coordinate the office systems and routine as well as procedure of these branch offices with the functions of the General Office, and I undertook an important part of this work. . . . In 1921 after my first year with the Society, the gross income of the Society was $250,000."

20 *Sustaining ASCAP in its first years*: Coinage of the phrase "the Great White Way" is credited to Shep Friedman, a columnist for the *New York Morning Herald*, in 1901 in *Broadway: An Encyclopedic Guide to the History, People and Places of Times Square*, by Ken Bloom (New York: Facts on File, 1991), p. 499, and *Gotham: A History of New York City to 1898*, by Edwin G. Burrows and Mike Wallace (New York: Oxford University Press, 1999), p. 1063.

But a perhaps much stronger case can be made for the sign builder O. J. Gude, known as "the Napoleon of publicity" (Charyn, *Gangsters and Gold Diggers*, p. 47). In an essay in *Inventing Times Square*, edited by William R. Taylor (Baltimore: Johns Hopkins University Press, 1996), p. 235, William Leach cites *The Business Man and the Amusement World*, by Robert Grau (New York: Broadway Publishing, 1910), pp. 247–248, in support of the Gude attribution.

Originally used to describe lower Broadway, the term traveled uptown to the glitzy theater district with the opening of the Times Square subway station in 1904. In *Incredible New York* (Syracuse, NY: Syracuse University Press, 1951), p. 259, Lloyd Morris refers to the area as "the Gay White Way," a short-lived alternative nomenclature based on the 1907 musical of the same name ("Gay White Way (Broadway)," barrypopik.com, January 13, 2010).

20 *"The most important thing"*: Quote from Jerome Charyn is from a personal interview with the author on January 13, 2011.

20 *"ASCAP was one of the great central things"*: Quotes from Mary Ellin Barrett are from a personal interview with the author on January 20, 2011.

20 *"he certainly didn't sit around deploring swing"*: The pleasures of swing are described in *Since Yesterday: The 1930s in America*, by Frederick Lewis Allen (New York: Harper Collins, 1975), p. 267. "The appreciation of the new music was largely vertebral. A good swing band smashing away at full speed, with the trumpeters and clarinetists rising in turn under the spotlight to embroider the theme with their several furious improvisations and the drummers going into long-drawn-out rhythmical frenzies, could reduce its less inhibited auditors to sheer emotional vibration, punctuated by howls of rapture."

21 *The period starting in 1914*: Among the many authors in agreement on the Golden Age is Donald Clarke in *The Rise and Fall of Popular Music* (London: Viking Press, 1995), pp. 95–122, who offers an especially illuminating and balanced view.

21 *"During the first years of Prohibition"*: For a great description of Broadway, see *The Night Club Era*, by Stanley Walker (Baltimore: Johns Hopkins University Press, 1933), p. 199.

22 *One place where blues and jazz were conspicuously missing*: According to the arbiters of radio, during the early years of the Depression, "there was little interest in hot jazz" (Frederick Lewis Allen, *Since Yesterday*, pp. 266–267). Allen credits the popular heyday of jazz in the 1920s to the dance crazes kicked off by "Alexander's Ragtime Band," circa 1911–1916, but acknowledges that "even during this time there were obscure jazz bands, mostly of Negro players, which indulged in a mad improvisation, superimposing their own instrumental patterns made up on the spur of the moment (and sometimes later committed to writing)." Jazz sold well overseas, but not well enough to distract the attention of ASCAP from what was happening on Broadway.

22 *In the first category, Noble Sissle and Eubie Blake*: All song credits from *Popular Music: An Annotated Index of American Popular Songs*, Volume 5, 1920–29, by Nat Shapiro (New York: Adrian Press, 1969).

23 *The ASCAP members who benefited most*: This description of jazz's triumphs and tribulations, written in 1969 by Frank Driggs to introduce Nat Shapiro's *Popular Music* volume on the 1920s, is apropos (p. 22): "Basically every style of jazz was either initiated or anticipated during the 1920s, when the classic patterns were established for the big bands, for arrangers, and for soloists. Since that first blues record nearly 50 years ago, jazz led the way to swing and bebop, influenced the development of rhythm and blues and its successor, rock and roll. If no one made any fantastic sums of money out of it then, it was only because the means for its exploitation were not yet sufficiently developed."

23 *Gene Buck, who took over for George Maxwell*: Gene Buck replacing Maxwell is fuzzily recounted by Hubbell in *From Nothing to Five Million a Year* (pp. 81–82). But the details of the scandal were heavily reported in the *New York Times*, from May 11, 1923, to July 26, 1923, when all charges against Maxwell were dropped. Mention of Maxwell not being a US citizen was made in the very first *Times* article in May of 1923.

24 *As profiled in the* New Yorker: ASCAP's second president was worthy of a two-part profile in the *New Yorker*, December 17 and 24, 1932, entitled "Czar of Song," written by Alva Johnston.

24 *Not that he was hurting for money*: Special mention is made in the

profile of Buck's relationship with one of his Great Neck, Long Island, neighbors, the humorist Ring Lardner, and the relationship of both of them to frequent Great Neck visitor F. Scott Fitzgerald. Said Jonathan Yardley in his Lardner biography, *Ring* (Lanham, MD: Rowman & Littlefield, 2001), p. 239, "As a local publication of the day put it: 'Nowhere in America, probably, are there so many widely known celebrities as are located here. To live in Great Neck is synonymous to being a national success.'" At the time, Buck was one of the biggest of these celebrities. Lardner satirized his extravagant home in a short story called "The Love Nest," in which it is called "a white house that might have been mistaken for the Yale Bowl" with "a living room that was five laps to the mile and suggestive of an Atlantic City auction sale. . . . Friends of Gene Buck report that Gene made a big mistake not leasing his living room for the six-day bicycle race, as the new Madison Square Garden could not begin to accommodate the devotees of this soul-stirring pastime. Gene wired that he wanted to keep the room neat for the Olympic Games of 1932. Gene Jr. is entered in the Marathon that year and is already a top heavy favorite, having circled the room twice in practice in 2 days, 4 hours, 20 minutes and 3.25 seconds with two stops for engine trouble and milk" (pp. 259–260).

25 *"In the summers the house in Great Neck"*: From *Man of the World: Herbert Bayard Swope: A Charmed Life of Pulitzer Prizes, Poker and Politics*, by Alfred Allan Lewis (Indianapolis, IN, and New York: Bobbs-Merrill, 1978), p. 110.

25 *the arrival of the talking pictures*: Along with "Blue Skies," the pop songs Jolson sang in *The Jazz Singer* included his 1923 hit from *Bombo*, "Toot Toot Tootsie (Goo'bye)"; the 1921 hit from *Sinbad*, "My Mammy"; and a cover of Marion Harris' "Dirty Hands! Dirty Face!" The only original song debuted in the film was "Mother of Mine (I Still Have You)," written by Louis Silvers and Grant Clarke, which spent three weeks at number two. The power of the big screen to sell songs (and vice versa) was duly noted.

26 *"The Alley had had a long relationship with the movies"*: Ben Yagoda, "Lullaby of Tin Pan Alley."

27 *It started in 1933*: The Hollywood Gold Rush actually started as a trickle in 1929, which yielded three number one movie tunes: "Am I Blue" from *On with the Show*, "Tiptoe Through the Tulips" from *Gold Diggers of Broadway*, and "Singin' in the Rain" from *Hollywood*

Revue. Nineteen thirty picked up the pace a bit, with several hits that lasted coming from movies that didn't, including "Happy Days Are Here Again" from *Chasing Rainbows,* "Puttin' on the Ritz" from *Puttin' on the Ritz,* and "Three Little Words" from *Check and Double Check.* But during the next three years the Hollywood bonanza may have seemed like nothing but a typical Tinseltown mirage, with only one number one hit in 1931 ("Out of Nowhere" from *Dude Ranch*) and one in 1932 ("A Shanty in Old Shanty Town" from *The Crooner*). Nineteen thirty-three was a different story.

27 *From 1934 through 1937:* Song titles culled from *The Great Song Thesaurus,* by Roger Lax and Frederick Smith (New York: Oxford University Press, 1984). From 1934 through 1937, nearly half the number one hits in America started in the score of a Hollywood film, written by the country's greatest songwriting teams, chief among them Mack Gordon and Harry Revel ("Did You Ever See a Dream Walking" from *Sittin' Pretty,* "Stay as Sweet as You Are" from *College Rhythm,* and "Goodnight, My Love" from *Stowaway*) and Dorothy Fields and Jimmy McHugh ("I'm in the Mood for Love" from *Every Night at Eight,* and "Lovely to Look At" [with Jerome Kern] and a revision of "I Won't Dance"—originally written by Oscar Hammerstein II, Otto Harbach, and Jerome Kern—both from *Roberta*). Jerome Kern and Dorothy Fields wrote the Oscar-winning "The Way You Look Tonight" for *Swing Time.* Dubin and Warren continued their run with "I'll String Along with You" from *Twenty Million Sweethearts,* the Oscar-winning "Lullaby of Broadway" from *Gold Diggers of 1935,* "September in the Rain" from *Stars over Broadway,* "With Plenty of Money and You" from *Gold Diggers of 1937,* "She's a Latin from Manhattan" from *Go into Your Dance,* and "Remember Me" from *Mr. Dodd Takes the Air.* The team of Arthur Freed and Nacio Herb Brown scored with "All I Do Is Dream of You" from *Sadie McKee,* "You Are My Lucky Star" from *Broadway Melody of 1936,* and "Alone" from *A Night at the Opera.* George and Ira Gershwin accounted for "They Can't Take That Away from Me" from *Shall We Dance* and "Nice Work If You Can Get It" from *A Damsel in Distress.* Rodgers and Hart contributed "It's Easy to Remember" and "Soon" from *Mississippi,* as well as "There's a Small Hotel" from *On Your Toes.* Cole Porter hit the top with the title tune from *Rosalie.* Irving Berlin contributed "Cheek to Cheek" from *Top Hat,* "This Year's Kisses" from *On the Avenue,* and "I'm Putting All My Eggs in One Basket" from *Follow the Fleet.* Leo

Robin had two hits with William Rainger, "June in January" from *Here Is My Heart* and "Love in Bloom" from *She Loves Me Not*, and one hit with Frederick Hollander, "Whispers in the Dark" from *Artists and Models*.

The above partial list does not even include future standards that lapsed just short of number one, like "Let's Call the Whole Thing Off" from *Shall We Dance*, "Temptation" from *Going Hollywood*, "Isn't It Romantic" and "Lover" from *Love Me Tonight*, "Beyond the Blue Horizon" from *Monte Carlo*, "Love Is Just Around the Corner" from *Here Is My Heart*, "I Only Have Eyes for You" from *Dames*, "Shuffle Off to Buffalo" from *42nd Street*, "You Are Too Beautiful" from *Hallelujah I'm a Bum*, "Let's Face the Music and Dance" from *Follow the Fleet*, "I've Got My Love to Keep Me Warm" from *On the Avenue*, "Hooray for Hollywood" from *Hollywood Hotel*, and "Lydia the Tattooed Lady" from *A Day at the Circus*.

27 *"It was a great period"*: Interview with Harold Arlen from *They're Playing Our Song*, by Max Wilk (New York: Atheneum, 1973), pp. 156–157. In addition to Harry Warren and Harold Arlen, Wilk spoke with a veritable Songwriters Hall of Fame, including Dorothy Fields, Richard Rodgers, Ira Gershwin, Betty Comden, Yip Harburg, and Johnny Mercer.

28 *"The publishing houses were acquired primarily"*: From "Performing Rights Societies in the United States," by Lucia S. Schultz, *Notes: The Quarterly Journal of the Music Library Association*, Volume 35, No. 3, March 1979 (pp. 511–536), which offers a good account of ASCAP's troubles with Hollywood, including the defection of Warner Brothers Publishing (p. 519) and the activities of the Justice Department (p. 520).

28 *Warner Brothers bought out the great Witmark imprint*: The sale of Witmark to Warner Brothers in 1929 is reported in Goldberg and Witmark, *From Ragtime to Swingtime* (p. 421).

28 *"Hollywood brought Tin Pan Alley to its knees"*: From Yagoda, "Lullaby of Tin Pan Alley."

29 *But the case went nowhere*: "The Passing of Buck," in *Time Magazine* (May 4, 1942), published in the aftermath of the radio wars, details Buck's ouster, in which he was "eased out, not kicked out." Replacing him as president at no pay, Deems Taylor quipped, "I hope to get the presidency to a point where I will earn my salary."

29 *"would have had the effect of nullifying the Supreme Court decision"*:

Hazel Meyer discusses the implications of joining the Berne Convention (*The Gold in Tin Pan Alley*, pp. 86–87). A thorough discussion of the Berne Convention, and America's relationship to it, is presented in *Copyright's Highway: The Law and Lore of Copyright, from Gutenberg to the Celestial Jukebox*, by Paul Goldstein (New York: Hill & Wang, 1995), pp. 150–161.

30 *the judge put out a warrant for Buck's arrest*: There are differing accounts as to the length of Gene Buck's stay in prison in Arizona, ranging from six hours ("ASCAP" at Answers.com) to four days (Schultz, "Performing Rights Societies in the United States," p. 521). Schultz has him there on vacation, while Leonard Allen, reporting in *Harper's Magazine*, who also has Buck remaining in custody for four days, states, "Gene Buck was arrested in Phoenix, Arizona, where he was recovering his health, after two deaths and a near-fatal illness in his family."

30 *Deems Taylor described the situation this way*: Deems Taylor's letter to the ASCAP membership about the lawsuit by the Department of Justice is from *Deems Taylor: A Biography*, by James Pegolotti, p. 265.

31 *"The allegation was that ASCAP"*: Quote from Richard Reimer is from a personal interview with the author on April 1, 2010.

31 *"After that, we could no longer get paid"*: Quote from Nancy Knutsen is from a personal interview with the author on April 20, 2010.

31 *"In most cases the studio or production company"*: Quotes from Richard Bellis are from a personal interview with the author on August 17, 2011.

32 *"This year will either see lasting peace"*: Buck's comment on the radio wars reported by Leonard Allen in "The Battle of Tin Pan Alley" (p. 523).

Chapter 3: Radio Waves

33 *In 1924, the National Association of Broadcasters (NAB) was formed*: The story of the "Dill Bill" was recounted by Hazel Meyer in *The Gold in Tin Pan Alley* (p. 84): "Dill . . . introduced a measure which would have nullified the 1917 Supreme Court decision by giving to radio the privilege of using music without cost on the grounds that the music so used was a public service. . . . Authors, composers, and publishers should be grateful to radio for 'free advertising.'" Raymond Hubbell offers his own account (*From Nothing to Five Million a Year*, pp.

91–96): "The Dill Bill died an early death from overexposure, but the users were back with another one in 1925 . . . in fact I can't remember a restful moment that they've allowed us since they discovered that music was their raw material. . . . As I said earlier, they haven't fooled Congress—yet!"

35 *Writing in his syndicated column*: A copy of Broadway chronicler Damon Runyon's syndicated column of 1938 was among the artifacts included in the ASCAP Collection at the Library of Congress, Washington, DC.

36 *Nevertheless, in a desperate attempt to control*: Letters from ASCAP's then general manager E. Claude Mills relating to issues of radio play from 1932 are from the ASCAP Collection at the Library of Congress.

37 *A lengthy letter written by Gene Buck*: Letter from Gene Buck to the ASCAP membership describing the Society's stance on the practice of "cut-ins" from 1931 is from the ASCAP Collection at the Library of Congress, as are the follow-ups from E. Claude Mills.

38 *a vociferous and impassioned defender*: E. Claude Mills experienced a career as checkered as any songwriter's. According to a profile of the Society published in the January 1933 issue of *Fortune*, "He ran away from home when he was fourteen, shipped aboard a freighter as a cabin boy, deserted the boat at Buenos Aires and hiked back to San Antonio. That hike took three years. Mills had a dozen jobs after that. He was a salesman, railroad train master, circus and carnival producer, promoter of automobile and airplane meets. He worked for three years with Colonel Goethals on the Panama Canal, for which the late Theodore Roosevelt medaled him."

38 *He summed up the organization's mission*: E. Claude Mills' essay "What Is ASCAP?" is in the ASCAP Collection at the Library of Congress.

39 *which drew a response from one of their directors*: Arthur E. Garmaize's letter is in the ASCAP Collection at the Library of Congress.

40 *As the decade neared its end, broadcasters' bickering*: Stories on the radio wars appeared regularly in the press in the late '30s and early '40s, with Leonard Allen's piece in *Harper's* being the most thorough. Of the 1934 suit, Allen wrote, "After ten days' trial in June 1935, the government asked for an adjournment in order that the parties might stipulate the facts. It later proved to be a pigeonholing, for the case has remained dormant since."

Time Magazine reported on the earlier case in "*US v. ASCAP*"

(July 1, 1935): "Round No. 3, which ended last week, was a victory for ASCAP. Though the Government had insisted on beginning the trial this month, its witnesses wavered so under cross-examination that it was glad to adjourn to bolster up its case."

An editorial in the *Bridgeport Post* from April 4, 1938, also leaned in ASCAP's favor: "The plain fact of the matter is that in this case the Department of Justice has moved, not to break up a combination in restraint of trade, but to help its friends the radio barons escape paying for what they use."

Hazel Meyer devotes significant space to ASCAP's troubles with radio and the Justice Department (*The Gold in Tin Pan Alley*, pp. 84–90), as does Schultz ("Performing Rights Societies in the United States," pp. 515–522).

41 *Since jukebox plays were unaccountably excluded*: This is the wording of the notorious jukebox exemption granted by the Copyright Act of 1909: "The reproduction or rendition of a musical composition by or upon coin-operated machines shall not be deemed a public performance for profit unless a fee is charged for admission to the place where such reproduction or rendition occurs."

41 *An unlikely ASCAP ally*: Mark Coleman introduces James Petrillo into the battle between records and recording (and radio) with the phrase "Enter the dragon" in his book *Playback: From the Victrola to MP3, 100 Years of Music, Machines, and Money* (New York: Da Capo Press, 2004), pp. 40–41. Later he talks about Petrillo's role in the musicians' strike of 1942 (pp. 47–49). He also spends quality time analyzing the jukebox industry and ASCAP's inadequate response to it in the run-up to the advent of BMI (pp. 42–46).

41 *"There was the implicit assumption"*: Dave Sanjek's comments are from a telephone interview with the author on January 24, 2011.

41 *"The company I was with"*: Quote from Hank Ballard is taken from a personal interview for my book *When Rock Was Young: A Nostalgic Review of the Top 40 Era* (New York: Holt, Rinehart and Winston, 1981), p. 110.

42 *Buck wrote an introduction for the program*: Gene Buck's preface to the 25th Anniversary Concert is in the ASCAP Collection at the Library of Congress.

43 *However, the San Francisco concerts survived*: The recording of the San Francisco concert, entitled *Carousel of American Music*, was released on May 30, 1997. It was reviewed by Scott Yanow of *All Music*

Guide: "On September 24, 1940, a concert took place that was not only unique but can accurately be called incredible." Unfortunately, the set is currently out of print.

44 *"As Berlin launched into a creaky version"*: Cary Ginell, "A Gathering of Giants: The 1940 ASCAP 25th Anniversary Concert," June 2004, Musicreports.com.

44 *The government, however, did notice*: A much more exhaustive account of the radio wars is given by Leonard Allen in *Harper's* (pp. 514–523). Hazel Meyer also extensively charts the rise of BMI (*The Gold in Tin Pan Alley*, pp. 90–100), leading to ASCAP's signing of the consent decree, and veers into a short history of SESAC (pp. 93–94).

44 *"The logic of ASCAP's operations"*: Goldstein, *Copyright's Highway*, p. 57.

45 *One of the first orders of business*: A recap of the San Francisco concert and the subsequent unpleasant aftermath of the radio wars appears in Pegolotti's Deems Taylor biography (pp. 266–269), which also treats the rise of BMI (p. 265) and Taylor's mellifluous cordiality with the broadcasters, as witnessed by *Variety* (p. 269).

46 *Although ASCAP lost a few members to BMI*: Anything and everything else you need to know about the formation and history of BMI, especially in relationship to ASCAP, can be found in *American Popular Music Business in the 20th Century*. David Sanjek edited this volume based on his late father Russ' massive three-volume work. Sadly, David passed away shortly after I interviewed him by telephone from England on January 24, 2011.

46 *Jimmie Davis wrote "You Are My Sunshine"*: All ASCAP and BMI song information from Shapiro, *Popular Music*, Volumes 1 and 2, on the 1950s and the 1940s, respectively.

47 *this story told by Duke Ellington's lyricist*: From *The World of Duke Ellington*, by Stanley Dance (New York: Scribner, 1970), p. 33.

48 *Still smarting from their battles with radio*: For more on the rise of BMI, see Schultz, "Performing Rights Societies in the United States" (pp. 520–526). Schultz also delves into the ramifications of the *Alden-Rochelle* decision (pp. 527–528).

Chapter 4: TV vs. Rock 'n' Roll

49 *In 1953, for example*: This case was called *Schwartz v. BMI*, after lead songwriter Arthur Schwartz. It dragged on through the courts

for more than ten years before being thrown out (Sanjek and Sanjek, *American Popular Music Business*, p. 127).

51   *Thus, while ASCAP's legal team*: ASCAP's continuing battles with BMI led to hearings by the House Anti-Trust Subcommittee on Television Broadcasting, the opening day of which was covered by three of New York's major newspapers on September 18, 1956. The *New York Herald Tribune* published the figures detailing how much money ASCAP writers had lost due to BMI's affiliation with the radio stations. The *New York Times* noted that the chairman of the committee was none other than ASCAP-leaning Emanuel Celler, Democrat of New York. Also mentioned was the fact that "writers who work for publishing houses associated with BMI receive no performance fees for their work." A week later the trade paper *Broadcasting/ Telecasting* chimed in (September 24, 1956) with ASCAP songwriter Jack Lawrence's doleful quote: "We fear a repetition of the 1941 blackout."

51   *Which is probably why ASCAP*: Designations of BMI publishing companies are from Shapiro, *Popular Music*, Volume 1, 1950–1959.

52   *But the song of the most interest*: As a precursor to the hip detective series *Miami Vice*, *77 Sunset Strip* was the first of the TV detective shows to make use of colorful scenery, colorful characters, and pop music. Edd Byrnes, playing Kookie, became a breakout star, singing the future hit "Kookie, Kookie (Lend Me Your Comb)" on the show's debut episode on October 10, 1958. Perhaps the first pop hit for the upcoming rock 'n' roll generation to emanate from television was Fess Parker's "The Ballad of Davy Crockett," from *Disneyland* (December 15, 1954). Tommy Sands and Sal Mineo owe their careers to *Kraft Television Theatre*, with Sands' "Teenage Crush" coming from a production called "The Singing Idol" (January 30, 1957) and Mineo's "Start Movin'" being featured in "Drummer Man" (May 1, 1957). And then there was Ricky Nelson, whose version of "I'm Walkin'" became a big hit after an April 1957 airing on *The Adventures of Ozzie and Harriet* (Ozzie and Harriet Nelson, both former big band singers, were, of course, his parents).

The above information as well as everything else about the formative years of music on TV is culled from *The Compete Directory to Prime Time Network TV Shows, 1946–Present*, by Tim Brooks and Earle Marsh (New York: Ballantine Books, 1979).

52   *"One day Jack came to me and said"*: The recollections of Arthur

Hamilton are from an interview with the author on November 12, 2010.

53   *One of his biggest personal crusades*: Among the many users of music who claimed they should be exempt from paying ASCAP, because, after all, their exposure of a given song helped boost its sales, the jukebox industry had perhaps the best argument. Built for a dancing crowd, the jukebox is given credit for establishing swing and helping to revive a dormant industry in the late '30s. It was the jukebox industry that sustained country music and R&B in the years when neither genre was getting much radio play, paving the way for rock 'n' roll (Mark Coleman, *Playback*, pp. 32–36). ASCAP's quixotic battles with the jukebox industry, as well as Alan Freed's relationship to the BMI/ASCAP debate, are detailed in John A. Jackson's *Big Beat Heat: Alan Freed and the Early Years of Rock & Roll* (New York: Schirmer Books, 1991), p. 75.

54   *ASCAP's performance income dropped 23 percent*: BMI's dominance of the record charts of the '50s in the context of the upcoming payola scandal is from "Same Old Song and Dance," by Cliff Doerksen, *The Chicago Reader*, October 10, 2002.

55   *One prize ASCAP witness*: Vance Packard's incendiary quote on country music and Tennessee's response are reported by Sanjek and Sanjek in *American Popular Music Business* (p. 167).

55   *Overlooked in the process*: From Sanjek and Sanjek, *American Popular Music Business* (p. 173), in which the quote from Herm Schoenfeld appears.

56   *"While the payola hearings did not directly inhibit"*: John A. Jackson, *Big Beat Heat*, p. 333.

56   *"To be honest, it did look like an antitrust thing"*: John A. Jackson's comments on ASCAP's case against BMI are from an interview with the author on January 19, 2011.

57   *By 1964, BMI controlled 80 percent*: *Variety* covered ASCAP's move to give advances to new writers (August 31, 1966), followed by *Billboard* (September 3, 1966), both mentioning that ASCAP members could collaborate with other writers, provided they weren't members of BMI.

58   *Most ASCAP writers had been enrolled*: Discussions of the Four Funds are from interviews by the author with Paul Adler (on April 12, 2011) and Todd Brabec (on December 30, 2011).

59   *"there was a committee you had to go to, chaired by Leon Brettler"*:

The role of Leon Brettler comes from interviews by the author with Brettler's son, Michael, and Paul Adler on April 12, 2011.

59 *"Lou Levy, top man of Leeds Music Publishing"*: Quote from Bob Dylan is from his memoir, *Chronicles* (New York: Simon & Schuster, 2004), pp. 3–4.

60 *"I once asked my father"*: Quotes from Leeds Levy about Dylan are from a personal interview with the author on August 1, 2011.

60 *Dylan's mentor at Columbia Records*: Quotes from John Hammond are from his memoir, *John Hammond on Record* (New York: Summit Books, 1988), pp. 354–355. Of interest to the music historian reading the Dylan and Hammond memoirs is the size of Dylan's initial advance, which differs much in the two accounts. It's also significant that Dylan's move from Leeds to Witmark meant changing affiliates from BMI to ASCAP.

61 *"By the late '60s"*: Quote from Dave Sanjek is from a telephone interview with the author on January 24, 2011.

62 *Neither could most ASCAP board members*: Yip Harburg interview is from Max Wilk's *They're Playing Our Song.*

62 *the Society would first have to weather*: The CBS TV lawsuit challenging the blanket license was first reported by Jack Gould in the *New York Times* (December 22, 1969). The story of the Supreme Court decision in the case was reported by John Rockwell in "Decade-Old TV Music Question Still Open" in the *New York Times* (April 18, 1979).

63 *"Organizations that rely on an enforced consensus"*: From *The Production of Culture in the Music Industry: The ASCAP-BMI Controversy*, by John Ryan (Lanham, MD: University Press of America, 1985), p. 147.

Chapter 5: The Comeback

65 *"In the '50s and early '60s"*: Quotes from Connie Bradley are from a personal interview with the author on February 9, 2011.

66 *"It was easier for me to get into the White House than it was to get into ASCAP"*: This famous quote was reported in *Gene Autry, His Life and Career*, by Don Cusic (Jefferson, NC: McFarland, 2007), p. 86. The quote comes from Autry's testimony recorded in *To Amend the Communications Act of 1934: Hearings Before a Subcommittee of the Committee on Interstate and Foreign Commerce*, 80th Congress, 1st

session, 1947: "While country music could not get me into ASCAP, it did get me invited to the White House." Pitching since 1930, Autry finally gained ASCAP membership in 1939.

66 *"God knows what Frances Preston would do to them"*: Quote from Paul Adler is from a personal interview with the author on April 12, 2011. Preston, who died on June 13, 2012, was hired from radio station WSM in Nashville to run BMI's first office in Nashville in March 1958. She was president of BMI from 1986 to 2004.

67 *"I think Ed Shea had been the mayor"*: Quote from Nicholas Firth is from a personal interview with the author on March 30, 2011. Not quite mayor of Nashville, Ed Shea was formerly the director of the Nashville Area Chamber of Commerce and head of the Nashville Human Rights Commission (Gerry Wood, *Billboard*, December 27, 1986).

67 *Bradley's earliest triumphs were with . . . Wayland Holyfield and Bob McDill*: Bob McDill has written 31 number one country hits, including "Gone Country" for Alan Jackson and "Good Ole Boys Like Me" for Don Williams.

68 *"It can be punitive if you switch"*: Quote from Wayland Holyfield is from a personal interview with the author on January 17, 2012.

69 *"We wouldn't have jobs here today"*: Owen Bradley and Ralph Peer I were two pioneers of modern country music. Bradley produced future Country Music Hall of Fame artists like Patsy Cline, Bob Wills, Brenda Lee, and Webb Pierce. See *The Encyclopedia of Country Music*, Paul Kingsbury, ed. (New York: Oxford University Press, 1998), pp. 50–51. Ralph Peer I was an important talent scout and music publisher who discovered Jimmie Rodgers and the Carter Family. At his company, Southern Music, he published Fats Waller, Jelly Roll Morton, Louis Armstrong, and Count Basie. During the emergence of BMI, Peer founded Peer-International and helped establish BMI's base in country music. See *Deep Blues*, by Robert Palmer (Harmondsworth, UK: Penguin Books, 1991), p. 109.

69 *One of these hit-makers was Don Schlitz*: Quotes from Don Schlitz are from a personal interview with the author on April 23, 2010. "Amanda" was originally the B-side of Don Williams' 1973 hit "Come Early Morning." Waylon Jennings recorded it the next year. When he re-released it in 1979, it went to number one, with only one lyric changed—"I made it to forty / still wearing jeans . . ." (from "thirty")— to reflect the passage of time. *The Billboard Book of Number One*

Country Hits, by Tom Roland (New York: Billboard Books, 1991), pp. 235–236.

70 *Not too long after that first meeting*: At the time of "The Gambler," Schlitz was working the graveyard shift as a computer operator at Vanderbilt University in Nashville. His version of the song only made it to number 65. Kenny Rogers' version was number one for three weeks in December 1978 (Roland, *The Billboard Book of Number One Country Hits*, pp. 224–225).

71 *"That's when they knew they had to change"*: Comments from Irwin Z. Robinson are from a personal interview with the author on May 19, 2010.

71 *"If you look at the charts at the end of the '60s"*: Quote from Todd Brabec is from a personal interview with the author on December 30, 2011. As an example of this "strange mix," on the *Billboard* Hot 100 of the week ending November 1, 1969, ASCAP had 18 tunes on the chart, including three by Bacharach and David ("Raindrops Keep Fallin' on My Head," "Baby It's You"—cowritten by Bacharach and Hal's older brother Mack—and "Walk On By"), two by Bob Dylan ("Tonight I'll Be Staying Here with You" and "She Belongs to Me"), John Denver's "Leavin' on a Jet Plane," Robbie Robertson's "Up on Cripple Creek," "Jean" by Rod McKuen, "Easy to Be Hard" from *Hair*, and "Tracy" by Pockriss and Vance. *Joel Whitburn Presents the Billboard Hot 100 Charts: The Sixties*, by Joel Whitburn (Menomonee Falls, WI: Record Research, 1990).

72 *Breaking entirely new ground*: The great Motown leap from BMI to ASCAP was described by Paul Adler (on April 12, 2011) and Todd Brabec (on December 30, 2011) in separate interviews with the author. A key part of the Motown music empire, Jobete Publishing was established in 1961.

73 *"I started at ASCAP right after"*: Quote from Richard Reimer is from a personal interview with the author on April 1, 2010.

74 *As recently as the late '80s*: The story about collecting from licensees in Milwaukee is from an interview with Keith Mardak by the author on June 10, 2012.

74 *This was nothing new*: Zelma Wooten showed potential as a writer, opening her article like so: "Reno, 'The biggest little city in the world,' the place where married women throw their wedding rings in the river and the single men fish them out after dark" (The *ASCAP Journal*, 1937).

76   *Debbie Rose joined the A&R team*: Quotes from Debbie Rose are from a personal interview with the author on April 12, 2011.

Chapter 6: Seeding the Garden of Creativity

79   *"That's when we started rolling out"*: Quotes from Debbie Rose are from a personal interview with the author on April 12, 2011.

80   *"I went to the board and I said"*: Quotes from Charles Strouse are from a personal interview with the author on September 12, 2011.

80   *"What BMI does is more like a prescribed lesson plan"*: Quotes from Ted Chapin are from a personal interview with the author on June 12, 2012.

81   *"They're usually two very distinct types of writing"*: Quotes from Stephen Schwartz are from a personal interview with the author on March 11, 2011.

Concerning the previous popularity of theater songs: in an advertisement probably placed by ASCAP in *Variety* in the mid-'50s, called *Variety's Golden 100*, "based on performances, sheet music and disk sales," 62 percent of the songs on the list were either written for or interpolated into a Broadway show. All the songs on the list were written or published by ASCAP members. Information collected from Lax and Smith, *The Great Song Thesaurus*.

82   *The team behind* Elf: Quotes from Chad Beguelin and Matt Sklar are from personal interviews with the author on December 23, 2010.

82   *ASCAP's assistant vice president of musical theater*: Quotes from Michael Kerker are from a personal interview with the author on May 18, 2010.

84   *"You work for IMDb credit"*: Quotes from Richard Bellis are from a personal interview with the author on August 17, 2011. "We also give them all the nonmusical stuff that really counts more than just writing good music," he said, "all of the sophisticated aspects of putting a budget together, getting it done. They only have 16 minutes to record their three-minute cue, and while that is a little unrealistic in the real world, if you can't do it in that amount of time then it's wrong. You have to work with the circumstances that you have, so getting along with the filmmaker and realizing that this is a job and not a concert, and all of those things that go along with being a successful film composer, is what we give them that most schools don't offer."

84   *This is more than confirmed by Nancy Knutsen*: Quotes from Nancy

Knutsen are from a personal interview with the author on April 20, 2010.

86 *Dan Foliart has made his living*: Quotes from Dan Foliart are from a personal interview with the author on March 17, 2011.

87 *As the current head of ASCAP's film and TV*: Quote from Shawn LeMone was provided by ASCAP on November 1, 2013.

88 *"Hans Zimmer, for instance"*: Hans Zimmer has composed music for over 100 films, including award-winning film scores for *The Lion King* (1994), *Crimson Tide* (1995), *The Thin Red Line* (1998), *Gladiator* (2000), *The Last Samurai* (2003), *The Dark Knight* (2008), and *Inception* (2010).

88 *"We've built a reputation filtering talents"*: Quotes from Michael Todd are from a personal interview with the author on April 20, 2010. "In order to build a career you have to be where the action is and it's predominantly here in LA," he added. "That's your first goal. Your second goal is to do whatever it takes to get closer to finding work, so if that means being an orchestrator or musician for a working composer or assisting them and answering phones, do anything to get closer to that position. Find someone to work with. Typically, you go out and find young directors who are good. Ultimately, it's about building that relationship and keeping it, because when the next film comes around, they don't want to have to relearn the process; they've already developed a shorthand with you. That's because time is money and you have to be quick and communication has to be fast on a musical level. It's a wake-up call for many people. One thing about this business: you can have all the goods and you can be out there pounding the pavement, but there is still this element of luck. The same two people with the same set of skills, one could hit the first year, another could hit in ten years. But you increase your odds if you're out there more."

90 *ASCAP's own history shows*: On an early 2013 edition of the *Billboard* Hot 200 Album Chart, there were eight soundtrack albums, including *Pitch Perfect*, *Les Misérables*, *Django Unchained*, and *Rock of Ages*.

90 *"You get your shades of hope"*: Quote from Jonathan McHugh is from a personal interview with the author on April 23, 2010.

91 *As an example of how television*: Comments from Jason Mraz are from a personal interview with the author on January 18, 2011.

91 *"If you look at what television and film pay now"*: Quotes from Barry Coburn are from a personal interview with the author on April 22, 2010.

92   *"When you're asked to give away your music"*: Quote from Earl Rose is from a personal interview with the author on April 21, 2010.

92   *"He listened to our music"*: Quote from Jenn Bostic is from a personal interview with the author on December 22, 2010.

93   *Now known as the ASCAP Foundation Lester Sill Songwriters Workshop*: Lester Sill (1918–1994) "is primarily credited with shepherding the fledgling career of the influential songwriting team of Jerry Leiber and Mike Stoller before teaming with the legendary producer Phil Spector to found Philles Records. . . . In 1964 Sill was instated as a consultant to Screen Gems-Columbia Music. He remained there for 21 years, serving for 14 years as President. In April of 1985, Mr. Sill became the President and Chief Operating Officer of Jobete Music Company Inc. and served on the Board of Directors of both ASCAP and The National Music Publishers Association (NMPA)" ("Lester Sill" at sillmusic.com).

93   *"The kind of guests we bring in"*: Quotes from Brendan Okrent are from a personal interview with the author on March 11, 2013.

93   *Another notable ASCAP program*: In the interest of full disclosure, I am a past winner of the Deems Taylor Award, for my articles in *Rock Magazine* in 1972–73.

94   *Lauren Iossa, then a ten-year ASCAP veteran*: Quotes from Lauren Iossa are from a personal interview with the author on March 16, 2010.

95   *Iossa's boss at the time*: Quotes from Phil Crosland are from a personal interview with the author on March 16, 2010.

96   *"The Expo works on two levels"*: Quote from John LoFrumento is from a personal interview with the author on November 16, 2011.

97   *"Not one single unknown songwriter"*: Quote from Randy Grimmett is from a personal interview with the author on January 23, 2012.

99   *"There was one writer I knew"*: The Mariah Carey tune from *Oz the Great and Powerful*, "Almost Home," peaked at number 18 on the *Billboard* R&B charts. The writers credited are Mariah Carey, Simone Porter, Justin Gray, Lindsey Ray, Tor Erik Hermansen, and Mikkel S. Eriksen.

Chapter 7: New Blood, Nashville, and Capitol Hill

101   *Toni Winter worked as an executive assistant*: Quotes from Toni Winter are from a personal interview with the author on April 7, 2010.

Aside from the Society's first president, George Maxwell (1914–1924), all ASCAP presidents have been composers or songwriters: Gene Buck (1924–1942), Deems Taylor (1942–1948), Fred Ahlert (1948–1950), Otto Harbach (1950–1953), Stanley Adams (1953–1956 and 1959–1980), Paul Cunningham (1956–1959), Hal David (1980–1986), Morton Gould (1986–1994), Marilyn Bergman (1994–2009), and Paul Williams (2009–).

101 *he hosted the Victor Herbert 100th anniversary celebration*: ASCAP held at least two 100th anniversary tributes to Victor Herbert in 1959, one in March after the 45th annual membership meeting, at the Hotel Astor, where the entertainment was supplied by Vincent Lopez and his band, and by Johnny Nash (*Billboard*, March 14, 1959). The second was in Washington, DC, in front of 17 senators and 32 congressmen, where Paul Cunningham spoke with passion about Herbert and his service to songwriters (*Billboard*, April 27, 1959). Unfortunately, President Cunningham is referred to as Arthur in the article, probably a mix-up with Arthur Schwartz, ASCAP's then vice president.

101 *penned a tribute to W. C. Handy*: Paul Cunningham's "Eulogy to William C. Handy" (Handy Brothers Music, 1951) is collected at the Watkinson Library of Trinity College, Hartford, CT.

101 *and signed a major TV rights agreement*: ASCAP's first TV agreement was negotiated by Fred Ahlert in 1949 (Sanjek and Sanjek, *American Popular Music Business*, p. 112). Paul Cunningham presided over the extension of the TV rights agreement negotiated by Stanley Adams, from 1954 to 1961 (p. 156).

102 *"he was already married and living in Great Neck"*: Adams was obviously following in the tradition of Gene Buck, the great ASCAP president who also lived in Great Neck.

102 *Known primarily as Burt Bacharach's lyric-writing partner*: Here are all the Top Five hits credited to the team of Burt Bacharach and Hal David: "(They Long to Be) Close to You," "This Guy's in Love with You," "Raindrops Keep Fallin' on My Head," "Only Love Can Break a Heart," "One Less Bell to Answer," "Blue on Blue," "Magic Moments," "I Say a Little Prayer," and "The Man Who Shot Liberty Valance."

102 *"I used to listen to other writers"*: This quote from Hal David and the next are from *In Their Own Words*, by Bruce Pollock (New York: Macmillan, 1975), pp. xiii, xviii.

103 *"They tried to get me to take the presidency"*: Further quotes from Hal

David are from a personal interview with the author on March 25, 2011.

103 *Much of the credit for that also belongs to Connie Bradley*: Quotes from Connie Bradley are from a personal interview with the author on February 9, 2011.

104 *At ASCAP he met Bob Doyle*: Quotes from Bob Doyle are from a personal interview with the author on March 11, 2013.

104 *"I made a decision to go out on my own"*: Bob Doyle's publishing company is called Major Bob Music.

104 *"We went back and demoed this one song"*: "I'm Much Too Young to Feel This Damn Old" was Doyle's first charting single, reaching number eight on the country charts; his second charting single, "If Tomorrow Never Comes," went to number one.

105 *"When it was time to renew"*: Quote from Ricky Skaggs is from a personal interview with the author on April 2, 2011.

106 *the indefatigable Karen Sherry*: Quotes from Karen Sherry are from a personal interview with the author on April 1, 2010.

106 *It was David who appointed Gloria Messinger*: Quotes from Gloria Messinger are from a personal interview with the author on June 14, 2010.

107 *"one of her roommates was a black woman named Alice Randall"*: Alice Randall published three novels after *The Wind Done Gone*: *Pushkin and the Queen of Spades*, *Rebel Yell*, and *Ada's Rules*. Her best known song is "XXX's and OOO's (An American Girl)," a number one country hit for Trisha Yearwood, written with Matraca Berg.

107 *"There was a lot of rancor among a couple of very activist members"*: Hans Lengsfelder was a Viennese composer (1903–1979) whose best-known work was a collaboration with Ervin Drake on the English lyric to Juan Tizol's "Perdido." He fought the ASCAP powers that be for many years, trying to overturn the weighted vote, eventually succeeding to a small extent. As reported by Lucia Schultz: "The result, two years later, was further amendment of ASCAP's consent decree. The weighted vote was not eliminated, but it was modified to the extent that no member would be able to hold more than 100 votes" ("Performing Rights Societies in the United States," pp. 530–531).

109 *"A gentleman named Michael Koontz"*: Quote from Roger Greenaway is from a personal interview with the author on March 14, 2011.

110 *In his farewell essay to the membership*: Hal David, "Reflections," *ASCAP in Action*, spring 1986, p. 2.

Among the ASCAP rank and file who joined David in this fight against the new bills was its most senior living member, Irving Berlin, who wrote to the Honorable Robert Kastenmeier, Democrat from Wisconsin: "I am told that if H.R. 3521 becomes the law, it would end blanket licenses for local television stations. As a member of ASCAP since it was organized, I know that the present system works. This system has been beneficial for the songwriters, the broadcasters, and the public. A new method of licensing would be an attempt to change something that does not need changing and would threaten the livelihood of American songwriters" (ASCAP Archives at the Library of Congress).

111 *Palumbo was aware of the controversy surrounding his hiring*: Quotes from Ben Palumbo are from a personal interview with the author on February 16, 2012.

112 *One such senator, Palumbo said, is a songwriter*: Orrin Hatch's best-known song, "Everything and More," was released as a single by country singer Billy Gilman in 2005, but it didn't chart.

112 *Tracing her lineage from Nathan Burkan*: Some winners of the annual Nathan Burkan Copyright Awards: "Public Performance for Profit: Past and Present," by Frank D Emerson (Western Reserve University, Cleveland, OH, 1940); "The Author and the State: An Analysis of Soviet Copyright Law," by Marion Lozier Woltmann (Columbia University School of Law, New York, NY, 1966); "Copyright Misuse: Thirty Years of Waiting for the Other Shoe," by Frank Gibbs (Harvard University School of Law, Cambridge, MA, 1977); "The Creative Commissioner: Commissioned Works Under the Copyright Act of 1976," by Robert Penchina (New York University School of Law, New York, NY, 1990).

113 *"I had a record deal"*: Quote from Robert Ellis Orrall is from a personal interview with the author on April 23, 2010.

114 *When ASCAP honored Stevie Wonder*: Stevie Wonder's quote is taken from a special 2007 issue of *Playback, ASCAP in Washington, DC,* detailing the tribute.

Chapter 8: Gridlock, Grants, and Gigabytes

115 *Taylor, in 1943, arranged for the Hungarian composer*: The Béla Bartók story, related by Fran Richard, is also found in *Deems Taylor: A Biography,* by James Pegolotti (p. 270).

115 *Fran Richard, ASCAP's former director of concert music*: Quotes from
     Fran Richard are from a personal interview with the author on June
     23, 2010.
116 *In a diary entry from early in his tenure*: A detailed account of the
     shake-up at the top of ASCAP in 1993 can be found in *Morton Gould:
     American Salute,* by Peter W. Goodman (Portland, OR: Amadeus
     Press, 2000), pp. 309–321.
116 *Fred Koenigsberg, now counsel to the ASCAP board*: Quotes from Fred
     Koenigsberg are from a personal interview with the author on June
     3, 2010.
117 *The internal organizational battles he faced*: Gould himself summed
     up the changes he'd been trying to implement since 1986 in a memo
     to the membership dated September 15, 1993: "Several months ago
     the ASCAP Board of Directors initiated a top-to-bottom review of
     ASCAP—including our domestic and international operations. The
     Board sought to get an honest review of ASCAP's strengths and to
     identify areas where improvement was possible. . . . With our new
     agenda, ASCAP will enjoy a better present and an even better future.
     To express the new spirit, I paraphrase the lyrics of one of our great
     members, Bob Dylan. 'We were so much older then, we're younger
     than that now.' I look forward to working with you as we continue
     to represent your interests and build a better ASCAP" (*Playback*,
     Fall 1993). Within two years, Gould would be retired and Bob Dylan
     would be a member of SESAC.
117 *"The shake-up came more from the board"*: Quotes from Irwin Z.
     Robinson are from a personal interview with the author on May 19,
     2010.
117 *Seated outside the often closed door*: The Booz Allen report, delivered
     by media and entertainment practice chief Michael Wolf, was never
     captured in print form. Like ASCAP, Booz Allen was founded in 1914.
     "Today, it is one of the world's leading international management and
     technology consulting firms, with more than 10,000 employees in
     over 100 offices worldwide. Booz-Allen's Media and Entertainment
     Practice has worked alongside senior management of many of the
     most successful media and entertainment companies in developing
     strategies and helping implement change" (Booz Allen & Hamilton
     eInsights: "Windows into the Future: How Lessons from Hollywood
     Will Shape the Music Industry").

117 *"From its very founding"*: Quote from Gloria Messinger is from a personal interview with the author on June 14, 2010.

118 *Early in 1994, they tapped someone from the broadcasting industry*: Daniel Gold served as president and director of Century Communications, Inc., president of Knight Ridder Broadcasting, Inc. and president of Comcast Cable, Inc., as well as vice president and general manager of CBS and Post-Newsweek Stations' radio and television stations in Washington, DC, Philadelphia, and Hartford, Connecticut. He also served as general counsel of Westinghouse Broadcasting Company (profile at Forbes.com).

118 *"Before John LoFrumento came in"*: Quotes from Marilyn Bergman are from a personal interview with the author on March 14, 2011.

118 *"I came from a different world"*: Quotes from John LoFrumento are from a personal interview with the author on November 16, 2011.

119 *"I was hired by ASCAP in September of '95"*: Quotes from Vincent Candilora are from a personal interview with the author on March 8, 2011.

121 *in the mid-1990s, ASCAP found small business owners*: The Digital Millennium Copyright Act (DCMA) of 1998 (also known as the Fairness in Music Licensing Act) was signed into law by President Clinton on October 28, 1998.

121 *The run-up to H.R. 789*: Comments from Russ Hauth and Brandt Gustavson are from the Music Matters column by Chuck Merritt in the September 1996 issue of *Religious Broadcasting* (p. 70).

121 *"What hypocrisy!"*: Michael Kosser's comments are from the Street Smarts column in the September 1996 issue of *American Songwriter Magazine*.

Originally the DMCA was supposed to provide "the administration's blueprint bill for its information superhighway plan." Its three key features were: 1) it clarified that under existing law, a copyrighted work can be distributed by transmission; 2) it offered protection against circumvention of copyright protection systems; 3) it provided protection against the removal or alteration of copyright management information. That is, until several other interested parties began attaching their concerns to it. "For example, the redrafted House version . . . now contains sections that deal with the controversial issue of music licensing exemptions for 'background music' used by restaurateurs and bar owners. Such sections would also exempt religious broadcasters from having to pay music fees" ("Congress Mulls Over Entertainment Issues," by Bill Holland, *Billboard Magazine*, September 14, 1996).

Answers.com provided further perspective on the issue: "Restaurateurs became the subject of increased music licensor attention." Sources include "Paying the Piper," by Joseph Conlin, *Successful Meetings*, October 1992; "All Keyed Up," by Steve Brooks, *Restaurant Business*, November 1, 1993; "Congress Could Turn Table on Music Licensers," by Melinda Jensen, *Successful Meetings*, April 1995; "ASCAP and BMI Are Turning Up the Volume," by Steve Brooks, *Restaurant Business*, July 1, 1995; "ASCAP Restructuring Rates," by Donna Petrozzello, *Broadcasting and Cable*, August 12, 1996; and "Dinner Music," by Brian Breuhaus, *Restaurant Business*, October 10, 1993 ("ASCAP" at Answers.com).

122 *"It used to be all radio"*: Quote from Peter Boyle is from a personal interview with the author on February 13, 2013.

123 *"In the view of the Copyright Office"*: From Statement of Marybeth Peters, Register of Copyrights, before the Subcommittee on Courts and Intellectual Property, Committee on the Judiciary, July 17, 1997.

124 *ASCAP's man in Washington, Ben Palumbo*: Quotes from Ben Palumbo are from a personal interview with the author on February 16, 2012.

125 *Needless to say, ASCAP was not pleased*: Quotes from Marilyn Bergman and Frances Preston are from a joint press release issued October 9, 1998, the day after passage of the DMCA.

126 *"We had negotiated an agreement"*: Quotes from Richard Reimer are from a personal interview with the author on April 1, 2010.

127 *On August 25*: David Brinkley commented on the Girl Scouts controversy on *This Week with David Brinkley*, August 25, 1996.

127 *It took until August 29*: Comments from Charles Osgood are from *The Osgood File*, August 29, 1996.

128 *"The first years we underwrote this project"*: Quotes from Karen Sherry are from a personal interview with the author on April 1, 2010.

128 *She also spearheaded the Children Will Listen program*: ASCAP's Summer 2008 issue of *Playback* reported: "In keeping with the mission of 'Children Will Listen,' to bring the musical theater experience to young students nationwide, The ASCAP Foundation brought 500 eleventh-grade students from various Los Angeles inner city schools to the Reprise! Broadway's Best production of Stephen Sondheim's

Sunday in the Park with George. . . . Other recent beneficiaries of our 'Children Will Listen' program were students from P.S. 115, which is located in Washington Heights, New York. Over 100 sixth graders enjoyed a matinee performance of . . . *In the Heights.* Free orchestra level seats, transportation and CD's of the cast recording were also provided."

128 *In 2011, board member Valerie Simpson:* Quotes from Valerie Simpson are from a personal interview with the author on May 29, 2012.

129 *"We got involved in the Foundation":* Quotes from Caroline Bienstock are from a personal interview with the author on February 27, 2013.

ASCAP Foundation Awards include: the Robert Allen Award to an aspiring ASCAP pop and/or jazz songwriter participating in ASCAP's New York Paul Cunningham Songwriters Workshop; the Louis Armstrong Scholarship at the University of New Orleans for a talented jazz musician to study music in a formal academic environment; the Richard Rodgers New Horizons Award to encourage promising young composers of musical theater; the Boosey & Hawkes Young Composer Award to a senior at LaGuardia High School of Music and Art for excellence in music composition; the Leonard Bernstein Award to aspiring composers for career-related expenses, such as travel to important performances or music copying; the Joe Raposo Children's Music Award to support emerging talent in the area of children's music; and the Jay Gorney Award for an original song honored for its message of social conscience / social significance as well as overall craft, artistry, and compositional elements.

A list of The ASCAP Foundation fellowships, grants, and awards can be found in appendix C of this book.

130 *"For some reason it was a key":* Quote from Mary Ellin Barrett is from a personal interview with the author on January 20, 2011.

130 *held during the annual South by Southwest festivities:* Launched in 1987, the South by Southwest music festival, held each spring in Austin, Texas, has become one of the most influential events of its type in the world.

130 *"Either I wasn't big enough":* Quotes from John Mayer are from a personal interview with the author on April 22, 2010.

131 *"The ASCAP Foundation touches the lives":* Comments from Doug Wood were provided by ASCAP on July 24, 2013.

131 *"My first introduction to ASCAP":* Quotes from Kenny Burrell are from a personal interview with the author on May 5, 2010.

132 *"We'd been sending out numerous requests"*: Quotes from Hans Schuman are from a personal interview with the author on December 21, 2010.

132 *The much-recorded bassist Rufus Reid*: Quotes from Rufus Reid are from a personal interview with the author on March 6, 2012.

133 *"When I did* Horses"*: Quote from Patti Smith is taken from the transcript of her appearance at the ASCAP Founders Award Ceremony in Los Angeles, April 21, 2010. In addition to Stevie Wonder, Paul McCartney, and Bob Dylan, recipients of the ASCAP Founders Award to date include Jule Styne, Smokey Robinson, and Berry Gordy (1988); Jerry Leiber and Mike Stoller (1991); Burt Bacharach and Hal David (1993); Tito Puente and Don Henley (1994); George Martin and Ashford & Simpson (1996); Billy Joel (1997); Garth Brooks, Joni Mitchell, and Stephen Sondheim (1999); Steely Dan (2000); Tom Waits, Arturo Sandoval, and Elmer Bernstein (2001); James Taylor (2002); Elvis Costello (2003); Emmylou Harris and Jackson Browne (2004); Neil Young and Ruben Blades (2005); Annie Lennox (2006); Melissa Etheridge (2007); Alan and Marilyn Bergman (2008); Ann and Nancy Wilson of Heart (2009); Patti Smith, Dr. Dre, and Alan Jackson (2010); P. Diddy and Rod Stewart (2011); Carly Simon (2012); and Steven Tyler and Joe Perry of Aerosmith (2013).

Chapter 9: A Common Cause

136 *"We are going through the most drastic change"*: Quote from Dean Kay is from a personal interview with the author on August 20, 2012.

137 *Nicholas Firth was the head of publishing at BMG*: Quote from Nicholas Firth is from a personal interview with the author on March 30, 2011.

137 *ASCAP publisher vice chair Irwin Z. Robinson was on the board*: Quote from Irwin Z. Robinson is from a personal interview with the author on May 19, 2010.

138 *Former board member Jay Morgenstern*: Quote from Jay Morgenstern is from a personal interview with the author on March 11, 2011.

138 *Warner Brothers Records is now run by Cameron Strang*: Quotes from Cameron Strang are from a personal interview with the author on March 25, 2013.

139 *Film/TV composer Bruce Broughton*: Quote from Bruce Broughton was provided by ASCAP on July 24, 2013.

140 *Veteran ASCAP board member publisher*: Quote from John Eastman was provided by ASCAP on August 18, 2013.

141 *Jimmy Webb, author of "MacArthur Park"*: Quotes from Jimmy Webb are from a personal interview with the author on January 5, 2012.

143 *"In a world where music content"*: Quote from Laurent Hubert was provided by ASCAP on August 18, 2013.

143 *"There's a whole group of people"*: Quotes from Valerie Simpson are from a personal interview with the author on May 29, 2012.

144 *Wayland Holyfield ("Could I Have This Dance")*: Quote from Wayland Holyfield is from a personal interview with the author on January 17, 2012.

145 *ASCAP board member Barry Coburn*: Quotes from Barry Coburn are from a personal interview with the author on April 22, 2010.

145 *Succeeding Marilyn Bergman*: Quotes from Paul Williams are from a personal interview with the author on November 16, 2011.

From *Playback*, Summer 2009: "As a passionate voice for the rights of music creators, Bergman . . . helped lead ASCAP to several major legislative victories, including most notably the Supreme Court's decision in 2003 to uphold the Sonny Bono Copyright Term Extension Act of 1998, which extended copyright protection an extra 20 years—to the life of the author plus 70 years" (p. 12). In the same issue, Bergman added: "I have worked closely with Paul during his eight years as a member of the ASCAP Board of Directors, and particularly since he assumed the post of Vice Chairman . . . I have no doubt that he will be a powerful and vigorous advocate for our needs and rights" (p. 8).

Chapter 10: Follow the Dollar

149 *Although ASCAP's current payment system is painstakingly explained*: "The ASCAP Payment System," ASCAP.com.

149 *"It's fun to look at the ASCAP statements"*: Quote from Billy Steinberg is taken from a personal interview with the author on April 30, 2010.

150 *"Having thrown the original system"*: Quotes from Raymond Hubbell are from his history of ASCAP's early years, *From Nothing to Five Million a Year* (pp. 59–65).

150 *It was ASCAP founder and legal genius*: A printout entitled "Classification of Publisher Members as of the Fourth Quarter 1932" included 100 publishers, divided into 15 classes, ranging from AA to

X. Up at the top in AA were Irving Berlin, Inc., Leo Feist, Inc., and Harms, Inc.

In 1931, writer members were divided into 16 categories, with revenues distributed as follows: *Permanent A*: $30,000 (split among 12 writers); *AA*: $248,613 (split among 51 writers); *A*: $77,557 (split among 19 writers); *Permanent B*: $10,500; *BB*: $52,620; *B*: $48,970; *Permanent C*: $13,500; *CC*: $51,646; *C*: $40,409; *Permanent D*: $750; *DD*: 0; *D*: $1575; *1*: $31,400; *2*: $20,050; *3*: $14,800; *4*: $1,370 (*Fortune*, January 1933, pp. 29–30).

Twenty-seven years later, in *The Gold in Tin Pan Alley*, Hazel Meyer reported on what had changed, namely the advent of the Four Funds: the Sustained Performance Fund (30 percent), the Accumulated Earnings Fund (20 percent), the Availability Fund (30 percent), and the Current Performance Fund (20 percent). "Of these four funds, the last named is the only one which . . . is based on the compilation of performance credits amassed during the preceding calendar year" (p. 104).

152 *Said ASCAP senior vice president and longtime chief economist*: Quotes from Peter Boyle are from a personal interview with the author on February 13, 2013.

152 *"Earnings-wise you can get"*: Quotes from Todd Brabec are from a personal interview with the author on December 30, 2011.

152 *When Brabec worked with Paul Adler*: Commenting on the much-maligned Four Funds during a personal interview with the author, Todd Brabec said, "You couldn't all of a sudden get rid of it, because a lot of these older writers had a lot of money tied up in it, their five- and ten-year averages, so they would have lost money."

One of the most significant changes to the process came into effect in 1966. According to then president Stanley Adams: "Under ASCAP's present payment system, members have a choice of being paid for their performances all in one year or averaging their performances over a period of years" (*Cashbox*, September 3, 1966).

153 *The smallest among American performing rights organizations*: SESAC was purchased in 1993 by Freddie Gershon, Ira Smith, and Steve Swid. According to David Hinckley in *The Daily News*, "Reports circulating in the industry this week suggested the deals will triple their [Dylan's and Diamond's] previous songwriting earnings" ("Moving Up to Majors SESAC Gets Dylan, Diamond," February 3, 1995).

153 *"The business plan was to identify"*: Quotes from Vincent Candilora are from a personal interview with the author on March 8, 2011.

153 *While members frequently switch alliances*: From "When Composers and Publishers Switch Performing Rights Societies? Effects on Per Program License Reporting," by Doug Brainin in Music Reports, LLC, June 2001. "Eagles members Glenn Frey and Don Henley switched from ASCAP to BMI in 1996. James Taylor, formerly a BMI writer, joined ASCAP in 1997, as did Joni Mitchell. Effective October 1, 2000, the publishing for the Beatles' former Northern Songs catalog, now owned by Sony/ATV Music Publishing, switched from BMI to ASCAP. . . . Jonathan Wolff, the composer for the music of such hit TV shows as *Seinfeld* and *Caroline in the City*, recently switched his affiliation from ASCAP to SESAC."

154 *"The fellows who run SESAC"*: Quote from Fred Koenigsberg is from a personal interview with the author on June 3, 2010.

154 *"We would get sheets of paper"*: Quote from Dorothy Gullish is from a personal interview with the author on May 4, 2011.

156 *ASCAP board member and SONGS Music*: Quote from Matt Pincus was provided by ASCAP on August 18, 2013.

157 *Longtime television composer Alf Clausen*: Quote from Alf Clausen was provided by ASCAP on August 18, 2013.

157 *ASCAP's senior vice president for special projects, Seth Saltzman*: Quotes from Seth Saltzman are from a personal interview with the author on April 1, 2010.

158 *"Judge Conner's expertise"*: "William Conner, Judge Expert in Patent Law, Dies at 89," by Douglas Martin, The *New York Times*, July 19, 2009.

159 *"ASCAP's income reached $995 million"*: From Todd Brabec's newsletter *Music and Money*, December 10, 2010.

160 *ASCAP's Richard Reimer referred*. Quotes from Richard Reimer are from a personal interview with the author on April 1, 2010.

162 *"Traditionally, we've paid the top 300 grossing concert venues"*: Quote from Brendan Okrent is from a personal interview with the author on March 11, 2013.

164 *"I was just with my financial advisor"*: Quote from Jason Mraz is from a personal interview with the author on January 18, 2011.

164 *"We are underrepresented on radio, for sure"*: Quotes from Stephen Paulus, "one of the most prominent and prolific composers of our time, [who] has written over 400 works which have received premieres

and performances throughout the world" ("Board of Directors: Stephen Paulus," ASCAP.com), are from a personal interview with the author on January 20, 2012.

164 *The Oscar- and Pulitzer Prize–winning composer John Corigliano*: Quote from John Corigliano Jr. is from a personal interview with the author on February 7, 2012. "Since the mid-1960s, when he won an award for his professional debut, Sonata for Violin and Piano, Corigliano has worked in a diverse number of classical music forms, including oratorios for large-scale stage productions, orchestral works for symphonies and smaller ensembles, movie soundtracks, and even a full-scale opera. Long respected by critics and audiences in the classical music community, Corigliano earned wider public recognition in 2000–01, when he won an Academy Award for the soundtrack to *The Red Violin* and a Pulitzer Prize for his Symphony No. 2" (Timothy Borden, "John Corigliano Biography" at MusicianGuide.com).

165 *Fran Richard, former vice president of concert music*: Quotes from Fran Richard are from a personal interview with the author on June 23, 2010.

167 *Jim Kendrick pointed to the ASCAP awards ceremonies*: Quotes from James Kendrick are from a personal interview with the author on February 25, 2013. "Trained as an oboist at the Manhattan School of Music and The Juilliard School, Jim Kendrick began his publishing career in 1977 helping to establish European American Music before studying law. . . . Kendrick is also Secretary and a Director of The Aaron Copland Fund for Music, Inc., The Amphion Foundation, Inc., the Virgil Thomson Foundation Ltd., The Koussevitzky Music Foundation, and The Charles Ives Society, Inc. He is counsel to the Music Publishers Association of the United States and the American Academy of Arts and Letters" ("James M. Kendrick" at ASCAP.com).

Chapter 11: Playback and Fast Forward

171 *"The price of liberty is eternal vigilance"*: Quoted by Fred Koenigsberg in a personal interview with the author on June 3, 2010. This famous quote is often mistakenly attributed to Thomas Jefferson, but goes much further back in history. According to the official Web site of the Thomas Jefferson Foundation, "Several nineteenth-century sources claim that this was a quotation from Junius, an anonymous political writer who wrote a series of letters to the London *Public Advertiser*

between 1769 and 1772, but we have not found this exact statement in his writings" ("Spurious Quotations," Monticello.org).

172 *"Music is performed in more ways"*: "ASCAP Delivers Strong 2009 Financial Results," *Playback*, Summer 2010, p. 8.

172 *LoFrumento delivered those figures*: John LoFrumento's comments are from the transcript of the 2010 "I Create Music" Expo.

173 *"I continued to do the Democrats"*: Quote from Ben Palumbo is from a personal interview with the author on February 16, 2012.

173 *"I was on the board when we changed our attitude"*: Quote from Nicholas Firth is from a personal interview with the author on March 30, 2011.

174 *"We have a very recognizable name now"*: Quotes from Harriet Melvin are from a personal interview with the author on March 11, 2013.

174 *"We're fortunate to have some chairmen"*: Quote from Marilyn Bergman is from a personal interview with the author on March 14, 2011.

174 *Alec French, ASCAP's current Democratic lobbyist*: Quote from Alec French is from a personal interview with the author on December 23, 2010.

175 *Without a doubt the best champions*: Quotes from David Israelite are from a personal interview with the author on February 12, 2012. According to its Web site, the National Music Publishers Association represents over 3000 American music publishers, working "to interpret copyright law, educate the public about licensing, and safeguard the interests of its members" ("About NMPA," NMPA.org).

176 *Josh Kear, coauthor of several Grammy Award–winning hits*: Quotes from Josh Kear are from a personal interview with the author on March 14, 2013.

178 *"Earlier this week I attended"*: Quote from Senator Mel Watt is from a May 16, 2013, hearing before the House Subcommittee on Courts, Intellectual Property, and the Internet.

178 *ASCAP board member Bruce Broughton*: Quote from Bruce Broughton provided by ASCAP on July 24, 2013.

179 *"We have a tremendous grassroots network"*: Quote from Karen Sherry is from a personal interview with the author on April 1, 2010.

181 *"This is a complicated subject"*: Bill Keller's article, "Steal This Column," appeared in the *New York Times*, February 6, 2012.

181 *Former ASCAP board member Jimmy Jam*: Quotes from Jimmy Jam are from a personal interview with the author on June 20, 2012.

183 *LoFrumento commented*: Quotes from John LoFrumento are from a personal interview with the author on November 16, 2011.

184 *"Like ASCAP, PRS has writer members"*: Quote from Roger Greenaway is from a personal interview with the author on March 14, 2011.

184 *"It was a big deal when we were able"*: Quote from Paul Adler is from a personal interview with the author on April 12, 2011.

185 *"We have Society visits to make sure"*: Quotes from Bob Candela are from a personal interview with the author on February 25, 2013.

Further on the issues in China: at the 2010 "Music Matters" conference in Hong Kong, Bill Zang, vice president at Shanghai Synergy Culture & Entertainment Group, presented the outlines of a plan whereby the Chinese government will be using watermarking technology to aid in tracking performances for royalty collections to songwriters. Until 1990 all copyright in China was illegal. "It is the fact that the government is publicly outlining a strategy and process to tackling the problem which is a watershed. . . . Even more encouraging was the emphasis on using the technology not just to fight piracy, but also properly compensate rightsholders for the use of their music" ("Music Matters Scoop: China's Plan to Fight Piracy," Eric de Fontenay, *MusicDish*, June 1, 2010).

186 *ASCAP publisher board member*: Quote from Zach Horowitz was provided by ASCAP on August 18, 2013.

187 *Veteran music publisher Martin Bandier*: Quote from Martin Bandier is from a personal interview with the author on June 14, 2012.

188 *"The way I see it"*: Quote from Paul Williams is from a personal interview with the author on November 16, 2011.

188 *"I would say that ASCAP is the Magna Carta"*: Johnny Mercer's thoughts on ASCAP may have come from a BBC interview in the 1960s, according to Mercer's grandson Jim Corwin, but could be even older.

SELECTED BIBLIOGRAPHY

Allen, Frederick Lewis. *Since Yesterday: The 1930s in America*. New York: Harper Collins, 1975.

Armitage, Merle. *George Gershwin, Man and Legend*. New York: Duell, Sloan and Pearce, 1958.

ASCAP Biographical Dictionary. New York: ASCAP, 1966.

Atkinson, Brooks. *Broadway*. New York: Macmillan, 1970.

Belz, Carl. *The Story of Rock*. New York: Oxford University Press, 1971.

Bloom, Ken. *Broadway: An Encyclopedic Guide to the History, People and Places of Times Square*. New York: Facts on File, 1991.

Breslin, Jimmy. *Damon Runyon*. New York: Ticknor & Fields, 1991.

Brooks, Tim, and Earle Marsh. *The Compete Directory to Prime Time Network TV Shows, 1946–Present*. New York: Ballantine Books, 1979.

Brown, Les. *Television: The Business Behind the Box*. New York: Harcourt Brace Jovanovich, 1971.

Burrows, Edwin G., and Mike Wallace. *Gotham: A History of New York City to 1898*. New York: Oxford University Press, 1999.

Cahn, Sammy. *I Should Care*. New York: Arbor House, 1974.

Carmichael, Hoagy, and Stephen Longstreet. *Sometimes I Wonder*. New York: Farrar, Straus and Giroux, 1966.

Chapple, Steve, and Reebee Garofolo. *Rock 'n' Roll Is Here to Pay: The History and Politics of the Music Industry*. Chicago: Nelson-Hall, 1977.

Charyn, Jerome. *Gangsters and Gold Diggers: Old New York, the Jazz Age and the Birth of Broadway*. New York: Thunder's Mouth Press, 2005.

Christgau, Robert. *Any Old Way You Choose It: Rock and Roll and Other Pop Business*. Baltimore: Penguin Books, 1973.

Churchill, Allen. *The Great White Way: A Re-Creation of Broadway's Golden Era of Theatrical Entertainment*. New York: Dutton, 1962.

Clark, Dick, and Richard Robinson. *Rock, Roll and Remember*. New York: Crowell, 1976.

Clarke, Donald. *The Rise and Fall of Popular Music*. London: Viking Press, 1995.

Cohan, George M. *Twenty Years on Broadway and the Years It Took to Get There*. New York: Harper and Brothers, 1924.

Coleman, Mark. *Playback: From the Victrola to MP3, 100 Years of Music, Machines, and Money*. New York: Da Capo Press, 2004.

Conrad, Earl. *Billy Rose, Manhattan Primitive*. Cleveland, OH: World Publishing, 1968.

Crawford, Richard. *America's Musical Life*. New York: W. W. Norton, 2001.

Cusic, Don. *Gene Autry, His Life and Career*. Jefferson County, NC: McFarland, 2007.

Dance, Stanley. *The World of Duke Ellington*. New York: Scribner, 1970.

Denisoff, R. Serge. *Solid Gold: The Popular Record Industry*. New Brunswick, NJ: Transaction Books, 1975.

Dietz, Howard. *Dancing in the Dark*. New York: Quadrangle, 1974.

Douglas, Ann. *Terrible Honesty: Mongrel Manhattan in the 1920s*. New York: Farrar, Straus and Giroux, 1995.

Dylan, Bob. *Chronicles*. New York: Simon & Schuster, 2004.

Eisen, Jonathan, ed. *The Age of Rock: Sounds of the American Cultural Revolution*. New York: Vintage Books, 1969.

Ewen, David. *The Life and Death of Tin Pan Alley: The Golden Age of American Popular Music*. New York: Funk & Wagnalls, 1964.

Farnsworth, Marjorie. *The Ziegfeld Follies*. New York: Putnam, 1956.

Freeland, Michael. *Irving Berlin*. New York: Stein and Day, 1974.

Friedlander, Paul. *Rock and Roll: A Social History*. Boulder, CO: Westview, 1996.

Gillett, Charlie. *The Sound of the City: The Rise of Rock and Roll*. New York: Outerbridge and Dienstfrey, 1970.

Goldberg, Isaac. *Tin Pan Alley: A Chronicle of American Popular Music*. New York: Frederick Ungar, 1930.

Goldberg, Isaac, and Isidore Witmark. *From Ragtime to Swingtime: The Story of the House of Witmark*. New York: Lee Furman, 1939.

Golden, Eve. *Anna Held and the Birth of Ziegfeld's Broadway*. Lexington, KY: The University of Kentucky Press, 2000.

Goldstein, Paul. *Copyright's Highway: The Law and Lore of Copyright, from Gutenberg to the Celestial Jukebox*. New York: Hill & Wang, 1995.

Goldstein, Richard. *Goldstein's Greatest Hits*. New York: Tower, 1970.

Goodman, Peter W. *Morton Gould: American Salute*. Portland, OR: Amadeus Press, 2000.

Grau, Robert. *The Business Man in the Amusement World*. New York: Broadway Publishing, 1910.

Hamm, Charles. *Yesterdays: Popular Song in America*. New York: W. W. Norton, 1983.

Hammond, John. *John Hammond on Record*. New York: Summit Books, 1988.

Harris, Charles K. *After the Ball: Forty Years of Melody*. New York: Frank-Maurice, 1926.

Howe, Irving. *World of Our Fathers*. New York: Harcourt Brace Jovanovich, 1976.

Hubbell, Raymond. *From Nothing to Five Million a Year: The Story of ASCAP by a Founder*. Typescript. Washington, DC: Library of Congress, 1937.

Jablonski, Edward. *Irving Berlin: American Troubadour*. New York: Henry Holt, 1999.

Jackson, John. *Big Beat Heat: Alan Freed and the Early Years of Rock & Roll*. New York: Schirmer Books, 1991.

Jahn, Mike. *Rock: From Elvis Presley to the Rolling Stones*. New York: Times Books, 1973.

Jasen, David A. *Tin Pan Alley: The Composers, the Songs, the Performers, and Their Times*. New York: Donald I. Fine, 1988.

Kingsbury, Paul, ed. *The Encyclopedia of Country Music*. New York: Oxford University Press, 1998.

Lax, Roger, and Frederick Smith. *The Great Song Thesaurus*. New York: Oxford University Press, 1984.

Leiter, Robert. *The Musicians and Petrillo*. New York: Bookman Associates, 1953.

Levine, Faye. *The Culture Barons: An Analysis of Power and Money in the Arts*. New York: Crowell, 1976.

Levine, Robert. *Free Ride: How Digital Parasites Are Destroying the Culture Business, and How the Culture Business Can Fight Back*. New York: Doubleday, 2011.

Lewis, Alfred Allan. *Man of the World: Herbert Bayard Swope: A Charmed Life of Pulitzer Prizes, Poker and Politics*. Indianapolis, IN, and New York: Bobbs-Merrill, 1978.

Lydon, Michael. *Flashbacks: Eyewitness Accounts of the Rock Revolution, 1964–1974*. New York: Routledge, 2003.

Marks, E. B. *They All Sang: From Tony Pastor to Rudy Vallee*. New York: Viking, 1934.

Meyer, Hazel. *The Gold in Tin Pan Alley*. Philadelphia: J. B. Lippincott, 1958.

Michel, Trudi. *Inside Tin Pan Alley*. New York: Frederick Fell, 1948.

Miller, James. *Almost Grown: The Rise of Rock*. London: Arrow, 2000.

Morris, Lloyd. *Incredible New York*. Syracuse, NY: Syracuse University Press, 1951.

Morris, Ronald L. *Wait Until Dark: Jazz and the Underworld, 1880–1940*. Bowling Green, OH: Bowling Green University Press, 1980.

Nite, Norm N. *Rock On: The Illustrated Encyclopedia of Rock 'n' Roll*. New York: Crowell, 1974.

Nolan, Frederick. *Lorenz Hart: A Poet on Broadway*. New York: Oxford University Press, 1994.

Palmer, Robert. *Baby, That Was Rock & Roll: The Legendary Leiber & Stoller*. New York: Harcourt Brace Jovanovich, 1978.

———. *Dancing in the Street: A Rock and Roll History*. London: BBC Books, 1996.

———. *Deep Blues*. Harmondsworth, UK: Penguin Books, 1991.

Pegolotti, James A. *Deems Taylor: A Biography*. Lebanon, NH: Northeastern University Press, 2003.

Pollock, Bruce. *In Their Own Words*. New York: Macmillan, 1975.

———. *When Rock Was Young*. New York: Holt, Rinehart and Winston, 1981.

Rodgers, Richard. *Musical Stages: An Autobiography*. New York: Random House, 1975.

Roland, Tom. *The Billboard Book of Number One Country Hits*. New York: Billboard Books, 1991.

Roxon, Lillian. *Rock Encyclopedia*. New York: Grosset & Dunlap, 1969.

Ryan, John. *The Production of Culture in the Music Industry: The ASCAP-BMI Controversy*. Lanham, MD: University Press of America, 1985.

Sanjek, Russell, and David Sanjek. *American Popular Music Business in the 20th Century*. New York: Oxford University Press, 2000.

Sarlin, Bob. *Turn It Up! (I Can't Hear the Words)*. New York: Simon & Schuster, 1973.

Shapiro, Nat. *Popular Music: 1920–1929*. New York: Adrian Press, 1969.

Shaw, Arnold. *The Rockin' '50s*. New York: Hawthorn, 1974.

Spitz, Robert Stephen. *The Making of Superstars: Artists and Executives of the Rock Music Business*. New York: Doubleday, 1978.

Stagg, Jerry. *A Half-Century of Show Business and the Fabulous Empire of the Brothers Shubert*. New York: Random House, 1968.

Taylor, Deems. *Some Enchanted Evenings*. New York: Harper, 1953.

Taylor, Theodore. *Jule: The Story of Composer Jule Styne*. New York: Random House, 1979.

Taylor, William R., ed. *Inventing Times Square*. Baltimore: Johns Hopkins University Press, 1991.

Walker, Stanley. *The Night Club Era*. Baltimore: Johns Hopkins University Press, 1933.

Waters, Edward N. *Victor Herbert: A Life in Music*. New York: Macmillan, 1955.

Whitburn, Joel. *Joel Whitburn Presents the Billboard Hot 100 Charts: The Sixties*. Menomonee Falls, WI: Record Research, 1990.

————. *Joel Whitburn's Pop Memories 1890–1954*. Menomonee Falls, WI: Record Research, 1986.

Whitcomb, Ian. *After the Ball: Pop Music from Rag to Rock*. New York: Simon & Schuster, 1973.

Wilder, Alec. *American Popular Song: The Great Innovators, 1900–1950*. New York: Oxford University Press, 1972.

Wilk, Max. *They're Playing Our Song*. New York: Atheneum, 1973.

Woollcott, Alexander. *The Story of Irving Berlin*. New York: Putnam, 1925.

Yardley, Jonathan. *Ring: A Biography of Ring Lardner*. Lanham, MD: Rowman & Littlefield, 2001.

INDEX

ABC television, 86
Acuff, Roy, 46
Adams, Lee, 80
Adams, Stanley, 49, 54, 58, 101, 106, 135
Adele, 176
Adler, Paul, 58, 66, 152, 184
advances, 71–72, 79
AFM. *See* American Federation of Musicians
"After the Ball," 3–4, 151
Ahlert, Fred, 101
Aiken, George, 34
"Ain't Misbehavin'," 23
"Ain't No Mountain High Enough," 128
Aladdin, 82
Alden-Rochelle, Inc. v. ASCAP, 31, 48, 85
"Alexander's Rag Time Band," 4
ALF, 157
"Alice's Restaurant," 61
Allan, Lewis, 46
"All She Wants to Do Is Rock," 46–47
"All the Things You Are," 43
"All the Way," 130
Almond, Marc, 109
Alpert, Herb, 132
Amalfi Resolution, 108–9
"Amanda," 70
"Amapola," 46
American Bandstand, 57
American Camp Association, 126
American Federation of Musicians (AFM), 1–2, 11, 15–16, 45
American Gramophone Company, 10
American Heritage, 26
American Idol, 91

American Popular Music Business in the 20th Century (Sanjek, R.), 55–56
American Society of Composers, Authors and Publishers (ASCAP). *See also* income; lawsuits; membership; royalties; workshops; *specific topics*
  as bipartisan, 179
  history of formation, 1–17
  1920 bylaws amendment, 17
  1950s and 1960s overview, 49
  1960s highlights, 61
  1980s, 76
  100 years overview, 169–71
  reorganization, 117, 118–20, 171, 183
  stability factor, 156
  testimonials on impact and importance of, 130–33
  transferring from BMI to, 68–69
  underworld figures' support of, 21
American Songwriter Magazine, 121
Anderson, Melvin, 51
Annie, 80
antitrust lawsuits, 29–30, 44–45, 56–57, 73–74, 76–77, 123
AOL, 145, 158, 162
Applause, 80
Arlen, Harold, 27–28, 43, 53, 89
Armstrong, Harry, 43
Armstrong, Lillian Hardin, 23
Armstrong, Louis, 23, 47, 132
Arthur Godfrey and His Friends, 50
Arthur Godfrey's Talent Scouts, 50
Articles of Association, 14, 38

ASCAP. *See* American Society
     of Composers, Authors and
     Publishers
The ASCAP Foundation, 79, 80, 82, 89,
     92, 93, 94, 97, 127–30, 131, 132,
     166, 177, 178, 188
Ashford, Nickolas, 128, 177
The Autocrat of the Breakfast-Table
     (Holmes, Sr.), 16
Autry, Gene, 66

"Baby It's You," 103
Bacharach, Burt, 51, 71, 102, 103
background music, 155–56, 160–61
"Back o' Town Blues," 47
Bagdasarian, Ross, 51
Ballard, Hank, 41–42
The Band, 61
Bandier, Martin, 187
Band Perry, 94
Barrett, Mary Ellin, 20–21, 130
Barry, Jack, 55
bars, 152, 161
Bartók, Béla, 115
Bartók, Peter, 115
Barton, Eileen, 50
Basie, Count, 47
the Beatles, 154
"Beat Me Daddy, Eight to the Bar," 47
Beauty and the Beast, 81
"Because the Night," 133
"Before He Cheats," 176
Beguelin, Chad, 82
Bellis, Richard, 32, 84, 85
Bennett, Tony, 114, 132
Benny, Jack, 50
Bentsen, Lloyd, 111
Bergman, Alan, 120, 177
Bergman, Marilyn, 118, 120–21, 125–
     28, 143, 144, 145, 146, 171, 174, 177
Berlin, Irving, 1, 4, 5, 14, 20–21, 27, 28,
     81, 135, 187
     God Bless America Foundation of,
     127
     on Sullivan's show, 50
     writing of "God Bless America," 44
Bernstein, Louis, 135
Berry, Chuck, 51, 61–62
"Besame Mucho," 46
Betsy, 25

"Better Dig Two," 94
Bienstock, Caroline, 129
Bienstock, Freddy, 129
Big Beat Heat (Jackson, John), 54
Billboard, 57–58, 98, 109, 138
Bill Haley & His Comets, 59–60
"Birmingham Breakdown," 23
Bishop, Walter, 47
Black, Clint, 105
"Black and Tan Fantasy," 23
Blake, Eubie, 22, 23
blanket license, 22, 38, 40, 44, 62
     continuing threats to, 121
     unreasonable restraint of trade
     allegation, 73, 76
Bleyer, Archie, 50
Blige, Mary J., 181
"Blowin' in the Wind," 60, 61
blues, 22, 161
"Blue Skies," 25
BMG Music North America, 142–43
BMI. *See* Broadcast Music Incorporated
board of directors, 66, 135–48
     crusade of, 135–36
     disenchantment of, 116
     issues facing, 140
     makeup of, 95
     meetings, 119
     1960s music viewed by, 62
     operational changes and, 136
     reelection to, 135
     songwriters and publishers on, 135,
     140
The Bodyguard, 93
Bon Jovi, Jon, 96
"Boogie Woogie Bugle Boy," 47
Boone, Pat, 50
Booz Allen, 117, 120
The Borgias, 88
Bornstein, Saul, 28
"Born Too Late," 51
Bostic, Jenn, 92
Bourne Music, 28
Boyle, Peter, 122–23, 152, 155–56, 165
Brabec, Jeff, 152, 163
Brabec, Todd, 58, 71–72, 152, 159, 163
Bradley, Connie, 65–68, 69, 103–5
Bradley, Jerry, 67
Bradley, Owen, 66, 69
"Brazil," 46

"The Breeze and I," 46
Brettler, Leon, 59, 65, 71, 92
Brettler, Michael, 59
bribery, 56–57
Bridgewater, Dee Dee, 132
Brigati, Eddie, 61
Brinkley, David, 127
British court system, 12
Broadcasting-Telecasting Magazine, 54
Broadcast Music Incorporated (BMI),
    33, 40, 105, 109, 159
    ASCAP members from, 154
    battle with, 49, 53–54
    collaboration between songwriters of
        ASCAP and, 72
    lawsuit against, 44, 49, 54–57
    markets cornered by, 46–47, 66, 163
    membership, 41–42, 46
    Nashville office, 65–66
    1967, 58
    presidents, 66
    radio ally of, 54
    transferring to ASCAP from, 68–69
Broadway, 5, 6, 14, 16, 20, 22, 23, 26, 27,
    36, 37, 53, 81
Broadway Open House, 50
"Broken Hearted Melody," 103
Brooklyn Dodgers, 53
Brooks, Garth, 104–5, 114
Brooks, Harry, 23
Brooks, Harvey O., 50
Brooks, Tim, 49–50
"Brother, Can You Spare a Dime?," 62
Broughton, Bruce, 139–40, 177, 178–79
Brown, James, 51, 132
Brown, Lew, 25
Brown, Roy, 46–47
Browne, Jackson, 96
Buck, Gene, 14, 24, 25, 30, 32, 37–38,
    42–43, 45, 135
Buffalo Broadcasting Co. v. ASCAP, 76,
    79, 109, 110, 112
Burkan, Nathan, 8, 9, 14–17, 19, 29, 150
Burke, Billie, 24
Burnett, Ernie, 43
Burrell, Kenny, 96, 131–32
Butler, Larry, 70
Bye Bye Birdie, 80
Byrnes, Edd ("Kookie"), 52
"By the Time I Get to Phoenix," 141

cable television, 146, 157–58
Caesar, Sid, 50
Cagney and Lacey, 88
Cahill, Marie, 13
Cahn, Sammy, 130
Cale, J. J., 70
Cameron, S. T., 10
Candela, Bob, 185–86
Candilora, Vincent, 119–20, 153,
    157–59
"Can't Help Falling in Love," 51
Cantor, Eddie, 24
Capitol Hill, 176–79
Capone, Al, 21
Carey, Mariah, 99, 181
Carlin Music, 129
Carmichael, Hoagy, 27, 43, 50
Carolina Chocolate Drops, 178
Carter, A. P., 46
Carter, June, 65
Cash, Johnny, 70
Cashbox Magazine, 57
Cason, Buzz, 66
Cavaliere, Felix, 61
CBS. *See* Columbia Broadcasting
    System
CBS Television Network, 73, 77–78,
    86, 91
Celler, Emanuel, 53–54
Chapin, Ted, 80, 81
Chapin Carpenter, Mary, 96
Chaplin, Charlie, 8
Charles, Ray, 51
"The Charleston," 23
Charyn, Jerome, 5, 20, 21, 22
"Cheek to Cheek," 27
Chicago Reader, 54, 56
Child, Desmond, 96
Children Will Listen program, 128
China, 185
"The Chipmunk Song," 51
"Choo Choo Ch' Boogie," 47
Chordettes, 50
Christy, June, 132
Chronicles (Dylan), 60
CISAC. *See* Confédération
    Internationale des Sociétés
    d'Auteurs et Compositeurs
Citadel, 144
Clark, Brandy, 94

Clark, Dick, 57
Clarke, Donald, 21
classical (concert) music, 115, 129, 133, 140, 164–67
Clausen, Alf, 157
Clear Channel, 144
Clinton administration, 174
Clooney, Rosemary, 114
Coburn, Barry, 91, 145
Coca, Imogene, 50
coffeehouses, 2, 161
Cohan, George M., 24, 43–44
Cohen, Philip, 19
Cole, Nat King, 47
Coleman, Cy, 53
Coleman, Mark, 40–41
collaboration, 72, 139, 163
collections, 74
    field representatives for, 67, 75–76, 170
Collins, Judy, 96
Colt, LeBaron Bradford, 12
Coltrane, John, 132
Columbia Broadcasting System (CBS), 36, 40, 44, 56, 62–63, 73
Columbia Records, 39, 56
Colvin, Shawn, 76
Como, Perry, 46
compilations, 90, 164
The Complete Directory to Prime Time Network TV Shows, 1946–Present (Brooks, T., and Marsh), 49–50
composers, 108, 132, 166, 167
    contemporary, 164
    film, 84, 85, 88, 89
    foreign, 31
    jazz and classical, 129
concerts, 161–62, 164–67
Confédération Internationale des Sociétés d'Auteurs et Compositeurs (CISAC), 108, 109
Congress, 110–14, 176–77, 179
Conner, William C., 158
Connie's Hot Chocolates, 23
consent decree, 57, 73, 109–10, 112, 123, 154, 160, 171, 174
contemporary composers, 164
contracts, BMI-ASCAP comparison, 71
Cook, Roger, 109

Copyright Act
    of 1897, 3
    European laws, 123
    Gagliardi reversal, 76–78
    jukebox exemption, 53
    1909 revision, 3, 7, 8, 12–13, 169
    1976 amendment to, 74
    radio application of, 35
    small rights and, 26
Copyright Office, 123
Copyright's Highway (Goldstein), 45
Corigliano, John, 164–65
"Corner of the Sky," 81
"Could I Have This Dance," 144
country music, 46, 50, 55, 58, 59, 66, 92, 103–4, 163
Country Music Association Hall of Fame, 66
"Coward of the County," 66
"Cow Cow Boogie," 47
Creamer, Henry, 22–23
Creativity in the Classroom, 128
Crenshaw, Marshall, 96
Crosby, Bing, 146
Crosland, Phil, 95, 96, 97
Crowder, Bob, 47
Crudup, Arthur ("Big Boy"), 46–47
"Cry Me a River," 52
cue sheets, 86, 155–56, 185
Cunningham, Paul, 101–2
Currier, Frank, 11
cut-ins, 37–38

"Daddy Has a Sweetheart and Mother Is Her Name," 24
Dance, Stanley, 47
dance music, 79–80
David, Hal, 51, 69, 71, 101–3, 106–7, 109, 110–11, 113, 114, 146
David, Mack, 103
Davis, G. Howlett, 10
Davis, Jimmie, 46
"Day by Day," 81
The Dean's List, 136
deejays, 41, 46, 55, 90
Deems Taylor: A Biography (Pegolotti), 115
Deems Taylor Awards Competition, 93–94

Def Jam, 90
DeJohnette, Jack, 132
De Knight, Jimmy, 51–52
De Koven, Reginald, 10–11
Dempsey, Jack, 60
Depression, 27
The Desert Song, 101
DeShannon, Jackie, 96
De Sylva, Buddy, 25
Dexter, Al, 46
Diamond, Neil, 71, 153, 154
digital downloads, 138, 141, 158, 164, 173, 181
Dill, Clarence, 33–34
DiMucci, Dion, 51
Dion and the Belmonts, 51
Disney, Walt, 81
Doerksen, Cliff, 54, 55, 56
Domino, Antoine ("Fats"), Jr., 51
Donaldson, Walter, 43
Dooley, Jim, 88
the Doors, 61
Dorsey, Tommy, 20, 37
"Down the Road a Piece," 47
"Down Where the Wurzburger Flows," 4
Doyle, Bob, 104–5
"Do You Know the Way to San Jose," 102
DreamWorks, 81
dress code, 102
Dreyer, Dave, 25
Dreyfus, Louis, 135
Dreyfus, Max, 42, 135
Dr. Luke, 98
Dubin, Al, 27
Duffy, Ryan, 29
Dupri, Jermaine, 96
Dylan, Bob, 59–61, 65, 153–54

The Earl and the Girl, 5
"Early Morning Rain," 61
Eastman, John L., 140–41
Easy Rider, 89
Eckstine, Billy, 47
Edwards, Sherman, 103
Elf, 81, 82
Ellington, Edward ("Duke"), 21, 23, 47, 132

Engel, Lehman, 80
Enright, Dan, 55
ER, 86
"Eulogy to William C. Handy," 101–2
Europe, 185–86
    copyright laws, 123
"Evergreen," 188
"Everlasting Love," 66
Everly Brothers, 50
Expositions, 42, 94–98, 188

Fairness in Music Licensing Act, 121, 123–26
La Fanciulla del West, 7
Fariña, Richard, 61
FCC. *See* Federal Communications Commission
feature performances, 160
Federal Communications Commission (FCC), 45
Feist, Leo, 6, 28
female executives, 105–6, 108, 118, 120
El Fey club, 22
field representatives, 67, 75–76, 170
Fields, Dorothy, 27
Fields, W. C., 24
film and TV/visual media department, 84–85, 87–88
films, 31–32, 89–91
    advent of talkies, 25, 26
    budget for music in, 86
    composers for, 32, 84, 85, 88, 89
    radio songs from, 27
    royalties from, 85, 87
    silent, 26
film scoring workshops, 84–91
"Fine and Mellow," 46
Finkelstein, Herman, 107, 112
Firth, Nicholas, 66–67, 137, 173–74
Fitzgerald, Ella, 52, 146
Fitzgerald, F. Scott, 24
FM radio, 157–58
Foliart, Dan, 86–87, 89–90, 92, 177
folk music, 61, 65, 161
Follow That Dream, 103
Follow the Fleet, 27
foreign composers, 31
foreign songwriters, 108–9
"For Lovin' Me," 61

42nd Street, 27
Foster, Stephen, 2, 3
Four Funds, 58, 152–53
FOX television, 86
Freed, Alan, 54, 55
Freedman, Max, 51
free music, 91, 113, 136–48, 169
French, Alec, 174–75
Fricker, Sylvia, 61
"From Maine to Oregon," 14–15
"From the Vine Came the Grape," 101

Gabler, Milt, 47
Gagliardi, Lee P., 76–78
"The Gambler," 70
Gansgsters and Gold Diggers (Charyn),
    20, 21
Garland, Judy, 43
Garmaize, Arthur E., 39
Gaye, Marvin, 72
Gayle, Crystal, 104
the Gaylords, 101
"Gee, Baby, Ain't I Good to You," 23
"Geek in the Pink," 91
Geibel, Adam, 11
GEMA, 109
general counsel, 107, 116, 118
Generalissimo Snowflake, 59
Germany, 109
Gershon, Freddie, 153–54
Gershwin, George, 21, 27, 28, 43, 53, 108
"Get Your Kicks on Route 66," 47
Gillespie, Dizzy, 47, 132
Gingrich, Newt, 124, 125
Girl Scouts of America, 126–27
Gladys publishing, 51
Glenn, John, 113
"God Bless America," 44, 50
"God Bless the Child," 46
Goddard, Henry W., 44
Godfrey, Arthur, 50
Godspell, 81
Going Places, 27
"Going to Chicago Blues," 47
Gold, Dan, 118
Golden, John, 14
Golden Age, 21, 22, 33, 48, 78
Golden Gate International Exposition,
    42
Goldenthal, Elliot, 79

The Gold in Tin Pan Alley (Meyer), 29
Goldstein, Paul, 44–45
"Good Luck Charm," 51
Goodman, Benny, 21
Goodman, Peter W., 116–17
"Good Rockin' Tonight," 46–47
Gordon, Dexter, 132
Gordon, Mack, 27
Gordy, Berry, Jr., 51, 72
Gossip Girl, 90
Gould, Jack, 62
Gould, Morton, 53, 114, 116–18, 120,
    135, 166
Grainger, Porter, 23
Grand Ole Opry, 69
grand rights, 26
The Great Gatsby (Fitzgerald, F. S.), 24
Great Motown Switch, 72
Great Neck, NY, 24–25, 102
"The Great Pretender," 51
Greenaway, Roger, 108–9, 184
Greenberg, Herman, 19–20, 32
Grimmett, Randy, 97–98
Grossman, Albert, 60
Guinan, Mary Louise Cecilia ("Texas"),
    22
Gullish, Dorothy, 154–55
Gustavson, Brandt, 121
Guthrie, Arlo, 61
Guthrie, Woody, 61

Haley, Bill, 51, 59–60
Hall, Bill, 67–68
Hamilton, Arthur, 52–53
Hammer, Jan, 89
Hammerstein II, Oscar, 28, 50, 53, 80,
    170
Hammond, John, 60–61
Handy, William Christopher, 23, 43,
    101–2
Harbach, Otto, 42, 101, 135
Harburg, E. Y. "Yip," 27, 62
Hard, Courtney, 130
"Hard Lovin' Loser," 61
Hard to Get, 27
Harms, T. B., 4–6, 15, 28
Harold Arlen Film & TV Award, 89
Harper's Magazine, 32
Harris, Charles K., 3–4, 14, 15, 151
Harris, Oren, 55

Harris, Wynonie, 46–47
Hartman, Manny, 19
Hatch, Orrin, 112, 124–25
Hauth, Russ, 121
Hedgeland, F. W., 10
Hein, Silvio, 13, 16
Held, Anna, 5
Henderson, Fletcher, 23
Henderson, Ray, 25
Herb Alpert Young Jazz Composer
    Awards program, 132
Herbert, Victor, 1–17, 9–10, 28, 43, 101,
    135, 151
Herbert v. Shanley, 16, 33–34
Herrmann, Bernard, 32
Herzog, Arthur, Jr., 46
Hickenlooper, Smith, 34
hillbilly music, 40–41
Himber, Richard, 37
Hinckley, David, 153–54
Hines, Earl, 47
Hirsch, Louis A., 13
history, ASCAP formation, 1–17
Hoffman, Al, 50
Holiday, Billie, 46
Holly, Buddy, 51
Hollywood, 27, 28, 53
Holmes, Oliver Wendell, Jr., 2, 12–13,
    16–17, 158–59, 170
Holmes, Oliver Wendell, Sr., 16
Holyfield, Wayland, 67–69, 96, 144, 177
Home Improvement, 86
"Home Is Where the Heart Is," 103
"The Honeydripper," 47
"Honeysuckle Rose," 23
Hoover, Herbert, 29
Horne, Lena, 114, 132
Horowitz, Zach, 186–87
Horses, 133
Houdini, Wilmoth, 47
Hour Glass, 50
"The House of Blue Lights," 47
"House of the Rising Sun," 60
House of Witmark, 3, 6, 15, 28
Howard, James Newton, 86
"How'd You Like to Spoon with Me," 5
Hubbell, Raymond, 13, 16, 17, 135, 150
Hubert, Laurent, 142–43
Hurt, Henry, 67
Hyde, Henry, 173

"I Create Music" Expo, 94–98
"I Don't Care If the Sun Don't Shine,"
    102–3
"If I Knew You Were Comin' I'd've
    Baked a Cake," 50
"If Tomorrow Never Comes," 105
"I'm a Yankee Doodle Dandy," 44
"I'm Every Woman," 128
"I'm Gonna Move to the Outskirts of
    Town," 47
"Immigration Blues," 23
"I'm Much Too Young to Feel This
    Damn Old," 104
"I'm Not the Marrying Kind," 103
"I'm Putting All My Eggs in One
    Basket," 27
"I'm Yours," 164
income
    decline, 136, 143–44
    membership dispersal of, 160
    1921, 20
    1960s largest source of, 51
    1980–1985, 109
    performance rights, 145
    radio, 154
    since 2009, 159
    2010, 172
    2012, 184
Intellectual Property subcommittee,
    111, 124
international distribution, 185–86
international relations, 108–9
Internet, 136–48, 152, 158, 168
    free music trend and, 113, 136–48,
        169
    licensing and rate calculation for,
        162–63, 172–73, 175
    performance tracking for, 156
    piracy, 179–81
Internet Movie Database (IMDb), 84
In the Heights, 82
Iossa, Lauren, 94–95, 97
Irving Berlin Summer Music Camp
    Scholarship, 130
Isham, Mark, 96
Israelite, David, 175–76, 179–80
"Is You Is or Is You Ain't My Baby," 47
"It's Now or Never," 51
iTunes, 141
"I Wonder Why," 51

"Jack, You're Dead," 47
Jackson, Alan, 105, 145
Jackson, Janet, 181
Jackson, John, 54, 56, 57
Jam, Jimmy, 96, 181–83
Japanese Society for Rights of Authors,
    Composers and Publishers
    (JASRAC), 108, 185
jazz, 21, 22–23, 129, 132–33
The Jazz Singer, 25
Jean, Wyclef, 96
"Jeepers Creepers," 27
Jennings, Waylon, 66
*Jerome H. Remick & Co. v. American
    Automobile Accessories*, 34
Jobete publishing, 72
Joel, Billy, 114, 154
John Church Company, 14–15
John Hammond on Record (Hammond),
    60
"Johnny Get Angry," 103
Johnson, Arlene, 50
Johnson, James P., 23
"The Joint Is Jumpin'," 47
Jolson, Al, 5, 8, 20, 25
Jonathan Larson Performing Arts
    Foundation, 82
Jones, Juanita, 65, 66
Jones, Quincy, 96, 143
Jones, Thad, 132
Joplin, Janis, 61
Jordan, Louis, 47
Judas and Me, 82
jukeboxes, 40–41, 53, 142, 171
Juno, 90
"Just A-Sittin' and A-Rockin'," 47

"Kansas City Stomp," 23
Kaplan, Steve, 89
Kay, Dean, 68–69, 136, 177
Kear, Josh, 176–77
Keller, Bill, 181
Kendrick, Jim, 167
Kennedy, Ted, 113
Kennedy v. McTammany, 12
Kerker, Gustave, 13
Kerker, Michael, 82, 83
Kern, Jerome, 1, 4–5, 14, 28, 42, 43, 135,
    187
Khan, Chaka, 96

Kid Galahad, 103
King, B. B., 132
Kittredge, Alfred, 11
Knight, Evelyn, 50
Knutsen, Nancy, 31, 84–88
Koenigsberg, Fred, 116–18, 154, 171
"Kookie, Kookie (Lend Me Your
    Comb)," 52
Koontz, Michael, 109
Korman, Bernard, 112
Kosser, Michael, 121
Kristofferson, Kris, 69

Lacombe, Emile, 15
Lady Antebellum, 176
Lady Gaga, 160
LaGuardia, Fiorello, 42
Lambert, Miranda, 94
Lardner, Ring, 24
La Rosa, Julius, 50
Larson, Jonathan, 80–81, 82
Lasca, Edward, 5
Lasker, Morris E., 73
Lawrence, Jack, 54
lawsuits, 2. *See also specific cases*
    antitrust, 29–30, 44–45, 56–57, 73–
        74, 76–77, 123
    AOL, 162
    against BMI, 49, 54–57
    CBS, 62–63, 73
    Congressional relations and, 110–14
    constant challenges and, 30
    continuance of, 57
    early, 14–15, 33
    Gagliardi reversal, 76–78
    Internet music, 162–63
    Messinger on importance of, 112–13
    movie theater, 30–31
    1982 local TV stations, 76–77
    overview of, 170–73
    radio, 33–34
    rate proceeding request, 110–11
    reason for, 183
    recent, 158, 159
    Shanley, 8, 15–16
Layton, Turner, 22–23
The Learning Channel (TLC), 86
Lee, Peggy, 114
Leeds Music Publishing, 59–60
legal department, 107

Leiber, Jerry, 129
Leiber and Stoller, 51, 113, 129
LeMone, Shawn, 87
Lengsfelder, Hans, 107–8
Lennon, John, 154
Lerner, Alan Jay, 54
Lester Sill songwriters workshop, 93, 98
Levy, Leeds, 60, 61
Levy, Lou, 59–60, 61
Lewis, Mel, 132
Lewis, Terry, 96, 181, 182
Libby, J. Aldrich, 6–7
licensing, 19–20. *See also* blanket
    license; Copyright Act; Internet;
    royalties; *specific legislation*;
    *specific licensees; specific music
    venues*
  cost and pricing, 31
  exemptions, 53, 74
  future requirements for, 183
  new media, 173
  payment collections, 67, 74–77, 170
  square footage and, 125, 142
  by telephone, 119
  weighting practice in, 122–23,
    160–61
Liggins, Joe, 47
Lightfoot, Gordon, 61
"Like a Rolling Stone," 61
"Like a Virgin," 149
The Lion King, 81
"A Little Bird Told Me," 50
"Little Boxes," 61
Littlefield, Merlin, 69, 70–71, 104
"Little Green Apples," 66
"The Little Lost Child," 4
"The Little Red Fox," 50
Little Richard, 51
Load of Coal, 23
lobbying, 111, 113, 173–76
Loeffler, John, 15, 16
Loesser, Frank, 27
LoFrumento, John, 95, 96, 118–19, 120,
    139, 172–73, 183–84, 186
Lombardo, Carmen, 50
London, Julie, 52
"London Blues," 23
Lorraine, Lillian, 24
Lott, Trent, 124–25
"Love for Sale," 50

"Love in Bloom," 43, 50
Lovett, Lyle, 179
Ludacris, 96
Lynne, Jeff, 96

"MacArthur Park," 141
MacDonald, Christie, 7–8
Mack, Cecil. *See* McPherson, Richard C.
Madama Butterfly, 7
"Mama's Broken Heart," 94
Mancini, Henry, 113, 114
Mandel, Johnny, 177
Manson, Marilyn, 122
Mardak, Keith, 74
"Maria Elena," 46
"Marie from Sunny Italy," 4, 20
Marks, E. B., 4, 46
Marrying Mary, 13
Marsh, Earle, 50
"The Marvelous Toy," 61
Marx, Groucho, 24
Marx, Harpo, 24–25
Maxwell, George, 7, 8, 13–15, 23–24,
    135
Mayer, John, 79, 96, 98, 130–31
McCartney, Paul, 140, 184
McChesney, Robert W., 56
McDill, Bob, 67–68, 69
McEntire, Reba, 104
McGuire Sisters, 50
McHugh, Jimmy, 27, 43
McHugh, Jonathan, 90
McKinney's Cotton Pickers, 23
McPherson, Richard C. ("Cecil Mack"),
    23
"Me and My Shadow," 34
"Moon to Me," 101
Melody Music, 55–56
Melvin, Harriet, 174
Member Access digital system, 162
membership, 22, 44
  bases, 103
  BMI, 41–42, 46
  department, 104
  difficulty enrolling in, 66
  former BMI affiliates in, 154
  goal of department, 99
  income dispersal among, 160
  Iossa's efforts to increase, 94
  for new and older songwriters, 58

membership *(Cont.)*
  1960s and 1970s, 58
  1960s changes, 58–62
  numbers, 166, 172
  publishers overlooked for, 51
  resignation, 68
  standards, 51
"Memories of You," 23
Mercer, Johnny, 27, 53, 188
Merrill, Bob, 50
Messinger, Gloria, 74, 105, 106–9, 112–13, 118
Metro-Goldwyn-Mayer, 28
Meyer, Hazel, 29
Miami Vice, 89–90
Midnight Frolic, 5, 24
Miller, Glenn, 21
Miller, Marilyn, 24
Miller, Steve, 96
Mills, E. Claude, 36–39
Milsap, Ronnie, 67
Miranda, Lin-Manuel, 79
Les Misérables, 82
mission, 2, 3
"Mister Five by Five," 47
Mitchell, Joni, 154
Modern Family, 93
Moffatt, Hugh, 70
Mogull, Artie, 60–61
Monroe, Bill, 46
"The More I See You," 34
Morgan, Corrine, 5
Morgenstern, Jay, 138
Morris, Trevor, 88
Morton, Ferdinand ("Jelly Roll"), 23
Morton Gould Young Composer Competition, 166
Motion Picture Theater Owners Association, 26
Motown, 72
MOVE program, 94–95
movie theaters, 26, 30–31
Mraz, Jason, 91, 96, 164
"Mr. Jelly Lord," 23
MTV, 157–58
"Much Too Young," 105
Murphy, Frank, 30
Murphy, Ralph, 105
music. *See also* films; *specific genres*
  background, 155–56, 160–61

as business, 129–30
concert, 164–67
free, 91, 113, 136–48, 169
outlets for accessing, 143
physical, 182
retail stores, 137
theme, 87, 161
underscore, 87, 89–90, 155–56
Musical Courier, 5, 8
musicals, 4, 5, 8, 21, 22, 23, 37, 82, 177–79
musical theater workshops, 80–83, 92
Music Choice channels, 157–58
musicians
  royalty payments through ranking of, 151–52
  strikes, 41, 45–46
Music Library Association, 28
Music Reports, 44
M. Witmark & Sons, 52, 61
"My Blue Heaven," 43
"My Melancholy Baby," 43

NAB. *See* National Association of Broadcasters
Nashville, 65–71, 75–76, 103, 105, 145
National Association of Broadcasters (NAB), 33–34, 40
National Music Publishers Association (NMPA), 175
National Religious Broadcasters (NRB), 121
NBC radio network, 36, 40, 44
NBC television, 50, 86
"Near You," 50
"Need You Now," 176
Nelson, Willie, 66, 69
Newman, Jon O., 77–78
Newman, Randy, 96
New Yorker, 24
New York Herald Tribune, 54
New York Times, 54, 62, 181
The Night Club Era (Walker), 21–22
"A Night in Tunisia," 47
Nixon, Richard, 158
NMPA. *See* National Music Publishers Association
Norworth, Jack, 43, 127
Notes, 28
Now That's What I Call Music, 90

NRB. *See* National Religious
   Broadcasters

"Oh, Promise Me," 10–11
Okrent, Brendan, 93, 98, 162
On Stage, 162
On the Avenue, 27
orchestra leaders, 38
Orrall, Robert Ellis, 92, 113
Osgood, Charles, 127
"Over the Rainbow," 27, 28, 43, 62
Owen, Randy, 67
Oz the Great and Powerful, 99

Packard, Vance, 55
Palumbo, Ben, 111–12, 124, 125, 173
Pandora, 156, 164, 175, 180
Panther Music, 51
Paramount, 87
Parker, Charlie, 47
Parker, Tom, 51
Parton, Dolly, 66
The Passing Show of 1912, 13
Paulus, Stephen, 164, 165, 166–67
Paxton, Tom, 61
payment and distribution, 85–86,
      107–8, 149–68. *See also* Internet;
   specific venues
   classification committees for, 150
   follow the dollar, 152
   Four Funds, 58, 152–53
   heart payment, 188
   international, 185–86
   musician ranking in, 151–52
   original system, 149–50
   payment collection, 67, 74–77, 170
   revamping of, 160
   for small-venue gigs, 162
   songwriter misconceptions about,
      159–60
   surveys and, 160
payola, 37, 49, 51, 55, 56
Peer I, Ralph, 46, 69
Pegolotti, James, 115
Pennington, Sam, 130
"Perfidia," 46
performance rights, 1. *See also* lawsuits
   early years, 11–13, 16–17
   forfeiting of, 6
   Internet era and, 138

movie theater, 31
need for income from, 145
for profit clause, 13, 74
small and grand, 26
performance rights organizations
      (PROs), 7, 131, 187–88
   international relations and, 108–9
   Japanese, 108
   switching, 68
performances, 34, 41
   Capitol Hill, 176–79
   digital downloads as, 138, 141, 158
   feature, 160
   symphonic and recital, 165
   television, 155–56
   for touring artists, 161–62
   tracking, 6, 152, 154–62, 186–87
Performing Right Society (PRS), 109, 184
Perry, Katy, 96
Pete Kelly's Blues, 52
Peter, Paul and Mary, 61
Peters, Marybeth, 123
Petrillo, James, 39, 45–46
Petty, Tom, 95
Philadelphia Music Project, 167
piano roll manufacturers, 8–12
The Pillars of the Earth, 88
Pincus, Matt, 156
Pinocchio, 28
PIPA. *See* Protect Intellectual Property
   Act
Pippin, 81
piracy, 179–81
"Pistol Packin' Mama," 46
Pitney, Gene, 109
the Platters, 51
Playback (ASCAP magazine), 171–72
Playback (Coleman, M.), 40
Poni-Tails, 51
pop songs, 21, 25, 81, 89, 90
   workshop, 92–93
Porter, Cole, 21, 27, 28, 53, 170
"Powder Your Face with Sunshine," 50
Powell, Teddy, 37
presidents, 30, 32, 45. *See also specific*
   names
   first, 13–14, 101, 135
   first female, 120
   lifestyle of, 148
   term of, 101

Presley, Elvis, 51–53, 102–3, 129, 146
Preston, Frances, 66, 67, 69, 126
prime time television, 85–86
Prince, Robert Graham, 23
printing press, 146
The Production of Culture in the Music Industry (Ryan, J.), 63
Prohibition, 19, 40, 170
PROs. *See* performance rights organizations
Protect Intellectual Property Act (PIPA), 179–80
PRS. *See* Performing Right Society
PRS Awards, for British songwriters, 114
publishers. *See also* lawsuits; *specific publishers*
    acquisition of, 28
    as board of directors members, 135, 140
    cut-in practice of, 37–38
    defection and return of, 169–70
    founding, 59
    overlooked, 51
    record company rivalry with, 139
    songwriters in business with, 3–4
    teams, 51–52
Puccini, Giacomo, 7–8
Pushing Daisies, 88

quiz show scandals, 55

Rabin, Buzz, 69–70
radio
    airplay monitoring, 154–55
    ASCAP music eliminated from, 44
    ban, 46–47
    battles, 28, 32–48, 49
    BMI alliance with, 54
    Copyright Act application to, 35
    FM, 157–58
    Hollywood domination of, 27
    income from, 154
    1920s, 22
    1930s, 32
    satellite, 144, 164–65
    stations, 36, 41, 157, 158
Radio City, 42
Radio Corporation of America, 29
Ragovoy, Jerry, 93

"Raindrops Keep Fallin' on My Head," 102, 111
Rainger, Ralph, 43
Ram, Buck, 51
RapidCue, 185
Rascals, 61
rate proceeding request, 109–10
Raye, Don, 47
Razaf, Andy, 23, 47
R&B. *See* rhythm and blues
RCA, 56, 67
RCA Victor Records, 56
"Reach Out and Touch" Award, 128–29
"Reach Out and Touch (Somebody's Hand)," 128
RealNetworks, 162
recitals, 165
recording industry
    1942 strike against, 45–46
    record companies, 39–42
    record sales, 25, 39
Redman, Don, 23
Reid, Rufus, 132–33
Reimer, Richard, 31, 73, 126–27, 160, 161, 162–63
religious broadcasting, 121–22
Rent, 80
reorganization, ASCAP, 117, 118–20, 171, 183
restaurants, 124, 125, 152, 161
restricted compositions, 38
Revel, Harry, 27
Reynolds, Malvina, 61
Rhapsody, 180
"Rhapsody in Blue," 21
rhythm and blues (R&B), 46–47, 50, 58, 109
The Rhythm Club, 82
Richard, Fran, 115, 165–66
Richardson, Chris, 91
right of continuing payment, 110
"Ring of Fire," 65
ringtones, 173
The Rise and Fall of Popular Music (Clarke), 21
Ritter, Tex, 46
Robbins, Marty, 51
Roberta, 101
Robertson, Robbie, 61
Robin, Leo, 43

Robinson, Irwin Z., 71, 72–73, 117, 135, 137–38
Robinson, Smokey, 72
Rochinski, Stanley, 50
"(We're Gonna) Rock Around the Clock," 51, 60–61
rock 'n' roll, 49, 50, 102
   antagonists, 54–55
   ASCAP in marketplace of folk and, 61
   first hit, 51
   initial view of, 56–57
   missed opportunity, 47, 48
   Tin Pan Alley and, 53, 61–62
Rockwell, John, 62
Rodgers, Jimmie, 66
Rodgers, Richard, 21, 50, 53
Rodgers and Hammerstein, 53, 80
Rodgers and Hart, 28, 53
Rogers, Kenny, 70
Rogers, Will, 24
Roosevelt, James, 107
Roosevelt, Theodore, 2, 9, 171
Rosalie, 27
Rose, Billy, 25
Rose, Debbie, 76, 79–80
Rose, Earl, 91–92
Rose, Fred, 66
Rose, Wesley, 135
Roseanne, 86
Rosenberg, Sylvia, 101
Rosenthal, J. C., 154
Rosenthal, Julius ("Rosey"), 16
Rossiter, Will, 3
royalties. See also Copyright Act; income; payment and distribution
   from abroad, 184–85
   advances on, 71–72, 79
   ASCAP membership required for, 22
   collaboration, 163
   cut-ins, 37–38
   film, 85, 87
   first system for allotting, 14
   to foreign composers, 31
   jukebox, 40–41, 53, 142, 171
   1900s, 4
   1966 revised schedule for, 57–58
   19th century, 3–4
   right of continuing payment for continuing use, 110
   television, 87

2012 total, 2
Runnin' Wild, 23
Runyon, Damon, 35
Rushing, Jimmy, 47, 70
Russell, Bobby, 66
Russell, Lillian, 24
Ryan, Charlie, 50
Ryan, John, 63
Ryan, Little, 50

SACEM. See Société des Auteurs, Compositeurs et Éditeurs de Musique
"Salt Peanuts," 47
Saltzman, Seth, 157, 159–61, 163
Sammy Cahn award, 130–31
"San Antonio Rose," 47
Sandoval, Arturo, 76
Sanjek, Dave, 41, 61–62
Sanjek, Russ, 41, 55–56
satellite radio, 144, 164–65
Saturday Night Review, 50
Schirmer, Gustav, 42
Schlitz, Don, 69–71, 96
Schoenfeld, Herm, 55
Schultz, Lucia S., 28
Schuman, Hans, 132
Schwartz, Arthur, 53
Schwartz, Stephen, 81–83, 82, 96
Scott, Jill, 96
Screen Composers Association, 32
Seeger, Pete, 51
Seger, Bob, 61
Seinfeld, 154
Selvin, Ben, 25
Sensenbrenner, Jim, 124, 125
SESAC. See Society of European Stage Authors and Composers
77 Sunset Strip, 52
Shanley's, 8, 15–17
Shapiro, Alex, 167
Shapiro Bernstein publishing company, 4, 6, 15, 59, 65
Shea, Ed, 66, 67
sheet music sales, 5–6, 7, 35–36, 169–70
Sherman Antitrust Act, 29, 30, 44
Sherry, Karen, 105, 106, 113, 127–28, 130, 179
Shuffle Along, 22
silent films, 26

Silver, Roy, 60
Silverado, 178–79
Simon, Carly, 96
Simone, Nina, 131
Simpson, Valerie, 128–29, 143, 177
The Simpsons, 157
Sinatra, Frank, 46, 54, 146
Sir Mix-a-Lot, 76
Sissle, Noble, 22
Skaggs, Ricky, 103, 105
"Skinny Minnie," 51–52
Sklar, Matthew, 82
Slack, Freddie, 47
Slay and Crewe, 52
slogans, 140
Small Business Association, 124
Small Business Committee, 107
Smith, Ira, 153
Smith, Kate, 44
Smith, Patti, 133
"Smoke Gets in Your Eyes," 43, 101
Snoop Doggy Dogg, 122
Snow, Mark, 88
Snow White, 28
soap operas, 91
Société des Auteurs, Compositeurs et
    Éditeurs de Musique (SACEM), 7,
    14
Society of European Stage Authors and
    Composers (SESAC), 40, 153–54,
    159, 184
"So Emotional," 149
"Someone Like You," 176, 177
"Something's Gotten Hold of My
    Heart," 109
"Something to Live For," 47
Sommers, Joanie, 103
Sondheim, Stephen, 80–81, 83, 128
SONGS Music Publishing, 156
songwriters. *See also specific*
    songwriters
  artists as partners of, 139
  ASCAP-BMI collaboration, 72
  on board of directors, 135, 140
  British, 114
  Congress visits by, 176–77
  courting new, 71
  Depression-era, 27–28
  early 1900s way of making money,
    5–6

foreign, 108–9
free music trend among, 91
misconceptions, 159–60, 176
non-performing, 144, 182
publisher rights from, 3
publishers in business with, 3–4
record label control of early, 41–42
religious, 122
royalty differences for new and long-
    term, 58
unknown, 97–98
Webb's counsel to future, 142
workshops for, 92–93, 98
Songwriters Hall of Fame, 147
Songwriters of America, 49, 54, 55
Sonny Bono Copyright Term Extension
    Act, 123
"Sonny Boy," 25
SOPA. *See* Stop Online Piracy Act
soundtracks, 90, 93
Sousa, John Philip, 9–10, 11, 14
South by Southwest, 130
speakeasies, 21
Special Edition, 132
special permissions, 36–37
Spotify, 156, 164, 180
Spring Awakening, 82
Springsteen, Bruce, 154
square footage, 125, 142
staff reduction, 119, 183
"Stardust," 43
Starr, Herman, 28
Steinberg, Billy, 149
Steiner, Max, 52
Stern, Joseph W., 4, 6
Stevens, Connie, 52
Stewart, Potter, 34
"St. Louis Blues," 43
Stoller, Mike, 51, 113, 129
"Stone Cold Dead in the Market," 47
Stookey, Paul, 61
Stop Online Piracy Act (SOPA), 179–80
"Stormy Monday Blues," 47
"The Story of My Life," 51
"Straighten Up and Fly Right," 47
Strang, Cameron, 138–39
"Strange Fruit," 46
Strayhorn, Billy, 47
strikes, 41, 45–46
Strouse, Charles, 51, 80–81

"Stuck on You," 51
Sullivan, Ed, 50
Sundance Film Festival, 98
"Sweet Adeline," 43
Swid, Stephen, 153
Swope, Herbert Bayard, 24–25
symphonic performances, 165
syndication, 76, 77–78, 110

"Tain't Nobody's Biz-ness If I Do," 23
Take Me Back to Oklahoma, 46
"Take Me Out to the Ball Game," 43,
    127
"Take the A Train," 47
talkies, 25, 26
Taylor, Deems, 30, 43, 45, 93–94, 115,
    135
Taylor, Irving, 52
Taylor, James, 154
technology owners, 143
Ted Snyder Company, 4
television, 49–63, 73, 77–78, 85–87, 91
    cable, 146, 157–58
    film songs as supplanted by songs for,
        90–91
    local, 152
    rate proceeding request from
        stations, 109–10
    tracking performances on, 155–56
Ten Ten Music, 91, 145
Thacher, Thomas Day, 29
Thanks for the Memory, 27
"That's All Right," 46–47
"That's Life," 136
"Theme from *A Summer Place*", 52
theme music, 87, 161
"There's a Rainbow 'Round My
    Shoulder," 25
They're Playing Our Song (Wilk), 27, 62
"This Year's Kisses," 27
Thomas, John Charles, 43
"Three Little Fishies," 50
Three Smoothies, 50
Thurmond, Strom, 112
tick . . . tick . . . BOOM!, 81
Tiffany's, 43
Timberlake, Justin, 96, 98
Time Magazine, 29
Tin Pan Alley, 3–4, 16, 23, 26, 29, 35,
    43, 45, 65

Hollywood defeat of, 28
    1970s Motown and, 72
    rock 'n' roll replacing, 53, 61–62
TLC. *See* The Learning Channel
Toast of the Town, 50
Todd, Mike, 88–89
Tonight Show, 90
Tootsie's Orchid Lounge, 69
Top Hat, 27
Treemonisha, 5
A Trip to Chinatown, 4
Troup, Bobby, 47
"True Colors," 149
Tucker, Tanya, 104
The Tudors, 88
*Twentieth Century Music Corp. v.
    Aiken*, 34
Twenty-One, 55
Twilight, 90
"The Twist," 41–42
"Two Sleepy People," 27
Tyson, Ian, 61

underscore, 87, 89–90, 155–56
Underwood, Carrie, 176
United Independent Broadcasters
    network, 36
Universal Music Publishing Group, 186
"(You Lift Me) Up to Heaven," 104
Urban, Joseph, 24
Urban, Keith, 145

The Vampire Diaries, 90
Vanderbilt Hotel lawsuit, 14–15
Van Doren, Charles, 55
Variety, 36, 55, 57
Vaughan, Sarah, 103
Vaughan, Stevie Ray, 132
video games, music for, 87–88
videola, 55
Virgil Thomson Foundation, 94
Von Tilzer, Albert, 43
Von Tilzer, Harry, 4

Wagoner, Porter, 66
Wainwright, Loudon, 96
Walker, Stanley, 21–22
"Walkin' My Baby Back Home," 101
Waller, Thomas ("Fats"), 23
Warner Brothers, 27–30, 60, 138

Warren, Diane, 79
Warren, Harry, 27
Washington Post, 127
Waters, Edward, 9
Watt, Mel, 178
Watts, Clem, 50
"Way Down Yonder in New Orleans,"
    22–23
Webb, Jack, 52
Webb, Jimmy, 61, 96, 141–42, 147, 177
The Wedding Singer, 82
The Wednesday Night Program, 50
Weeks, Ricardo, 51
"The Weight," 61
weighting practice, 122–23, 160–61
Welch, Elisabeth, 23
Welk Music, 68, 105
"We're Gonna Rock Around the Clock,"
    51
West, Mae, 8
Western swing, 47
"We've Only Just Begun," 145–46, 188
"We Write the Songs" musical shows,
    177–79
Wheeler, Billy Edd, 66
"A Whistling Tune," 103
White, Byron, 62, 73–74
Whiteman, Paul, 21–22
White-Smith v. Apollo, 11–12, 16
Wicked, 81
Wicked City, 82
WID. *See* Worldwide International
    Database
Wikipedia, 181
Wilk, Max, 27, 62
Williams, Bert, 13
Williams, Clarence, 22–23
Williams, Don, 70
Williams, Hank, 51, 66
Williams, John, 72, 84
Williams, Paul, 96, 139, 145–48, 171,
    177, 188
Willoughby, Jesse, 92
"Willow Tree," 23
Wills, Bob, 47

Wilson, Ann, 96
Wilson, Dan, 177
Wilson, Nancy, 96
Winter, Toni, 101–2, 117
"Witch Doctor," 51
Withers, Bill, 96
Witmark, Jay, 135
Witmark Music, 60
The Wizard of Oz, 27, 43
Wolff, Jonathan, 154
"Wolverine Blues," 23
Wonder, Stevie, 72, 114
Wood, Doug, 131
Wooten, Zelma, 75
workshops, 79–94, 98
The World of Duke Ellington (Dance),
    47
Worldwide International Database
    (WID), 185
Wynn, Ed, 24

The X-Files, 88

Yahoo, 145, 158, 162, 175
Yale Law School, 107–8
"Yankee Doodle," 9
Yarrow, Peter, 61
"You and Me Against the World," 145–
    46, 188
"You Are My Sunshine," 46
Youmans, Vincent, 21
"You Must Have Been a Beautiful Baby,"
    27
Young Composer awards, 167
"You're a Grand Old Flag," 44
"You're Getting to Be a Habit with Me,"
    27
Your Show of Shows, 50
YouTube, 156, 175, 180
"You Were on My Mind," 61

Zanuck, Darryl, 27
Ziegfeld, Florenz, 5, 24, 81
Ziegfield Follies, 5, 13, 24, 171
Zimmer, Hans, 88